Indian Tapestry

Syed Abdul Majid Quadri

Indian Tapestry is based on the author's memories of life in the 1940's in Central India. The incidents, names and characters are purely fictional. Any resemblance to actual people living or dead is purely coincidental.

Copyright © Syed Abdul Majid Quadri 2013.

ISBN-13:
978-0615807164 (Indian Tapestry)

ISBN-10:
061580716X

DEDICATION

On two separate occasions I nearly lost my life through being in the wrong place at the wrong time. I would like to thank the strangers who sprang to my rescue each time.

The first occasion was in 1949 when there were communal clashes between Hindus and Muslims in Bombay. Three of us from Ujjain, wearing Muslim hats, had wandered into a Hindu area. We swiftly found ourselves at the centre of a group of weapon-wielding Hindus, drawing closer to us in ever-decreasing circles. A tall, *dhoti* clad Hindu gentleman climbed on to a window ledge behind them and shouted, "Wait! Don't kill them, they are outsiders. You! Where do you come from?" "We are from Ujjain, Gwalior State," we replied. "You are in a Mahratta Hindu area," he told us, and shouted to the crowd, "They are from our Maharajah's state. Take them to the end of this street, and see that they cross the main road safely into the Muslim area." As soon as they saw us coming, some Muslim men appeared to welcome us. They guided us to our refugee hotel, "Mullah Jafar Musafir Khana," which was funded by local Muslims. Thank you, sir.

The second time was in 1953 when there was sectarian violence in Lahore, Pakistan. Three of us had come there from Karachi to take our Panjab University Matriculation examination. We were walking in an empty street when an open jeep stopped near us and a man in it pointed a gun at me. The bearded Muslim standing next to him put a hand on his arm and said, "Stop! Don't shoot, they are outsiders." Once again my life was saved.

CONTENTS

Acknowledgements

Thanks to my wife Ann: without her full support, this book would be incomplete. I would also like to thank my daughter Shabana for managing the editing and publication process. Thank you to my daughter Yasmin who spent many hours reading the chapters and helping me to clarify my thoughts. Rachel Schick Siegel provided invaluable assistance in proof reading this book – thank you. I also thank Elaine Michaud for creating our beautiful book cover. Thank you also to the rest of my family for their encouragement and support.

Introduction

Indian Tapestry is a historical novel set in the 1940's towards the end of the British Raj in Ujjain, a holy Hindu city in Gwalior state, Central India. It is based on the writer's memories of what he saw and heard during that time as seen through the eyes of Umer, a boy living in the Lawyers' Den. Much of this area and lifestyle has changed or disappeared since the partition of India in 1947.

The images on the Indian tapestry are set in Ujjain and the surrounding villages. They gradually reveal the everyday lives of some of the residents of Mirzawari, a Muslim locality in Ujjain. Activities included matchmaking, weddings, work, play, social gatherings, visits from *genies* and festivals. Muslim boys and girls played together until the age of 11. After that they led separate lives. Everyone learned to read the Quran at home. Muslim boys and girls were educated in separate Muslim schools. There was a private school for girls aged 5 to 12 in Mirzawari behind the Lawyers' Den and one Government school for boys outside Mirzawari.

Umer and his family lived in one of six houses facing a courtyard which was known as the Lawyer's Den. As can be seen in the book, only certain people entered this enclosed world through the single gate leading to it, which was called Elephant Gate. Most houses had no electricity, so people used candles or storm lanterns. However, there were street lights. When the schoolboys had their Middle School Examinations, they sat in the road beneath the street light, outside the headmaster's house, in the evening to study. They had to give way to a car on average twice in two hours.

From the age of 10, Muslim girls covered their heads in the house. When they went outside they wore a *burqa,* a veil covering the whole body from head to foot. They were not allowed to speak to any boys around their age or men who were not relatives, and their social lives were centred round activities with other women and girls in the community.

Parents, with the help of older friends and relatives, made every effort to find a suitable match for their sons and daughters in accordance with their family's status and standing in the community. Dark-skinned girls generally had fewer offers. Go-betweens, friends, and relatives visited the families seeking matches, and provided detailed verbal descriptions of prospective brides and grooms. People relied heavily on these descriptions, as photos were not exchanged at that time. Social family occasions, such as wedding feasts and festivals, also provided a rich source for possible future matches.

Most girls were married between the ages of 16 and 25. During the engagement ceremony, the bride and groom glanced briefly at each other when they exchanged rings beneath a sheet. However, they made their wedding vows in separate tents, and met for the first time on the wedding night as two complete strangers. This had consequences in some cases, as will be seen.

A glossary of italicized words and a list of characters can be found in the back of the book as a reference on the journey back to a bygone era in central India. Enjoy!

Chapter 1: Tapestry Background

"Your marriage has been arranged -- at last!" Tara Bibi's mother announced with satisfaction. "The wedding will take place in four weeks."

"What marriage? To whom?" asked her daughter, puzzled.

"He is a man with a good income who can give you a comfortable life," came the reply. "His name is Rauf Ahmed and he has his own farm just outside the village."

"I've heard about him. He is an old man and a widower," said Tara Bibi angrily. "How can you agree to this marriage without telling me?"

"You are already 24 years old," her mother pointed out. "I was married when I was 17. There is no other eligible man in the village of Ghanswara. All the suitable boys are already married or they live away from home."

"But I don't want to marry Rauf. He is an old man," Tara Bibi objected.

"He is only 40," replied her mother.

"He also has two children," said Tara Bibi. "I don't want to be their mother. I don't want to marry Rauf," she repeated.

"This is the best proposal you will ever get and your very last chance to get married at all," answered her mother.

"How did you hear about Rauf Ahmed?" asked Tara Bibi.

"The go-between came to see me a week ago. I discussed it with your father and we both agreed that this was the best possible future you could have here in the village."

"Ghanswara is just a small backwater," answered Tara Bibi. "I don't want to spend the rest of my life here. Couldn't you find someone for me in Aligarh?"

"We tried, we really did," her mother said. "It is ten years since we left the city of Aligarh. You were 14 then, when your father became head teacher in the school here. There aren't many people we can mix with socially in Ghanswara."

"Don't I know it!" Tara Bibi burst out. "Those village people don't have any other interests apart from their goats and their buffaloes and their cows and their hens. They still think of us as outsiders."

There was the sound of the house door opening and a moment later Tara Bibi's father entered the room. "What's the matter? You both seem to be very upset about something," he remarked.

"Our daughter doesn't want to marry Rauf Ahmed, the man the go-between found for her," answered Tara Bibi's mother.

Tara Bibi's father sat down and turned to Tara Bibi. "We've thought a lot about this," he told her. "Rauf Ahmed comes from a good family and we have already given them our word of honor that you will marry him."

"He's too old. He also has two children. I don't want to

marry him," came the reply.

"Rauf Ahmed is a most suitable match for you," said Tara Bibi's father. "The wedding date has been set and that's when you'll become his wife. No more arguments!"

Tara Bibi and her mother burst into tears. Her father stormed out of the house and went to see the go-between who had recommended the widower to them.

"We are only thinking of our daughter's future," Tara Bibi's father told the go-between. He had already described Tara Bibi's attitude to her forthcoming marriage. The go-between sighed.

"Perhaps you might have mentioned it to her before making a final decision on her behalf," she murmured. "However, I will see what I can do. Please ask her to come and see me."

When Tara Bibi's father returned home, Tara Bibi was in the kitchen silently helping her mother to start preparations for the evening meal. The eyes of both women were red.

"The go-between wants to speak to Tara Bibi now," he announced. Tara Bibi scowled.

"Go and see what she has to say to you," suggested her mother. "We both only want the best for you."

Tara Bibi washed her face, brushed her hair, and tidied her clothes. To her surprise, her mother joined her as she was leaving the house. Both women remained silent during the short walk to the go-between's house. The go-between opened her door with a smile.

"Tell my daughter that she must marry the man of our choice," Tara Bibi's mother burst out to the go-between. "Make her realize how important it is both for herself and for our family honor that she marries him."

"I need to speak to the girl alone and in complete privacy," came the reply. "Come inside, Tara Bibi, and have a cup of tea."

Tara Bibi was sitting on the sofa looking sullen when the go-between entered the reception room bringing tea and biscuits.

"It's not good when someone is forced to marry," the go-between told her. "It's not Islamic."

Tara Bibi looked at her in astonishment.

"Now, answer my question clearly," the go-between went on. "Do you want to marry Rauf Ahmed?"

"He's too old and I don't want to become the mother of his two children," muttered Tara Bibi sulkily.

"When you make your marriage vows the Qazi will ask you the same question three times. Each time you must answer loudly and clearly, 'Yes' or 'No.' Don't say more than that."

Tara Bibi's eyes lit up as she began to realize what the go-between was telling her.

"I will ask you again," said the go-between. "Do you wish to marry Rauf Ahmed?"

"No," answered Tara Bibi in a clear voice.

The go-between repeated the question two more times. Each time Tara Bibi gave the same reply.

"Now I will go with you and tell your parents to prepare for your wedding," said the go-between finally.

Tara Bibi's eyes widened in alarm. "Must I still go through with this?" she gasped.

"Your parents agreed to the proposal from the bridegroom's family and they must keep their word," answered the go-between. "It is a matter of honor. However," she added, "when you make your marriage vows you will be in a separate room together with the Qazi and me and a lawyer and two witnesses. When the Qazi asks you this question, you must give the same answer three times in a loud clear voice."

"I understand what you are saying," answered Tara Bibi.

"I must advise you to think very carefully about your reply to the Qazi's question," warned the go-between. "If you say 'no' to him, then it will be practically impossible to find another man for you later."

Soon afterward news went round the village of Tara Bibi's forthcoming wedding. During the early evening of the wedding day, loud drums announced the coming of the bridegroom. Many people lined the street to watch the wedding procession passing through the village. It was led by the bridegroom riding on horseback. The night was warm. The wedding guests were assembled in the men's and women's tents, sitting on the floor, which had been covered with white sheets.

The Qazi proceeded to the women's tent together with a lawyer and two witnesses to perform the wedding ceremony. The go-between led them to a small room, where Tara Bibi was sitting alone wearing her red wedding dress with her head covered, the anger in her eyes completely hidden by the veil over her face. The Qazi, the lawyer, the two witnesses and the go-between seated themselves on the floor near the bride.

"Do you take Rauf Ahmed to be your wedded husband of your own free will?" asked the Qazi loudly and clearly, looking directly at Tara Bibi. The go-between leaned forward and repeated the Qazi's question clearly in the bride's ear.

"No," answered Tara Bibi firmly in a loud, clear voice.

The Qazi, the witnesses, and the lawyer looked at each other in surprise. Then the Qazi and the go-between repeated the same question two more times. Each time Tara Bibi gave the same reply. When they had finished, the Qazi turned to the others in the room.

"Did you all hear the bride's reply to my question?" he

asked them. "She said 'No' three times loudly and clearly." All four people nodded in agreement.

The Qazi and the witnesses left the room, went to the men's tent, and climbed on to the stage at the far end, where the bridegroom was already sitting alone facing a large audience of wedding guests and relatives. The Qazi called for silence. "I have an important announcement to make," he said. "I am unable to issue a certificate of marriage for this wedding."

A hush fell. "Why, what has happened?" asked Tara Bibi's father. "What's wrong?"

"I asked the bride three times whether she would take the bridegroom of her own free will to be her wedded husband," the Qazi answered. "Each time, she answered 'No' loudly and clearly. These three people will confirm what I am saying."

The lawyer and the two witnesses nodded in agreement.

A collective gasp of astonishment rose up from the wedding guests. Then everyone rose and left the tent, murmuring quietly to each other. Tara Bibi's father had seated himself on the edge of the stage and was holding his head in his hands in shame. Meanwhile the go-between went to the people sitting in the ladies' tent and informed them that the bride had refused to make her marriage vows and the wedding had been called off.

Tara Bibi's mother gave a loud shriek and then, closely followed by the go-between, she rushed into the room where her daughter was sitting, still veiled, her face in her hands, sobbing quietly.

"What's this nonsense I hear?" shouted Tara Bibi's mother angrily. "Why are you bringing shame on your family by refusing to marry Rauf Ahmed?"

"I don't wish to marry him," answered Tara Bibi.

"Who do you think will marry you now?" her mother went on.

"Leave her alone with me," said the go-between. "I will speak with her."

"I don't know what you think you can do," Tara Bibi's mother replied and left, checking herself just in time to not slam the door.

"There are some ladies I want you to meet," the go-between said to Tara Bibi when they were alone. "I'll bring them here."

When the go-between returned with two ladies, Tara Bibi recognized the older one, who lived in Ghanswara.

"This is my niece," the older lady said, indicating her companion, who was wearing silk clothes in various shades of blue. "They call her the Blue Silk Lady. She visits Ujjain and the surrounding villages with her husband to sell cloth to the ladies living there."

"I don't only sell cloth," said the Blue Silk Lady. "I also bring news from outside to the ladies I meet and they in turn tell me what is happening in their localities. I am going to Ujjain shortly. Maybe I can find someone suitable for you there."

Tara Bibi looked up and pushed back her veil. "What sort of place is Ujjain?" she asked.

"Ujjain was once the capital of the whole of India," replied the Blue Silk Lady. "It is about 1,500 feet above sea level at the center of the Malwa Plateau and on the right hand bank of the river Shipra. It is ruled by the Maharajah of Gwalior state."

"We used to live in Aligarh," said Tara Bibi wistfully. "It's a beautiful city. I miss it."

"I'll come and see you when I have been to Ujjain," the Blue Silk Lady said. "Perhaps I will have some news for you then."

Tara Bibi nodded. "I look forward to seeing you."

Later the go-between stood a little apart together with the Blue Silk Lady and her aunt.

"I know of someone who might wish to marry the bridegroom," said the Blue Silk Lady quietly.

"Who is that?" asked her aunt.

"She is a young widow with a small child whose husband was mauled to death by a tiger some months ago in the jungle."

"Let me know if she is interested and I will see what I can do," said the go-between.

About a week later the Blue Silk Lady and her husband were in Mirzawari, a self-contained Muslim locality in Ujjain. She had passed through an Elephant Gate into Arithewaley, the Lawyers' Den, where six houses surrounded and faced on to an inner courtyard. Lawyers, solicitors, a rent collector, an estate manager, and a businessman lived there with their families.

The ladies from their families and families of similar standing were addressed according to their social status. Ladies from an upper class background were addressed as "Mrs.," whereas lower-ranking ladies were simply known by their first names. In the summer, the ladies would gather in the inner courtyard and sit on string beds, known as *charpoys,* to gossip and tell stories. This was called "*charpoy* chatter." They always welcomed the Blue Silk Lady with her silks, cottons, and news from other localities.

"Something most unusual happened recently in the village of Ghanswara," the Blue Silk Lady said as she set out her cloth samples. Mrs. Adiba Hassan, her mother, Mrs. Waheeda Begum; the Rent Collector's wife Kismet; and Kausar, a widow, examined the brightly colored pieces of material. "Tell us about it," urged Mrs. Waheeda Begum, looking up from the pale patterned cotton in her hand.

"Last week I went with my aunt to a wedding in Ghanswara," the Blue Silk Lady began.

"Who was getting married?" asked Kismet.

"The girl was 24 years old. She was also educated, intelligent, and very outspoken. Her family originally came from Aligarh so they were outsiders in the village. Her father is the head teacher at the school in Ghanswara."

"What happened at the wedding?" asked Mrs. Adiba Hassan.

"When the girl was asked to make her wedding vows, she said 'No' three times before the Qazi, two witnesses, a lawyer, and the go-between. The Qazi refused to issue a marriage certificate."

There was a stunned silence. "Why on earth did she refuse to marry?" asked Mrs. Waheeda Begum.

"The man was 40 and a widower with two children."

"A girl cannot be forced to marry against her wishes," said Mrs. Waheeda Begum sympathetically.

"She was an outsider," commented Kismet, "That was the problem."

"She was also intelligent and she knew her own mind," added Mrs. Adiba Hassan.

"Tara Bibi sounds like a really interesting person," Kausar mused.

"I'd love to meet her," remarked Kismet.

"My brother-in-law is coming here soon from Bhopal," said Mrs. Adiba Hassan. "He works in a government office there. He is about 30 years old and has never married. His father left him a bungalow in Mirzawari, Ujjain, and he hopes to settle down here. Perhaps Tara Bibi might agree to marry him and come and live in Ujjain."

"Let's talk to him first and see what he says," suggested Mrs. Waheeda Begum.

Mrs. Adiba Hassan's brother-in-law, Tara Bibi, and the families on both sides agreed to the match. The wedding took place in Ghanswara and was a quiet affair with few guests. Tara Bibi joined her new husband in Mirzawari, where she quickly made many friends among the local ladies. Some months later Tara Bibi's parents returned to Aligarh for good.

Tara Bibi's husband tried unsuccessfully for many months to find work in Ujjain. The money from his inheritance was running low. Three years after the Second World War started, Tara Bibi's husband joined the Bhopal regiment to fight on the war front. Tara Bibi felt lonely in the bungalow without him. Mrs. Adiba Hassan regularly invited her to visit her house in the Lawyers' Den, and Tara Bibi gradually became friends with some of the other ladies there.

As the Second World War continued, rumors quickly spread around Ujjain that wheat would be taken away for the armies, which would lead to wheat shortages. People began to buy up wheat and hoard it. Later, it was rumored that hoarded wheat would be confiscated and all hoarders jailed.

Kamal Hammal had started life in Gharib Colony, where poor people lived. His first job was carrying sacks of goods on his back. He became rich and successful and, like others, bought up and hoarded wheat when the rumors of possible wheat shortages started. His son was a full-time student at a local college and engaged to be married. Kamal Hammal made arrangements for his son to get married as soon as possible, in order to use up all his hoarded wheat for a wedding feast. This would prevent his wheat from being confiscated.

Before the wedding, two men with drums walked all around Gharib Colony. From time to time they stopped in the road, loudly beating their drums, and made the following announcement:

"Kamal Hammal's son is getting married next Sunday. Everyone in Gharib Colony is invited to the wedding feast. No one is to do any cooking on that day. Kamal Hammal Sahib does not want to see any smoke coming from any dwellings in Gharib Colony on that day. If anyone is unable to come to the wedding feast, let them send someone along to collect food for them."

That Sunday, no one in Gharib Colony did any cooking. Many people attended the wedding feast of Kamal Hammal's son and many men collected food for the ladies, children, and old people who were unable to be there.

When Prabhakar Sahib, the Governor of Ujjain, learned about the feast, he introduced food rationing, effective immediately. Police officers conducted searches for private hoards of wheat, which were then confiscated.

A black market in wheat started up. One day, two military men with a truck waited on the side of the main road outside Qazi Masjid and stopped an ox cart carrying brown wheat that was being driven by a *dhoti*-clad driver. "Your wheat will feed the hungry soldiers fighting for peace," they told the driver as they quickly loaded the wheat into their truck and drove off, leaving him wiping his tears away with one end of the white *safah* on his head.

Food rationing also forced families wishing to arrange marriages for their eligible sons and daughters to put their plans on hold. Everyone, even the richest and most influential people in Mirzawari, had to obtain permission from the Governor of Ujjain before they could invite people to attend feasts. A limit was set to the number of guests. Meat was a status symbol for both hosts and guests and was always served on special occasions in Muslim society, particularly at weddings.

- - - - - - - - - - - - - -

Toward the end of the Second World War, the rules governing food rationing were relaxed. This made it possible for families to think once again about arranging marriages. However it was still necessary to get the Governor's permission before giving a feast. There were also still restrictions on the number of guests that could be invited to a feast and food shortages meant that it was only possible to serve a limited number of dishes.

Tara Bibi awaited with anticipation the return of her husband from the front line. One afternoon she was sitting in her drawing room with Mrs. Waheeda Begum and her daughter Mrs. Adiba Hassan drinking tea when there was a loud knock at her front door. She raised her eyebrows in surprise and slowly rose from her seat. Her two guests also got up and followed her to the front door.

Tara Bibi opened the door a crack and peered out. Two tall military men in uniform were standing on her doorstep with a small boy in front of them. Tara Bibi backed away. "There are two soldiers here," she told Mrs. Waheeda Begum. "Can you talk to them?"

Mrs. Waheeda Begum moved forward and looked out the door. "What do you want?" she asked the men.

"We have a telegram for Tara Bibi," said one of them. "It comes directly from the War Office and is written in English."

"What does it say?" Mrs. Waheeda Begum asked. "Tara Bibi is here standing next to me."

The military man opened the envelope and translated the telegram into Urdu: "We regret to inform you that while traveling to Paris by train from the German front line your husband fell ill with a very high fever and died. He has been buried in a cemetery near Paris." He handed the telegram over to Mrs. Waheeda Begum and both men turned and left.

Tara Bibi stood there stunned with a hand to her mouth. Mrs. Adiba Hassan put her arms around her and helped her to her bed. At first, Tara Bibi was completely numb with shock. Then she began to wail and scream as the grief of her loss overwhelmed her. She started shivering as she realized that she now faced life without her husband at her side.

"What will happen to my life now?" asked Tara Bibi when the first shock of her grief had subsided somewhat.

"We are here for you," said Mrs. Waheeda Begum. "We will support you in any way we can."

"Come back with us now and stay in my house," said Mrs. Adiba Hassan gently.

For the next two weeks Tara Bibi stayed with Mrs. Adiba Hassan as she struggled to come to terms with the loss of her husband.

- - - - - - - - - - - - - - - -

Mrs. Adiba Hassan, Mrs. Waheeda Begum, and Tara Bibi had just had lunch and were sitting in the reception room drinking tea. "Tara Bibi, we are worried about what will happen to you when you leave us to return to your bungalow," said Mrs. Waheeda Begum.

"I still have a little money from my husband's savings," Tara Bibi answered.

"We will give you financial help," Mrs. Adiba Hassan put in. "After all, you are part of our family."

"I don't like to ask for help," stated Tara Bibi. "I will find some way of earning money."

Mrs. Waheeda Begum and Mrs. Adiba Hassan frowned and exchanged glances.

"I will speak to my husband tonight," said Mrs. Adiba Hassan quietly to her mother.

"Tara Bibi is very strong-willed and is determined not to be a burden on us," Mrs. Adiba Hassan told her husband later. Waqar Hassan was a solicitor and came across a wide variety of people in his work.

"From time to time, my brother, Police Inspector Afaq

Hassan, has cases where a woman's help is needed," said Waqar Hassan. "I will ask him to let us know more."

The following day, Waqar Hassan invited his brother for the evening meal with his family. Afterward, they joined his wife and Tara Bibi in the reception room to drink tea. "Would you be prepared to let part of your bungalow to earn some income?" Inspector Afaq Hassan asked Tara Bibi.

"I don't think I want to have strangers sharing my home," answered Tara Bibi.

"This is an extremely delicate matter," Inspector Afaq Hassan told her.

Tara Bibi looked interested. "Tell me more."

"I need to find secret accommodation for a woman from Gharib Colony. She is a witness against her husband in a murder case," came the reply. "Her husband has threatened to beat her up and kill her." Tara Bibi's eyes widened.

"This woman will be under police protection. A plainclothes policeman will be standing guard 24 hours a day. You will be paid well if you agree to let her have part of your bungalow."

Tara Bibi thought for a moment. She certainly needed to have some sort of steady income. "All right, the woman can come and stay with me," she said at last.

From that time onward, Tara Bibi obtained a regular income by providing part of her bungalow as a secret refuge for vulnerable women and girls under police protection.

One day there was a knock at Tara Bibi's door. When she opened it, two women were standing there. The older woman was sturdily built and plainly dressed. The younger woman's clothes were torn and crumpled and there were bruises on her face and arms.

"What has happened?" asked Tara Bibi with concern.

"This woman's husband has been beating her," the older woman replied. "It happens occasionally in Gharib Colony. Police Inspector Afaq Hassan sent us here"

"Come in," said Tara Bibi, and stood back to let both women enter.

"You're not from around here," the older woman remarked.

"No, I'm from Ghanswara. It's a village outside Ujjain." There was an unmistakable hint of a village accent when Tara Bibi spoke.

The older lady sized her up shrewdly. Then she smiled. "My name is Khatoon Bibi."

Over tea and biscuits Tara Bibi learned more about her visitors. They lived in Gharib Colony, a large area of small mud houses mainly inhabited by poor people. Khatoon Bibi was a widow and a go-between and also did voluntary social work among the women and children in Gharib Colony. She was sturdily built, had a determined personality, and worked part-time as a nurse in a hospital. The other woman needed to have somewhere to stay while she recovered from the effects of her husband's ill treatment. "You will be safe here," Khatoon Bibi told the other lady before she left. "Tara Bibi will look after you. I will come regularly to change the dressings on your wounds."

- -

Tara Bibi soon found that she and Khatoon Bibi shared a common interest in bringing people together and helping them to find happiness. People at higher social levels with unmarried daughters who were well-educated had few possibilities of finding men with a similar background. The girls from the well off families were educated locally, but the boys went overseas or away from home to Aligarh University for their higher education. The boys preferred marrying girls less well educated than themselves, so that they could have better control over them. In domestic arguments particularly, the boys always wanted to win or they felt insulted. The ladies in Mirzawari began to turn to Tara Bibi for help and advice on finding suitable partners for their eligible relatives who wished to get married. Gradually, she became known as a matchmaker and a go-between. When acting on people's behalf, Tara Bibi was always discreet in following the instructions she had been given. She soon became very knowledgeable on all family matters concerning the people in Mirzawari.

Tara Bibi had received a good education in Aligarh during the years she had spent there before moving to Ghanswara. She began to join the Mirzawari ladies for evenings of reading poetry or telling stories from the Arabian Nights. The drama classes she had attended in Aligarh had brought out her ability to copy the accents of upper class and working class people. This meant that she was able to move freely between all levels of society.

One day, Tara Bibi came to visit Mrs. Adiba Hassan and found her sitting with Kismet, Kausar, and Mrs. Waheeda Begum on *charpoys* in the courtyard of the Lawyers' Den.

"The Blue Silk Lady has been to visit us recently," said Kausar. "Mrs. Delara Begum has been buying cloth for wedding clothes for her daughter Shabnum."

"I have heard of Mrs. Delara Begum," remarked Tara Bibi. "Her husband is a rich landlord and they live in a large two-story house in one corner of Mirzawari."

"Her husband, Mirza Sahib, is highly respected by people at all social levels," Kismet put in. "Mrs. Delara Begum is well-informed and very upper class."

"I don't believe I've met her," said Tara Bibi. "How many children do they have?"

"Shabnum is their only child," answered Mrs. Adiba Hassan. "She is 20 years old. She is tall, beautiful, and elegant, with fair skin and long black hair. She teaches English part-time in the local girls' school and can also read and write French and Persian. In her free time, she meets other educated, wealthy young ladies like herself. She also goes horseback riding whenever she visits her uncle's country house."

"Who is her husband-to-be?" asked Tara Bibi.

"They have been making inquiries about my grandson Akhtar," Mrs. Waheeda Begum replied. "He is the eldest son of my son Shakil Sahib, the lawyer, and he has recently graduated. His parents would like you to convey their reply to Shabnum's parents."

Chapter 2: Shabnum's Wedding

Mrs. Delara Begum and her husband Mirza Sahib were sitting in the reception room after their evening meal drinking tea.

"How will we ever find a suitable husband for Shabnum?" There was despair in Mrs. Delara Begum's voice. "There are very few matches for her here in Ujjain."

"What's happened?" asked Mirza Sahib.

"The go-between Tara Bibi came to see me today with a message from Shakil Sahib and his wife Mrs. Farah Begum. Their son Akhtar is already engaged to another girl.

Mirza Sahib stroked his chin thoughtfully. "The families I meet through my work as a landlord are mainly farmers or small businessmen," he said. "None of their boys would really be a suitable match for our daughter."

The servant opened the door. "Talib Sahib and Mehboob the Messenger are here to see you," he announced.

"Show Talib Sahib in and send Mehboob to the servants' quarters," said Mirza Sahib. "Then bring more tea."

Talib Sahib was Mrs. Delara Begum's younger brother and worked as a lawyer in Ujjain. He lived some distance from Mirzawari in a large bungalow next to a main road. Beautiful trees lined the road on either side and it was always crowded with *tongas* carrying lawyers, solicitors, and clients, as it led to the only courthouse in Ujjain, which was outside the town,.

"These landlords," sighed Talib Sahib as Mrs. Delara Begum handed him a cup of tea. "All that land on the hill farms and they still have border disputes. I have just had such a case."

"Did you manage to persuade them to reach an agreement?" asked Mrs. Delara Begum.

"Yes, eventually," replied Talib Sahib. "Another lawyer and I were mediating. We told both parties that this matter would be much less costly if they settled out of court."

"We are trying to find a suitable husband for Shabnum," said Mrs. Delara Begum. "There's simply nobody for her here in Ujjain."

"My client Ahmed Ali Sahib has an unmarried son," her brother replied. "Shandar Ali is 28 years old, with a degree from Aligarh University, and an only son. He takes an active part in his father's business. Ahmed Ali Sahib also owns several properties in Daulatpur, which is the small town near his estate. I happen to know that he is looking for a suitable bride for his son."

"Shandar sounds very suitable," Mrs. Delara Begum remarked. "Could you speak to his father about our Shabnum?"

The following day Talib Sahib sent a message through Mehboob to arrange a meeting with Ahmed Ali Sahib regarding a possible match for his son. After discussion with their son, Shandar's parents invited Talib Sahib to come and see them. Following a favorable report from Talib Sahib, Mrs. Delara Begum went upstairs to see Shabnum .

When her mother entered her room, Shabnum was reading a book. "Your uncle Talib Sahib is here," said Mrs. Delara Begum.

"He has brought news of a suitable match for you. His name is Shandar Ali. He is 28 years old, unmarried, very tall and handsome, and is also well educated like you."

Shabnum lowered her eyes. A faint blush stole into her cheeks. "What does father say?"

"He will make the arrangements for your wedding if you agree."

"If you and father think he is suitable, then I agree," said Shabnum.

"Shabnum has agreed to marry Shandar," Mrs. Delara Begum announced when she rejoined Mirza Sahib and Talib Sahib.

In due course Mehboob delivered a letter from Mirza Sahib to Ahmed Ali Sahib suggesting a date for the engagement and wedding of Shandar and Shabnum and the proposed number of wedding guests to be invited by each side of the family. That same evening, Mehboob brought back a written reply from Shandar's father agreeing to all Mirza Sahib's suggestions. Due to food rationing restrictions, the number of guests at any one feast was limited. Wedding celebrations therefore continued for three days to enable the hosts to invite all their close friends and relatives.

On receiving the letter from Ahmed Ali Sahib, Mrs. Delara Begum, Mirza Sahib, and a couple of older relatives drew up a guest list for their side of the family. Mirza Sahib then sent a servant to ask Halim Nawaz, a teacher well-known for his neat Urdu handwriting, to write out the wedding invitations on behalf of his family.

"Let us also pay for weddings for two other couples, who are too poor to pay for themselves," Mirza Sahib told his wife.

"I will ask Tara Bibi, the matchmaker, to find us two poor couples prepared to get married at the same time as Shabnum," Mrs. Delara Begum answered.

The following day, Tara Bibi was shown into the reception room where Mirza Sahib and his wife were seated. Mrs. Delara Begum invited her to take tea.

"Our Shabnum's wedding will take place shortly," said Mrs. Delara Begum. "We also wish to bring happiness to two other couples who can't afford to marry. Can you find two such couples?"

"I will pay for all their wedding expenses," Mirza Sahib added, "and they may also invite some guests to join our guests for a wedding feast."

"That is a very generous offer," replied Tara Bibi. "I will have no difficulty in finding two such couples."

- - - - - - - - - - - - - - - - - - - -

The following morning, Tara Bibi took a *tonga* to the house of her friend Khatoon Bibi in Gharib Colony, a locality of mud houses in which poor people lived. Khatoon Bibi was an old lady and, like Tara Bibi, a widow and a go-between. She welcomed her friend with pleasure.

"I have been to Mirza Sahib's residence," said Tara Bibi. "His daughter Shabnum is getting married next month."

"What sort of man is her husband-to-be?"

Tara Bibi described him in detail.

"Mirza Sahib has also asked me to find two couples too poor to pay for a wedding," she added. "They will marry on the same day as his daughter. He will pay for all their wedding expenses including their silk wedding clothes and will even invite some of their relatives to join his own guests for the wedding feast afterward."

"That is very generous," said Khatoon Bibi. She thought for a moment. "I know two suitable couples," she said at last. "They both live quite near here."

"Tell me about them," said Tara Bibi.

"One girl is named Hasina. She is 17 years old. She can read and write Urdu and she is very pretty. Her father died in an accident and her widowed mother Fatima is unable to save enough money for her wedding as she only works part-time in the evenings. The girl's husband-to-be is named Samosa Khan. He is 18 years old and sells home-made *samosas* at the local market. His mother is a good cook but her health is poor and it will be a help to her if her son can get married. His father only works occasionally, earns very little, and mostly stays at home."

"What about the other couple?"

"Murad, the boy, is 22 years old and works in a cloth mill. He has to support his widowed mother, two younger brothers, and a sister. They live in a three-room house. One room has been reserved for Murad and his wife-to-be, Shakuri. She is 23 years old and the eldest of three sisters. Her father is unemployed and her mother washes dishes part-time in a local restaurant."

"Let us go and see both couples now," said Tara Bibi.

First they visited the widow Fatima, who invited them inside. "Hasina!" she called to her daughter in the next room. "Bring two glasses of water for our guests and put the kettle on." Then Fatima spread a white sheet on the floor and asked her visitors to be seated.

"We have good news for you," said Khatoon Bibi. "Your daughter's wedding can now take place."

"How is this possible?" asked the widow Fatima in surprise.

Tara Bibi told her of Mirza Sahib's offer to pay all wedding expenses for two couples. "He will pay for Hasina's wedding clothes and those of her husband-to-be and you can also invite some guests to the wedding," she added. "It will be on the same day as the wedding of Mirza Sahib's daughter."

"This is most generous," Fatima replied, struggling to keep back her tears of joy. "We are very grateful."

After Tara Bibi had measured Hasina for her wedding clothes, she and Khatoon Bibi went to visit Samosa Khan. He was not at home, but both his parents were there. They immediately accepted Mirza Sahib's offer. "We are so happy," his mother kept saying. "I have been praying to God for my son's wedding."

"*Allah mehrbaan ho to chhapper phaad kay daita hai* -- When God is kind, He will open your roof and shower you with gifts," said Khatoon Bibi.

"May I measure your son's clothes so that the tailor can make his wedding outfit?" asked Tara Bibi.

"Yes, of course you can," said Samosa Khan's mother. She quickly took out Samosa Khan's *Eid* clothes and laid them on a sheet on the ground.

The families of the second couple, Murad and Shakuri, were equally delighted to accept Mirza Sahib's generous offer. After taking the measurements for Murad's and Shakuri's wedding clothes, Tara Bibi left Gharib Colony. Later she gave the measurements to Mrs. Delara Begum at Mirza Sahib's residence and returned home.

- - - - - - - - - - - - - - - - - - - -

That evening, when Samosa Khan returned home, there was uproar.

"You agreed to my wedding without asking me!" he shouted angrily.

"Mirza Sahib is paying all wedding expenses including wedding clothes," said his mother.

"There will be a fine wedding feast," his father added, rubbing his belly. "You can bring your friends and family and eat as much as you like."

"I don't want to marry Hasina," Samosa Khan burst out. "I am fed up with selling *samosas*. There is no respect in such work."

"What do you want to do, son?" asked his mother quietly.

"I want to work with my uncle on the farm," replied Samosa Khan, calming down slightly.

"You can take Hasina with you to your uncle's farm after marriage," his mother pointed out.

"No, I don't want to marry Hasina," said Samosa Khan firmly. "She can read and write and I can't. I will marry Kulsum. She works on the farm."

"Tell us, Samosa, who is Kulsum?" asked his father. He looked grim.

"Don't call me Samosa," his son answered angrily. "I don't like this name. My name is not Samosa. I will never sell *samosas* again. Kulsum wants to call me Shikari -- the hunter -- so this will be my new name."

His father laughed. "Look at you, *haath paer agarbatti, munh mombatti* -- hands like sticks, face like a candle stump."

"Tell Hasina's mother I won't marry her daughter," shouted Samosa Khan. "Tell her that this Shikari is leaving Ujjain to work on a farm."

"Shame on you, Samosa," cried his mother. "I always thought you liked my *samosas*. You have been eating them since you were small. You used to crawl into the kitchen when I was sitting by the clay stove making *samosas*, pull my *dupatta*, and point at the *samosa* in my hand. The first word you spoke was 'samosa.' Get out of my sight!" She drew her *dupatta* over her head, covered her face and started to cry. "I will never be able to show my face in front of the neighbors again."

"I will go to the farm tomorrow," muttered Samosa Khan.

The next day Samosa Khan's mother, her face swollen with weeping, went to visit Hasina's mother.

"Why have you been crying?" asked the widow Fatima.

"It's our son, Samosa Khan. He says he no longer wishes to marry Hasina and he's gone away to his uncle's farm to wed some village girl."

Hasina came to stand behind the inner door and overheard Samosa Khan's mother. She slipped away to her room. "Why doesn't Samosa want to marry me?" she wondered, throwing herself on to her bed and starting to cry quietly.

"Who will want Hasina now when people learn that her husband-to-be has left Ujjain rather than marry her?" asked the widow Fatima in despair.

Samosa Khan's mother hung her head. "I have to see Khatoon Bibi," she said.

- - - - - - - - - - - - - - - - - - - -

"This is bad," said Khatoon Bibi when Samosa Khan's mother had finished speaking. "Let me think what to do. Hasina doesn't deserve to suffer. I will go and speak to the widow Fatima."

Later, Khatoon Bibi visited Tara Bibi to discuss this new development.

"I will inform Mirza Sahib immediately," said Tara Bibi.

Dusk was falling when Tara Bibi arrived at Mirza Sahib's residence, so Mrs. Delara Begum invited her to stay overnight. Later, Tara Bibi sat in the lounge, drinking tea, with Mrs. Delara Begum and her brother Talib Sahib. She had informed them of how Hasina's hopes of marriage had been dashed. "She is only 17 years old and very pretty," said Tara Bibi. "She can even read and write Urdu." Everyone sat in silence looking thoughtful.

"I think I know someone suitable," said Talib Sahib at last.

"Who?" asked the two ladies.

"My messenger Mehboob," came the reply. "He is unmarried. He's a good worker, most reliable, and he can also read and write Urdu."

"Please tell me about Mehboob," said Tara Bibi. "I don't want Hasina and her mother to be disappointed once again."

Talib Sahib related the details of Mehboob's background. The ladies were impressed by the way in which he had taken every opportunity to better himself.

"How old is Mehboob now?" asked Tara Bibi.

"He's about 18, of medium build and dark skinned," replied Talib Sahib. His father was a good storyteller and was often invited by a retired lawyer, Yousuf Ali Sahib, to gatherings in his bungalow to tell stories. This lawyer recommended Mehboob to me as my messenger. Mehboob lives in my servants' quarters and he may also take a wife there to live with him if he marries."

"I should like to go and see him now," said Tara Bibi.

"Let's both go and talk to him," said Talib Sahib.

"Bring him here and give him tea," said Mrs. Delara Begum.

Tara Bibi and Talib Sahib found Mehboob in the servants' quarters telling a story surrounded by all the household staff.

"Mehboob always creates a lively atmosphere wherever he goes," remarked Talib Sahib.

Everyone gaped in amazement when they saw Talib Sahib with Tara Bibi, aware, that as a matchmaker, her presence meant one thing. "Come with us," said Talib Sahib to Mehboob. "Tara Bibi has good news for you." An awed silence fell in the room behind them as they left.

Mehboob was wearing a colorful shirt and white *shalwar* and looked very smart when he entered the lounge with Tara Bibi and Talib Sahib. Delara Begum invited him to be seated and handed him a cup of tea.

"If you agree, I would like to arrange your marriage for you," said Tara Bibi.

Mehboob was speechless.

"There's a 17-year-old girl named Hasina and she is very pretty," Tara Bibi continued. "She can read and write Urdu. This will be a good marriage for you. If you agree, all wedding expenses, including the wedding clothes for you and your bride-to-be, will be paid for by Mirza Sahib. You will be married on the same day as his daughter Shabnum."

"Drink your tea and think about it. Take your time," said Talib Sahib.

Mehboob took a gulp of tea. A wide grin spread over his face. "I don't need time to think about this! I am very happy to accept," he said.

"I must go to Hasina and her mother next and see what they say," said Tara Bibi. "However, I am sure they will be pleased to accept you as Hasina's husband-to-be. I will return tomorrow and measure you for your wedding clothes."

"Kausar, Patwari Sahib's sister, has been like a mother to me for many years," said Mehboob. "Her two sons are like my brothers and they live in Arithewaley with Patwari Sahib and his family. If Hasina's mother accepts me as her future son-in-law, I should like my adopted mother Kausar to meet my future bride."

"I will take her with me to meet Hasina and her mother before the wedding," Tara Bibi promised.

"You can also invite Kausar and her sons to your wedding," said Delara Begum.

"Now you have another good story to tell," said Talib

Sahib with a smile as Mehboob left the room.

Early the next day, Tara Bibi went with Kausar to visit Khatoon Bibi and tell her about the new bridegroom she had found for Hasina. Khatoon Bibi immediately took both ladies to call on the widow Fatima and her daughter Hasina. The widow Fatima's face was pale and she had dark shadows under her eyes.

"We've heard about another boy who'd be pleased to marry your daughter," Tara Bibi told her.

"Who's that?"

"Mehboob, messenger to Talib Sahib the lawyer. He'll be happy to marry your daughter if you agree."

"Tell me about him," said the widow Fatima, brightening up. Hasina crept up behind the inner door to listen.

"Mehboob is the son of a storyteller. His father died when Mehboob was eight years old and his mother passed away a year later. Then his aunt took him in. From the age of 12, he worked full-time for a family with two sons -- shopping, washing clothes, and other domestic duties. He is a very intelligent and hard-working boy. When the family had to leave Ujjain, he got a job as messenger for a young lawyer, Talib Sahib, who is the brother of Mirza Sahib's wife, Mrs. Delara Begum. He is nicely spoken and has learned to read and write Urdu."

"Where would they live after marriage?" asked the widow Fatima.

"Talib Sahib said that Hasina could live with Mehboob in the servants' quarters," Tara Bibi replied.

The widow Fatima turned to Hasina, who had quietly entered the room while Tara Bibi was speaking. "Do you wish to marry this boy?" she asked.

"Yes, I do," answered Hasina.

That evening Tara Bibi went once again to Mirza Sahib's

house and measured Mehboob for his wedding clothes.

- - - - - - - - - - - - - - - - - - - -

Shabnum lay lounging luxuriously in her bed. Such moments would soon be rare when she took on the duties of a wife. The light scent of *agarbatti* lingered in the air. Asma and Salma, her two close friends and fellow teachers at the local girls' school, had arrived the previous evening and were sleeping in the guest bedroom nearby. They had spent the previous evening telling her all the latest gossip from the school and listening to Shabnum's mother's stories about her own wedding.

There was a knock at the door. "Come in!" called Shabnum.

Asma and Salma entered smiling. "We have one week to make you into the most beautiful bride that was ever seen," said Asma.

"Are you ready for your breakfast?" asked Salma.

"I will join you in a moment," replied Shabnum.

After breakfast, the three friends returned to Shabnum's room. Salma laid a white sheet on the floor. Shabnum sat on the sheet leaning back against the pillows heaped by the wall and rolled up her sleeves and the bottoms of her *shalwar* to bare her hands and feet.

Asma took a bowl of *mehndi*, a red dye. "Let me do your hands first," she said to Shabnum. "I will make some really special designs." She dipped her quill into the bowl of *mehndi* and carefully drew rings round the joints of each finger and thumb. Then she drew delicate patterns of dots all over the palms of both hands. "Now I'll do the backs of your hands," said Asma. She drew lines from the fingers to the wrists with small motifs between them to set off the overall pattern.

Then Asma handed the *mehndi* bowl to Salma. "Now I'll give you something from me as well for your wedding," said

Salma.

"Thank you," said Shabnum smiling.

Salma dipped her finger into the *mehndi* and swiftly drew several striking designs on the tops and soles of both feet. Then the friends sat and talked while Shabnum waited for the *mehndi* to dry.

"The patterns have come out really well," said Asma with satisfaction when Shabnum finally washed the dried *mehndi* from her hands and feet.

Three days before the wedding ceremony, the women in Mirza Sahib's house began to prepare *ubtan*. This was a yellow paste, which was freshly made each morning up to and including the wedding day. Salma and Asma helped Shabnum to rub it all over her body each day and then wash it off again, leaving her skin soft, clear, and sweet-smelling.

"You know the custom. I'll have to stay in my bedroom until my wedding day," Shabnum said to her friends. "Let me know what's going on in the rest of the house."

"Don't worry, we'll keep you informed," Salma assured her. "Here are some novels to pass the time."

"You look really pretty in those bright clothes," remarked Asma.

Just then they heard the loud rumbling of wooden wheels, the creaking of carts, and men shouting. "What's going on?" asked Shabnum.

Asma and Salma dashed out of the room to the balcony in front of the house. They looked down over the open ground. Two men were unloading food and cooking utensils from bullock carts. In one corner of the ground three other men were preparing for the coming wedding feast.

"The wedding caterers have arrived," said Salma when she and Asma returned to Shabnum's room.

"Oh yes, Riaz Brothers," said Shabnum. "They cater for most of the weddings around here."

"They provided the food for my sister's wedding," added Asma.

Later that afternoon, Asma and Salma came to Shabnum's room bursting with news.

"He's here! We've seen him! Your bridegroom has arrived," cried Asma.

"He came through the Elephant Gate," said Salma. "He was sitting in a beautifully decorated *victoria* drawn by two horses."

"Did you see his face?" asked Shabnum excitedly.

"No, it was all covered with garlands," answered Salma, smiling at her friend's happiness. "There was another open carriage behind his *victoria* with his parents and relatives in it."

The three friends remained in Shabnum's room while the servants carried the luggage for the bridegroom's party up the outer staircase to the second floor, where they would stay until after the wedding. Later, Asma and Salma went downstairs.

"They are delaying the evening meal a little until your relatives have arrived," Asma reported to Shabnum when they returned carrying trays with tea, snacks, and sweetmeats.

That evening, Mrs. Delara Begum and Tara Bibi sat in the reception room with some of the ladies from the bridegroom's family. They discussed the wedding preparations and Tara Bibi spoke about the two other couples who were marrying at the same time as Shandar and Shabnum.

"Who is the young man with Shandar?" asked Delara Begum.

"That is Akhtar," replied Shandar's mother Mrs. Khadeeja Begum. "He has recently graduated in law and is engaged to be married. He's staying with Shandar until after the wedding. They are old friends. While Shandar was learning about farm management and his father's property business, Akhtar went to Gwalior to study law. He will be joining the law practice of his father Shakil Sahib."

During the next two days leading up to the wedding, Shandar was often seen striding to and fro along the balcony outside his room, his head held high and his hands clasped behind him. He was deeply tanned and looked very smart in a silver silk *sherwani* --a long coat.

- - - - - - - - - - - - - - - - - - - -

Samosa Khan's parents were eating their evening meal when they heard a knock at the door. His father opened it to find Samosa Khan standing outside. "I suppose you'd better come in," he said grudgingly.

"Who is it?" asked his mother. She stared at the sad, bedraggled figure before her. "Why! Samosa, what has happened?"

"It all went wrong on the farm for me," muttered Samosa. Then he started sobbing.

"What happened?" his mother asked.

"Everything was fine at first. They all called me Shikari. Then one day during a break from work I was sitting next to Kulsum a little away from the others." Samosa Khan drew a deep breath. "I asked Kulsum to marry me."

His mother stared at him, astonished. "What did she say?"

"She burst out laughing. 'I am married and I have a five-year-old daughter at home with my mother,' she told me. The others came over and asked what the joke was. 'Shikari has asked me to marry him,' answered Kulsum. Everyone had a big laugh. I left at once. Uncle was angry that I hadn't consulted him before asking Kulsum to marry me. Now I want to sell *samosas* again."

"Well, your father has been selling *samosas* for me since you left. You can start again tomorrow. Oh dear, you have made things difficult for us." His mother shook her head sadly.

The next day, Samosa Khan left the house early to start selling *samosas* as usual. That afternoon, with some trepidation, his mother went to see Khatoon Bibi.

"What do you want?" asked Khatoon Bibi, surprised and angry. "Your son has already made one family very unhappy."

"He is very foolish and has been punished for it," replied Samosa Khan's mother. She could feel herself reddening, but forced herself to look up at Khatoon Bibi and continue, for her son's sake. "He's back home now and selling *samosas* again. Please find out if he can still marry Hasina."

"That's no longer possible," answered Khatoon Bibi, softening a little. "Hasina has found someone else, who is very suitable for her, and they will be marrying on the same day as Mirza Sahib's daughter. Your son will now have to wait until I can find a suitable bride for him."

- -

The preparations for the wedding guests were well underway. Three tents had been erected in front of Mirza Sahib's residence. There was a men's tent with two long dining tables and chairs for Mirza Sahib's special guests. The center seats had been reserved for the three bridegrooms and their close male relatives, as well as the Qazi and his assistant. Behind the men's tent and next to the residence was a smaller tent for the three brides and their close female relatives. Near it was a larger tent for the other ladies and the children.

Two men were busy building fires beneath three large cauldrons for meat *pulao*, meat curry, and *zardah* (sweet rice) on the open ground, a little way from the entrance to the men's tent. Another man was digging a shallow pit for a fire, over which a heavy, large, circular metal *tawa* shaped like an inverted shallow frying pan would be placed to prepare *maandey*, large thin round *chapatis* to be eaten with meat curry.

On the afternoon of the wedding day, the wedding guests from Ujjain started to arrive. Outside the men's tent, long white sheets were being laid out over the open ground for the male guests attending the wedding feast. Mirza Sahib had arranged for three *tongawalas*, Akram and his two friends Jugnu Khan and Hira Lal, to make several trips to Gharib Colony to fetch Hasina, Mehboob's bride-to-be, as well as Murad and Shakuri, the other couple about to be wed, together with their families and friends. Women stood outside their doors and a large crowd of men and boys followed the decorated *tongas* with cheers and laughter, as they drove round Gharib Colony to collect the people attending the weddings.

The widow Fatima, who had no close relatives of her own, had invited her next door neighbor in Gharib Colony to attend the wedding together with her husband Gulzar Khan, a big burly man.

On their arrival, Tara Bibi greeted them. "I want to ask you a favor," she said to Gulzar Khan. "As you know, a wedding feast like this always attracts uninvited guests. The regular security guards at Elephant Gate know everyone in this area. However, they will need your help to stop gatecrashers from Gharib Colony from attending the wedding feast."

"I am a retired security guard and I know everyone in Gharib Colony," replied Gulzar Khan. "I will be very pleased to perform this service."

Mirza Sahib had invited the Governor of Ujjain, Prabhakar Sahib, to attend Shabnum's wedding. However, the Governor was unable to attend due to official business, so he sent his secretary, Mr. D'Silva, to represent him on this auspicious occasion. Mr. D'Silva, was also a personal friend of Shakil Sahib, a lawyer and the son of Mrs. Waheeda Begum from the Lawyers' Den.

Mr. D'Silva arrived in an official *victoria*, its dark blue sides emblazoned in gold with the coat-of-arms of the Maharajah of

Gwalior state. He was immaculately dressed in a black suit, the trousers with knife-edge creases, and highly polished black shoes. Beneath the collar of his white shirt he wore a black tie, which was fitted tightly around his thick neck. Heavy gold cufflinks were visible beneath the sleeves of his jacket. He was middle-aged, short, stocky, and clean shaven with dark brown skin and a very serious expression.

Some small boys clustered round the horse-drawn *victoria* to touch its shiny sides and the gold painted coat-of-arms. They watched in awe as Mr. D'Silva got down from the *victoria*. He stood there, turned his head to the left, and lowered it slightly. Then, grasping his chin with one hand and holding his head with the other hand, he twisted his neck to give a good crack with a sound like someone cracking their knuckles. The boys stared open-mouthed.

Mr. D'Silva gave a small sigh of contentment. Shakil Sahib walked toward him and they shook hands. Then both men slowly made their way toward the men's tent, chatting together. Mr. D'Silva paused just outside the entrance, quickly turned his head to the left, gave his neck a twist to the right and cracked the bones once again, this time without using his hands. Then he moved forward. Deeply impressed by this unusual skill, the boys ran to the ladies' tents to inform them of the exhibition they had just witnessed. Soon after, the sound of laughter was heard coming from the ladies' tents.

Shakil Sahib introduced Mr. D'Silva to the other guests. They all greeted him and he nodded in acknowledgment. Then Mirza Sahib shook hands with Mr. D'Silva and invited him to sit opposite him for dinner, next to Shakil Sahib.

Inside the smaller of the two ladies' tents, the two brides prepared to celebrate their official engagement in the presence of their close female relatives. Shakuri, who was already engaged to her husband-to-be Murad, sat and waited quietly while Tara Bibi brought the two other bridegrooms into the tent one at a time.

Shandar came first, his head and face covered with garlands.

The garlands were made with scented flowers like roses, chambeli (jasmine) and mogra (double chambeli), which filled the room with a beautiful scent. Shabnum, her face also concealed by garlands, was brought in by her mother Mrs. Delara Begum and seated opposite Shandar. Next, Shandar's mother, Mrs. Khadeeja Begum, drew back the garlands over his head. At the same time Mrs. Delara Begum pushed Shabnum's garlands back from her face. Then she draped a white sheet over the heads of both bride and groom. After Shandar and Shabnum had exchanged engagement rings, Shandar removed the sheet and left the tent. The same ceremony was then repeated by Mehboob and Hasina. Their wedding garlands were pushed back by Mehboob's adopted mother Kausar and the widow Fatima.

Tara Bibi slipped out of the brides' tent and peered round the curtain at the back of the men's tent. "Mirza Sahib," she called quietly. "Please ask the Qazi to wait. One of the brides is not yet ready. I'll let you know when she has finished."

A few minutes later, a three-year-old boy entered the tent, went up to Mirza Sahib, and said something.

"I can't hear you," said Mirza Sahib. "Please be quiet," he requested the guests. Everyone watched in silence as Mirza Sahib lifted the boy on to the table. "Now, what do you want to say?" he urged the boy, gently pinching both his cheeks.

"The brides are ready to be wed," said the boy in a high clear voice. The guests cheered.

The Qazi performed all three wedding ceremonies, signing the marriage certificate after each one. The wedding celebrations began. Music was played in the men's tent. The *mirasan*, a woman singer, started her performance and the sound of singing came from the ladies' tent. Two musicians on the open ground outside the front of Mirza Sahib's residence began to play the flute very loudly. The sound of drums came from Elephant Gate. All over the neighborhood, people could hear the flutes and drums signaling the start of the wedding festivities. *Hijras* -- professional male dancers in women's clothes -- made their way to the open ground and began to sing and dance. They always came to large wedding celebrations and were given some money before they left.

Irresistible cooking smells were wafting toward the tents. Some boys wandered over to watch two men barbecuing kebabs. Nearby, a cook was roasting billy-goats' testicles. The boys looked on fascinated and the cook gave them each a piece. They found it very tasty.

"The meal will be ready shortly," the cook told them. "Go back to your tents."

Soon afterward an announcement came. "The wedding feast is ready to be served. After dinner, boxes of sweets will be distributed."

Bhishtis -- professional water carriers --stood just outside the tents where the guests were eating, each holding on his shoulders a *mashq* -- a large bag made of two goatskins sewn together that contained drinking water. Each *bhishti* held the open bag in his hands, ready to fill jugs when required. The attendants then brought the water jugs back to the tables in the tents. The men drank water from tumblers that were frequently refilled by these attendants, who were very attentive. Dinner was eaten against a background of flute music and singing.

Many male guests sat outside in two rows facing each other on white sheets laid across the open ground. Before taking their places, they went to large metal containers of water to wash their hands. Each container had a tap in its side with a man standing nearby holding two towels.

Male servants and family relatives waited on the men in the men's tent and on the open ground while female family relatives helped the women servants to attend to the guests in the women's tents. Two servants brought round ewers of water and basins to the guests sitting in the tents so that they could wash their hands. Then the wedding feast was served in the men's and ladies' tents.

The men sitting outside were served with food on large metal plates. They ate with their fingers, three or four people to one *thaal*, a large metal plate. The mouth-watering aromas of *pulao*, meat curry, kebabs, and *zardah* blended as they spread around the tents and all over the open ground. A little distance from the eating area, trays of *paan*, betel leaf, and betel nuts for chewing were provided to round off the meal, with spittoons strategically placed nearby.

- - - - - - - - - - - - - - - - - - - -

After the feast, the wedding procession began to form outside Mirza Sahib's residence. The three bridegrooms mounted their horses, each of which was being held by a man. The front leg of each horse was raised and an egg placed beneath its hoof. The leg was released and the horse broke the egg with its hoof to bring good luck. Then the procession set off.

First came men playing flutes together with several drummers. They were followed by the three bridegrooms on horseback, with some of the wedding guests walking behind them. The procession went around Mirzawari and some of the main roads just outside the locality.

The remaining wedding guests settled down to talk. In the men's tent, Mirza Sahib leaned forward and refilled Mr. D'Silva's water glass. "Has your official business ever brought you to Kaliadeh Palace?" he asked.

The other guests leaned forward and listened with interest.

"I was there when the Governor of Ujjain, Prabhakar Sahib, received His Highness Jivajee Rao Sindhya, the Maharajah of Gwalior, at the railway station in Ujjain," came Mr. D'Silva's reply. "The Maharajah was going to Kaliadeh Palace. He traveled in a Rolls Royce while the rest of us went in two horse-drawn *victorias*. We stopped at Bhairu Garh, where the villagers gave us a fine reception. Then the Maharajah rode a decorated and garlanded elephant for the rest of the way. He stayed for three days at the Palace. We also had rooms there." He smiled reminiscently.

"What did you do?" asked one of the guests.

"We went to see the bridge just opposite the palace," answered Mr. D'Silva. "That is truly one of the wonders of the world. The engineers have built arches beneath the bridge and constructed pools just above the bed of the river Shipra. Clear river water flows continuously through these pools and the water level there always remains ankle-deep. The Maharajah asked us to join him in these pools. We removed our shoes, raised our trousers above the ankles, and took a walk there. The cold water gently washing against our feet was most refreshing."

"Next the Maharajah went for a swim in the river Shipra." Mr. D'Silva continued. One of the men raised his hand. "Was the Maharajah wearing a *langot*, a loincloth?" he asked. Everyone smiled.

"That is a very intelligent question," replied Mr. D'Silva. "He was in fact wearing shorts with a pattern of large checks in different colors. These swimming shorts were presented to him when he visited Scotland in Great Britain. The Maharajah is a very good swimmer. He dove into the river from the bridge. We were most impressed."

In the women's tent, the talk turned to the subject of the food they had just eaten. All ladies from all levels of society learned how to cook, as the men never did the cooking at home. Upper class ladies did not do the cooking themselves, but used their cooking skills to ensure that the female servants prepared the food according to the family's requirements. Nevertheless, the professional cooks were men.

"The *pulao*, meat curry, and *zardah* were very tasty," remarked Mrs. Khadeeja Begum, Shandar's mother. "However," she continued, "that curry was definitely cooked too quickly."

"I noticed that the meat in the curry was slightly tougher than I like to eat," said Mrs. Delara Begum. "But it wasn't too bad, seeing that they had to cook for so many people."

"I could certainly feel the spices on my tongue," said

Khatoon Bibi.

Tara Bibi agreed. "The Riaz brothers did not keep an eye on their cooks. The spices should have been fried a little longer."

"At least these men brought the food, did all the cooking themselves, and finished the job on time," remarked Mrs. Khadeeja Begum. She was of medium height, rather plump, and older than the other ladies in the group. Since her marriage, she had lived on a hill farm outside Ujjain. She regularly visited her friends and relatives in the nearby village of Daulatpur, traveling there in her own sedan chair, carried by two tall strong servants.

"When my brother-in-law got married at our hill farm, the caterers messed everything up," she went on.

"What happened?" asked Mrs. Delara Begum.

"First of all, those useless cooks couldn't even bring the food and cooking pots up to our farm. The city bullocks pulled the cart half way up the hill. Then they sat down in the middle of the track and refused to take another step."

"What did the cooks do then?" asked Tara Bibi.

"They simply unloaded the bullock carts, left everything by the side of the track, turned around, and went back to the city. We had to get our own bullock carts and bring everything up ourselves to the top of the hill where our farm was."

"How did you manage to get the wedding feast prepared?" the other ladies asked.

"The ladies from the neighboring farms had already been invited to the wedding. I sent a servant around to explain what had happened and ask them if they could help me to prepare the wedding feast. They all came. We went to the yard at the back of the house to set everything out. I told two young boys to stand by the path leading to the yard and stop any men from coming that way. A little later, I was just coming out of the house when I spotted two older boys from a nearby village in our yard. They had simply pushed past the young boys and were standing there laughing quietly and watching the ladies cooking."

"What did you do?" asked Tara Bibi.

"I went back into the house, seized a big stick, crept up behind them, and hit them hard on their backsides. 'You know very well you are not supposed to be here,' I shouted. 'What would your mothers say if they could see you now? You should be ashamed of yourselves.' They ran away as fast as they could and we all had a good laugh."

"Did you manage to finish preparing the wedding feast on time?" asked another lady.

"Oh yes," replied Mrs. Khadeeja Begum. "It was all ready when the wedding guests arrived."

Everyone smiled with pleasure, fascinated by the story.

On the open ground, several groups of people were having lively conversations. Mehboob's friend Nazir was holding his audience spellbound with an account of a fishing trip he had once gone on, as a boy of eight, with Mehboob.

"Fishing is not allowed, so there are many fish and eels in the river Shipra," he began. "We borrowed a fishhook from our neighbor Lalu. He worked in the cloth mill, at least that's what he was supposed to do. He often took time off, though, without his father's knowledge. 'You can borrow two fishhooks if I can come with you as well,' he said to us. We agreed and promised not to tell his father that Lalu had been fishing with us instead of going to work.

"Four miles outside Ujjain, we came to a steep hill sloping down to the river bank. No policemen in sight. We looked down the river in both directions. No crocodiles to be seen. We left our clothes on the shore and swam out to a small island in the middle of the river to do some fishing. We had just caught some eels when Lalu spotted two policemen standing at the top of the hill. They saw us, quickly came down, and stood beside our clothes, smiling. 'Come on over here, boys,' one of them shouted. 'You know that fishing is illegal. Pay a fine or go to jail.' 'We don't have any money, but my father will pay the fine,' Mehboob shouted back. 'Where do you live?' 'We live in Mirzawari and my father is a lawyer,' replied Mehboob in an educated voice. He knew how to put on a good act. 'Who are you, big boy?' asked the policeman addressing Lalu. 'He is our neighbor Lalu,' answered Mehboob. 'Where do you work, Lalu?' 'I work in the cloth mill,' replied Lalu. 'OK, big boy, you know the law. You must pay a big fine.' 'No, no,' shouted Lalu and quickly swam to the other side of the river. The policeman picked up Lalu's clothes and waved them. 'I will count to ten and if you don't come, we will take your clothes to the police station,' he shouted. Lalu stayed where he was and the policemen disappeared with his clothes. 'You boys go home. I will come later,' shouted Lalu."

"Mehboob and I swam back to the shore, put our clothes on, climbed the hill, and hid behind a tree to see what Lalu would do. Darkness began to fall. Lalu swam over to our side and stood on the shore. He was almost invisible with his thick black hair, big black eyes, and dark skin, faintly lit at the waist by the white loincloth he was wearing.

"It was now completely dark. Lalu set off along the unlit track back to the town and we followed at a distance. We came to a locality with small mud houses on both sides of the track. Several women were sitting outside on *charpoys*. Lalu hid behind a tree. Suddenly he rushed out on to the track.

"'*Bhoot! Bhoot!* Ghost! Ghost!' the women shouted and ran into their houses as he streaked past them. Men and boys quickly came out to chase the ghost. As Lalu passed through the other localities, others started to pursue him. When Lalu finally got home, he was met by his father wielding a big stick."

Nazir's audience enjoyed the story, as many of them had made similar fishing trips themselves and knew some good secret fishing spots by the river.

A maidservant entered the women's tent to inform Mrs.

Delara Begum to that the wedding procession was returning. "Please excuse me, ladies," said Mrs. Delara Begum. "A man from Ram Das sweet caterers delivered some boxes of sweets earlier. I must go to the kitchen and show the servants how to package them."

Mrs. Delara Begum asked a maidservant to fetch silk scarves in different colors and led her into the kitchen. The table there was heaped high with brightly colored boxes. Each box contained *gulab jamons, laddus, jalebi*, and a piece of *ghaver*. This *ghaver* was a specialty of Ram Das. It was shaped like a crown, about six inches in diameter and one inch thick with raised edges and looked like an empty pastry case for jam tarts. However, it was much softer and tasted much sweeter.

"Please tie a silk scarf around each of these boxes," Mrs. Delara Begum instructed the servants. "I want you to make a really special knot." She showed three servants how to wrap the scarf around the sweet box and then knot it at the top, so that the two loops were exactly the same size and placed exactly at the center of the box. Each household received one of the boxes. Everyone admired the beautiful scarves wrapped round them.

"The knots on top of the boxes are quite remarkable," one of the guests commented. "Those loops - exactly symmetrical. Who did them?"

"That is Mrs. Delara Begum's knot," replied the servant. Word went round and Mrs. Delara Begum's knot became famous in Mirzawari.

The wedding guests began to take their leave, the men shaking the hands of all three bridegrooms. People living locally went on foot. Those from Gharib Colony left by *tonga*. Besides the boxes of sweets, the widow Fatima and the newly wed Murad and Shakuri were given large quantities of food left over from the wedding feast, so that they could continue the wedding celebrations with their other friends in Gharib Colony. Gulzar Khan also received sufficient food to feed himself and his wife for the next few days. Mehboob brought his new bride Hasina to the servants' quarters of Talib Sahib the lawyer. Shakil Sahib escorted Mr D'Silva to his *victoria*. Mr D'Silva cracked his neck one last time before climbing into the *victoria* and being driven away.

The following day, Shandar and his new wife Shabnum set off in a decorated *victoria* drawn by heavily garlanded horses to live on a hill farm near Daulatpur. They were followed by a second *victoria* carrying Shandar's relatives.

A few days after Shabnum's wedding, Tara Bibi went to visit her friends in the Lawyers' Den. They were seated on *charpoys* in the enclosed courtyard outside their houses. "The Blue Silk Lady and her husband are in Ujjain," said Tara Bibi after greeting them. "They have had to get more supplies. There have been so many people buying material for wedding clothes, now that there is less food rationing. She brought me a message from Bamboowala and Mrs. Jamila Begum in the village of Ghanswara."

"I remember them," remarked Kausar, leaning forward with interest. "My late husband was related to Bamboowala. We lived in Ghanswara for several years until he died and I came here with my two sons to live with my brother and his wife. They have children, I believe."

"Yes, two girls, Sara and Rani" answered Tara Bibi. "My parents and I were very friendly with their family when we lived in Ghanswara."

"How old are the girls now?" asked Mrs. Waheeda Begum.

"Rani is 18 and Sara is nearly 25 years old," Tara Bibi replied. "It's really difficult for their parents to find suitable matches for them in Ghanswara. I know the problem all too well. Bamboowala is a businessman of high standing. He buys and sells bamboos. His wife Mrs. Jamila Begum has done everything she can to prepare the girls to mix with people at their social level. There is no girls' school in the village, but she herself taught them to read the Quran and to read and write Urdu."

"I know just the right person for Rani," said Mrs. Waheeda

44

Begum suddenly.

"Who's that?" asked the others.

"Why, Anwar Ali, of course," came the reply. "He is 18 and he runs our local grocery shop. He lives with his widowed mother right here in the Lawyers' Den."

"Perhaps my husband Waqar Hassan might know of someone suitable for Sara," said Mrs. Adiba Hassan. "I'll speak to him."

Later that evening, Mrs. Adiba Hassan told her husband about Sara. "Do you happen to know of anyone who might be suitable for her?" she asked.

"I've had dealings with a businessman recently," replied Waqar Hassan. "His name is Adam Beg. He is a widower and his family is looking for a wife for him."

"I'll tell Tara Bibi about him and she can mention Sara to his family," his wife replied.

Some days later the Blue Silk Lady called on Tara Bibi at her bungalow. "I am going to Ghanswara," she said. "Do you have any message for Bamboowala and Mrs. Jamila Begum?"

"Yes, I have found very suitable matches for both their daughters," answered Tara Bibi.

When Bamboowala received Tara Bibi's message from the Blue Silk Lady, he invited Tara Bibi to come and stay in his house for a few days and sent a bullock cart to Ujjain to collect her.

Chapter 3: Bride Swap

"Adam Beg is not at all suitable for our Sara," declared Bamboowala.

"Why not?" asked Tara Bibi. "He is a well established businessman with a very good regular income. He has his own flour mill and employs two people. He also has his own house nearby."

"You say he is a widower. Does he have children?"

"A little girl," replied Tara Bibi. "She's only three years old. Her aunt looks after her."

"How old is he?" asked Jamila Begum.

"His family says he is 25, but he looks older," Tara Bibi answered.

"Please look for someone more suitable," requested Bamboowala.

"Your Sara is very pretty," replied Tara Bibi. "But she is 24 years old and time is running out for her. This man can look after her well and give her a good home. You must decide soon about her future."

"It's better that she doesn't marry a man who has already had one wife. There is also a small child," Bamboowala replied.

"Anwar Ali seems like a good match for Rani," remarked Jamila Begum. "It was very enterprising of him to start a grocery shop by himself when he was 16."

"He's been running it for two years now and it is very popular," Tara Bibi answered. "He even delivers groceries to people's homes. He lives with his widowed mother in a small, two bed room house in the Lawyers' Den."

"What does he look like?" asked Mrs. Jamila Begum.

"He is of medium height and has light brown skin. His face is round, and he has big brown eyes and curly black hair. He's really a very handsome young man."

Mrs. Jamila Begum and Bamboowala smiled with satisfaction.

"What shall I say to the family of Adam Beg?" asked Tara Bibi.

"My good friend Saeed Khan has an unmarried daughter. Her name is Nuri and she is 25 years old," answered Bamboowala.

"Oh yes, I remember," replied Tara Bibi. "The go-between found a suitable girl for her brother Wahid, but Saeed Khan refused her because he wanted Wahid and Nuri to be married at the same time, perhaps to a brother and sister."

- - - - - - - - - - - - - - - - - - - -

Sara and Rani were visiting their friend Nuri. Her father, Saeed Khan, owned a lot of land and lived with his second wife Latifa Bibi within walking distance of Bamboowala's house. Saeed Khan was tall, walked round the village with his head held high, and played a large part in village affairs. Nuri's mother had died when she was two years old and he had married his present wife a year later. She had given him a son, Wahid, Nuri's half brother.

Nuri had inherited her father's intelligence and interest in sports. However, she was short, stocky, and dark-skinned like her mother's side of the family. She dressed for comfort rather than fashion, had no interest in make-up, and generally wore fitted, plain, cotton trousers with a silk shirt and a pleated *dupatta*. Her stepmother frequently told her off for not covering her head when going out.

Latifa Bibi had been equally unsuccessful in teaching Nuri the more ladylike household skills. Nuri hated planning and preparing meals and particularly disliked sewing. However, she cooked *rotis* (thick *chapatis*) for the family, fed and milked the cows, and collected and dried *gober* (cow dung) to make fires so that she could cook *gaunkris* in the ashes, which she then served with yellow lentils Occasionally, she attended her stepmother's afternoon tea parties, bringing with her a faint aroma of cow dung. She would then be immediately sent out to change her clothes. Latifa Bibi was ready to consider anyone as a possible husband for Nuri.

Sara and Rani joined Nuri and her friend Shahida in the private grounds behind Saeed Khan's house. All four sat in two swings hanging from a couple of trees close together. After gently swinging to and fro for a few minutes, Sara stopped and rose to her feet. Standing in front of the other three, she took an exercise book from the cloth bag at her wrist, looked up at them, and gently cleared her throat.

"This is the first poem of the ladies' poetry reading," she announced.

"The taste of the spices plays a tune on my tongue.

Each spice, each separate flavor

Of the herbs, meat, and vegetables found in each dish

Blended to bring out its savor.

A concert of tastes with the cook to conduct it

Through a range of spices and heat

For the dishes presented throughout the meal

Moving from savory to sweet."

When the poem ended, Nuri rose. "Now I will show you the dance I am practising especially for your weddings," she announced. Moving her hands and wrists, she danced in a wide circle before them and then slowly swirled toward Sara and Rani and Shahida, swaying her hips and sinking before them with a flourish, before rising up and continuing to the music in her head.

Suddenly, Sara rose and joined in, the rhythm of her movements framing and developing the dance. When the dancers had finished, Shahida stood up, faced the others, and began to sing. She was very tall and thin with brown skin. Her long black hair streamed down her back, her brightly colored clothes fluttered round her. She dyed the cloth at home, using colors and patterns she had developed herself. The gestures of her hands and her long, multi-colored fingers brought out the message of her song.

More poetry was followed by more dancing. Finally, Rani said to Sara, "Read your special poem for us."

Sara stood up and read the following:

"Our women's world is one of wondering

When and what and where and why.

When will we marry, when will our lives change?

What towns, what people in the world outside?

Where will we go when finally we're wed?

Why can't we be free to do what we like?

Our thoughts will never cease their wandering."

There was a small orchard of fruit trees behind Saeed Khan's house with two tall *imli* (tamarind) trees among them. The *imli* pods grew on the upper branches and, when ripe, had brown, brittle shells containing a juicy, brownish, acid-tasting pulp with small hard shiny brown seeds. Ladies and girls were particularly fond of eating *imli* fruit and it was also added to curries and used for making chutneys.

"Let's eat some *imlis*," Sara suggested.

"What a good idea," said Nuri, jumping out of her swing. "I feel like taking some exercise."

Nuri threw off her *chappals* and went to the *imli* tree, giving Shahida her *dupatta* to hold. Grasping the tree trunk with hands and feet, she gradually eased herself up into the lower branches some distance from the ground and started to climb. She loved climbing trees and Sara and Rani often asked her to climb up and shake the top branches of the *imli* tree so that they could gather the ripe fruit from the ground.

Afterward, the four friends sat on the swings eating the *imli* fruit and spitting the seeds onto the ground.

"Tara Bibi has come to visit us from Ujjain," said Sara.

Nuri smiled. "What news does she bring?"

"She's sitting with our father and mother now, telling them her news."

"Maybe she has found fine husbands for you both," said Nuri.

"Whatever happens, wherever I go, I will always write letters to you," Sara promised.

"I also," said Rani. "We will never let our friendship die."

Nuri was silent for a while. Then she rose to her feet. "There are many *imlis* still left," she said. "Let us gather them all and make *imli* chutney together and I will show you my special recipe." Nuri's *imli* chutney was particularly good and very popular with her family and friends.

The day after speaking to Bamboowala and Mrs. Jamila Begum, Tara Bibi went to Saeed Khan's house. His wife Latifa Bibi greeted her and showed her into the reception room.

"I am here to talk about your daughter Nuri," said Tara Bibi. "I have some news that could be interesting for her."

"I will fetch my husband," replied Latifa Bibi.

Saeed Khan entered the room smiling. "I am pleased to hear that you have news for my daughter," he said. "Let my wife bring tea and then we will talk."

"Have you found a suitable man for our Nuri?" asked Latifa Bibi as she came into the room carrying a tray with tea and *namakpare*, small savory crisps.

"I came to make wedding arrangements for Bamboowala's two daughters," said Tara Bibi, "but Sara already had a proposal two years ago from someone studying at Aligarh University. I didn't know this. However, Bamboowala has accepted a proposal for Rani. Perhaps you will consider the other man for your daughter Nuri."

"Tell us about him," said Latifa Bibi.

"Well, his name is Adam Beg. He is a widower. He has his own house and a flour mill."

"How old is he?" asked Saeed Khan.

"I have been told that he is 25," replied Tara Bibi.

"That sounds just right for our Nuri," said Latifa Bibi with pleasure, looking across at her husband.

Saeed Khan hesitated. "Very well then," he said at last.

"Now I can arrange both weddings at the same time," Tara Bibi said as she left the house, relieved to have found a bride for Adam Beg.

Both weddings were fixed for the following month. During the next few weeks, wedding arrangements were made in Bamboowala's and Saeed Khan's houses. Many guests were expected to attend both ceremonies, which were to be held separately at each house.

- - - - - - - - - - - - - - - - - - - -

Ghanswara was by a river and was reached by a well-worn track through thick jungle inhabited by monkeys and snakes. The backyards of the mud houses faced onto narrow paths running around the whole village. Most people worked on the land, either for themselves or for a landowner. A couple of small shops and a weekly farmers' market supplied goods that people were unable to provide for themselves. Everyone knew everyone else in that village.

On the day before the weddings were due to take place, the rumble of heavy wheels coming along the track from Ujjain was heard in Ghanswara. It was afternoon and only the women and children were at home. The sound drew nearer and children ran from the houses to see what was happening. "It's a wedding procession!" they shouted. "Come and see!" They were joined by more children and women's faces appeared at the windows of the houses.

Two *tongas* decorated with garlands came into sight. In each *tonga* sat some men, one of whom was wearing wedding clothes, his face concealed by garlands of flowers. They were followed by two bullock carts with women and children sitting in them, wearing their best clothes and talking and laughing excitedly. Behind them came two more bullock carts carrying men and boys. The carts and the bullocks were also garlanded. As they passed, the children in them waved and smiled at the children and young boys standing by the houses lining the street. Behind the procession, several men rode bicycles, ringing their bells.

"It's the procession for the weddings of Rani and Nuri," said the women to each other as the carts rumbled past.

"Who are the bridegrooms?" asked one of the women.

"One of them is a mill owner," an older woman replied. "He also has his own house. He is to marry Nuri, the daughter of Saeed Khan."

"Nuri? That tree-climbing tomboy?" One of the younger women laughed. "She's lucky."

"I hear that the second bridegroom is young and handsome," the older woman went on. "He is Rani's husband-to-be."

The wedding procession arrived through a big gate leading to Camel Courtyard, a large yard in front of Bamboowala's house. His business friends from distant villages usually came there with bullock carts to deliver bamboos and his customers left their camels there when they came to collect their goods. Camel Courtyard had been cleaned up for the reception for both weddings and two large tents erected there for the male wedding guests.

The families of Bamboowala and Saeed Khan welcomed the bridegrooms and wedding guests with glasses of scented *sharbat* a sweet drink with rose petals floating in it, before taking them to the men's and ladies' tents. Then the carts were led to a large patch of ground by the trees to one side of Bamboowala's house. The bullocks were unharnessed, tethered to trees, and given fodder and water.

Mrs. Jamila Begum went to her kitchen to help with the last-minute preparations for a meal for the new arrivals. She sent the male relatives and family friends with food to the men's tent in front of the house. Her female relatives and friends served the ladies in another, larger tent that had been specially set up for ladies and children in an open space behind the house. A door opposite the ladies' tent opened onto a large living room with a window overlooking the courtyard. Another door next to it led to a narrow passage with two identical green doors next to each other on one side. These opened on to two small rooms for overnight guests. One of these rooms had been prepared for Rani and her new husband to spend the night together after the wedding ceremony.

When the ladies had eaten, Mrs. Jamila Begum invited them into the living room for tea. They complimented her on the meal and admired the furnishings.

"I am the mother of Anwar Ali," said one of the ladies to her. "We will be happy to welcome your daughter Rani into our house,"

"I am pleased to meet you," replied Mrs. Jamila Begum. "I hear your son is very successful with his shop."

"You have an older daughter, too?" asked another lady.

"She's upstairs with Rani," answered Mrs. Jamila Begum.

"She is still living at home?" the same lady enquired.

"She had a proposal of marriage, but the boy is still studying. We must consider it carefully." To Mrs. Jamila Begum's relief, the talk then moved on to other topics.

Some of the men and a few close female relatives of both brides, Sara and Nuri, had gone into one of the men's tents, so that they could see the bridegrooms Anwar Ali and Adam Beg before their marriages. The male relatives formed a small group near the stage that had been set up at one end of the tent. Tara Bibi lifted a tent flap and led both bridegrooms to the centre of the stage, their faces completely hidden by garlands.

She stepped before the first bridegroom and raised the garlands covering his face. "This is Anwar Ali," she said. Anwar Ali wore a golden *safah* on his head with a pale gold silk *sherwani* or long coat over a cream silk shirt and white *patloon* (wide-legged trousers). On his feet were Bata shoes. Everyone smiled to see his bright eyes and curly black hair. He bowed his head nervously.

Next, Tara Bibi moved over to Adam Beg. He was tall and wore a cream colored *sherwani*, white silk shirt, grey waistcoat, and white *shalwar* with Afghan *chappals* on his feet. Tara Bibi moved close to Adam Beg and jumped up a little to push back the garlands covering his face. His black fur hat fell off together with the garlands revealing straight black hair streaked with white above his dark skinned face. An awkward hush fell. Even allowing for the fact that most families took a few years off the real age when presenting possible brides and grooms, it was obvious to everyone that Adam Beg was much older than 25, the age his family had given for him.

Saeed Khan stepped forward to the stage and beckoned Tara Bibi to one side. "This man looks well over 30," he whispered. "Please ask Adam Beg his real age, which will go on the wedding certificate."

Tara Bibi obeyed. "I am 34," Adam Beg told her quietly.

"I refuse to marry my Nuri to this man," said Saeed Khan loudly when he heard this, and strode toward the tent entrance where his wife was standing with the other female relatives.

"Let's go," he muttered angrily to her and left the tent, followed by Latifa Bibi and his relatives. There were loud murmurs of astonishment.

Adam Beg was stunned when he saw them both leave. "He is a fool," said Tara Bibi quietly. She and Bamboowala went to Adam Beg and, together with Anwar Ali, they quickly took him to the guest room next to the bridal chamber. Leaving Adam Beg with Anwar Ali, Tara Bibi went to fetch a glass of water while

Bamboowala returned to the men's tent.

"Please remain where you are," he told the assembled relatives. Then he fetched Jamila Begum and went with her to the bridal chamber where they could talk in private.

"Adam Beg is a fine and honorable man," he told his wife. "We brought him here with the offer of a girl who will be a good match for him in every way. Saeed Khan's last-minute refusal to allow Nuri to marry Adam Beg is a great insult, not only to Adam Beg but also to us and to all our family."

"It's not as though Saeed Khan has had such a large choice of suitors for the girl," remarked Mrs. Jamila Begum who, like Latifa Bibi, was well aware of Nuri's lack of social skills. "Adam Beg is well established, he is also good, kind, and generous, so I have heard." She paused. "Maybe he might take our Sara as his bride instead of Nuri."

"Just what I was thinking," said Bamboowala. "Let's see what she says."

He asked Tara Bibi to join them and told her of their idea for saving the situation.

"That sounds good," said Tara Bibi. "I will suggest it to Sara."

Tara Bibi went to where Rani was sitting with Sara and the other bridesmaids. "Please come, I need your help," she said to Sara. Outside the tent she quietly told Sara about Saeed Khan's sudden last-minute refusal to marry Nuri to Adam Beg.

"What will happen now?" asked Sara.

"Your parents consider that Adam Beg is a good man and a very good match. They have asked me to find out whether you would agree to marry him yourself instead. If you are happy with this suggestion, then I will approach Adam Beg with a proposal."

Sara gasped and put a hand to her mouth. Her cheeks were pale. "Yes," she whispered.

"Go back to your sister," Tara Bibi told her. "We will speak to you again later."

Tara Bibi returned to Bamboowala and Mrs. Jamila Begum. "Sara has agreed to marry Adam Beg," she informed them.

"This is God's will," said Mrs. Jamila Begum. "He seems like a kind man."

"Please speak to Adam Beg," said Bamboowala to Tara Bibi. "If he agrees to marry Sara, then bring him here."

About ten minutes later there was a gentle knock at the door. "Come in!" called Bamboowala.

Tara Bibi entered the room together with Adam Beg, who still looked somewhat shaken.

"Please sit down," Bamboowala said to him. "We would like to apologize most sincerely for what has happened. We are very pleased that you have agreed to marry our daughter Sara instead. We will inform the guests and proceed with the engagement and wedding ceremonies."

Both men rose and shook hands. Then Adam Beg rejoined Anwar Ali next door.

- - - - - - - - - - - - - - - - - - - -

Saeed Khan strode through Camel Courtyard past the groups of men and boys, his face set with anger. Behind him Latifa Bibi drew her *dupatta* over her head, covering her face. They turned on to the road and started to walk back home.

"What do you mean by this refusal?" demanded Latifa Bibi, her voice choked with anger. "Who do you think you will find for Nuri now? Some prince, perhaps?"

"This man is far too old for her and he is a widower," answered Saeed Khan.

"Our Nuri will find nobody else now, especially when

news of this public refusal of her bridegroom-to-be gets around Ghanswara. Who will want to marry a woman of 25, especially one who has so little idea of how to run a house and prefers milking cows and collecting their *gober*?"

"There will be someone more suitable -- some rich landowner's son." However, Saeed Khan sounded uncertain.

"Some rich landowner's son? Some rich landowner will be ready to offer his son in marriage to the daughter of a man, who may well turn him down at the last moment? You have lost a golden chance here for Nuri to get married. She will stay on the shelf for the rest of her life. What will the neighbors say about our family?"

They went on walking, the silence between them broken only by Latifa Bibi's sobbing.

Meanwhile, Bamboowala asked both Adam Beg and Anwar Ali to come on to the stage with him. Then he strode to the front of the stage and made the following announcement:

"Adam Beg is an honest, hardworking businessman. We have invited him to come here to take part in a marriage ceremony. He will be an asset to any family. Nuri's father has refused to marry his daughter to this man. However, I myself will be happy to offer the hand of my own daughter Sara to Adam Beg. Let both weddings continue!" Everyone in the tent cheered and clapped.

Sara's female friends and relatives quickly prepared her to take part in her last-minute wedding. Some of the younger ones took Sara upstairs to one of the bedrooms and rubbed *ubtan*, a paste made of sandalwood, all over her body. Then they bathed her to wash it off, leaving the sandalwood perfume on her softened skin. Designs had already been painted on her hands with *mehndi* for her role as bridesmaid. All that remained to do was to find Sara a wedding dress from the large selection of unused wedding clothes in her mother's trunk, cover her head with a bridal veil and drape wedding garlands over her face. Her mother also provided her with engagement and wedding rings, which had belonged to Bamboowala, to be given to Adam Beg at the engagement and wedding ceremonies.

Meanwhile other women quickly transformed the bed in the room next to Rani's bridal chamber into a second bridal bed. A canopy resting on four posts was set up over the bed. Garlands of flowers were then draped over the canopy to hang down all around the bed, and rose petals were strewn over the fringed red and gold bedspread.

Both brides went to sit on the stage, their heads covered with wedding veils and their faces hidden by garlands. Adam Beg sat opposite Sara. The garlands were removed from their faces and a large silk *chadar* was draped over them. As they exchanged their engagement rings, Adam Beg caught a fleeting glimpse of his bride's face. He was only aware of her beauty, her flawless fair skin, and wide eyes before the *chadar* was removed and Sara was hidden once again beneath her veil and wedding garlands. At the same time, Anwar Ali and Rani were also exchanging engagement rings.

Next, details of the *mehr* or marriage gift payable by the groom to the bride were settled by intermediaries acting on behalf of Sara and Rani and their husbands-to-be. Generally, part of the *mehr* was paid on marriage and the rest after marriage.

When the Qazi arrived to start the wedding ceremony, the bridegrooms were in one of the men's tents, sitting on the stage well apart from each other. All the male wedding guests had crowded into the tent to watch from a distance. The Qazi climbed on to the stage and went toward Adam Beg. With him were two men acting as independent witnesses to ensure that the bride- and bridegroom-to-be were marrying each other of their own free will. A *vakil* (lawyer) acting on behalf of the bride was also present.

The Qazi turned to Adam Beg. "Do you take Sara, daughter of Bamboowala, to be your wedded wife?" he asked.

"I do," said Adam Beg in a clear voice.

The Qazi repeated the same question two more times. Each time Adam Beg answered very clearly, "I do." The Qazi then turned to the two witnesses and they nodded to show that they had heard Adam Beg.

Next, the Qazi went to one of the ladies' tents together with the same two witnesses and a *vakil* acting on behalf of Adam Beg. Tara Bibi took them to a separate room at the back, where Sara was sitting alone, her head and face veiled. Tara Bibi seated herself next to Sara with the two male witnesses, the bridegroom's *vakil*, and the Qazi nearby. The Qazi went through the wedding ceremony with Sara, asking her the same question three times through Tara Bibi, to which she replied, "I do" each time. Afterward the two witnesses and Adam Beg's lawyer nodded to confirm that they had heard Sara's response.

The Qazi then returned to the men's tent and the wedding ceremony was repeated with Anwar Ali before two different witnesses and a lawyer acting on behalf of Rani. Finally, he went with Tara Bibi to Rani and repeated the wedding ceremony once again in the presence of the same two witnesses and a lawyer acting on behalf of Anwar Ali, with Tara Bibi as an intermediary.

Afterward the Qazi returned to the men's tent and went on to the stage to conduct the *Khutbah-tun-Nikah* (marriage sermon) to conclude the solemnization of both marriages. He then issued a written *Aqd-e-Nikah* (marriage certificate) for each wedding. Each certificate was signed by the bride and groom together with the two witnesses of each marriage. Then, wedding rings were given to the brides and grooms.

Next the *walimah* (wedding feast) was served to the guests in the men's and ladies' tents. Male and female relatives brought kebabs freshly roasted over an open fire in the ground to the waiting guests. There was goats' meat curry with *roti* (thick chapati); *toor daal* (yellow lentils) swimming in *ghee* with bits of fried garlic floating in it; and *raitha*, yogurt mixed with finely chopped onions and cumin seeds, followed by *zardah* (sweet yellow rice). The playing of the *dholak* (drum) and *shahnai* (flute) and the singing of the *mirasan* (woman singer) formed a background to the celebrations. The guests lingered in the men's and ladies' tents drinking tea, chatting, and chewing *paan*.

Several men assembled in Camel Courtyard for the wedding procession. The bridegrooms mounted two horses and, after an egg had been broken beneath the front hoof of each horse for good luck, the wedding procession set off, led by the two bridegrooms. People cheered as it paraded around the main streets of Ghanswara and finally returned to Camel Courtyard.

When the wedding procession returned to Bamboowala's house, the bridegrooms, garlands still covering their faces, were led by Tara Bibi to the ladies' tent to exchange wedding rings with their brides.

- -

Tara Bibi took Sara and Rani to their rooms and left them seated on their marriage beds, each with her head covered and her face completely hidden by the wedding garlands. "Sara and Rani are ready and waiting in their marriage chambers," she told Mrs. Jamila Begum.

"Good," said Bamboowala's wife. "Call Anwar Ali first and send him to Rani's room."

Tara Bibi entered the house from the women's tent and went through the passage to the front door, passing the two bridal chambers on her right. Outside the house, she made for the men's tent where Anwar Ali was sitting on the stage.

"Your bride is ready for you now," she told him quietly.

Anwar Ali followed her out of the tent, nervously clearing his throat.

As they entered the house, one of the women called Tara Bibi from the kitchen. "It's the first door on the right," she told Anwar Ali, and quickly went away.

Anwar Ali stopped and stared at the two doors next to each other leading to the two bridal chambers. Both doors were painted green. However both doors were on the left hand side of the passage. The brides and bridegrooms had never seen or spoken to each other before their wedding day and had had only quick glimpses of each other's faces when exchanging engagement rings.

"Tara Bibi doesn't know her left hand from her right," muttered AnwarAli to himself. He knocked quietly at the first door on the left and entered the room, carefully bolting the door behind him. He found the bride sitting in the middle of the bed, her face hidden and a large scarf draped over her head, waiting to be unveiled by the bridegroom. Anwar Ali felt very shy indeed. He had never been alone in a room with a girl before, especially a complete stranger. He stood in silence and stared at her, wondering what to do. The veiled figure on the bed sat there not making a sound. Anwar Ali stood by the bed looking at her and then went and sat on a chair by the wall and began to think about his next move.

A little later Tara Bibi went to the men's tent to take Adam Beg to his bride. "This is your bride's room," she said, pointing to the door nearest the front of the house and went away. Adam Beg found the door bolted on the inside, so he tried the door of the room next door. This opened easily. As he expected, he found the bride sitting on the bed waiting for him to unveil her. He gently took the girl's hand from beneath her veil and looked at her fingers. The wedding ring she was wearing was not the one he had had specially made for his bride. "I think there has been some mistake," he murmured, releasing her hand, "I will find out what has happened."

In the next room, Anwar Ali was still sitting on his chair, staring at the silent figure on the bed and trying to work out how to make the first move. He was startled by the sound of a knock on the door. "Who is there?" he asked.

"It is I, Adam Beg. Open the door!"

Puzzled, Anwar Ali unbolted the door. "What's the matter?" he asked.

"Come outside a moment," came the reply.

In the passage Adam Beg leaned forward and whispered into Anwar Ali's ear, "I think we have been sent in to the wrong brides."

"How can you know this?" asked Anwar Ali in surprise.

"I looked at the bride's hand. The girl I was sent in to isn't wearing the wedding ring I gave my bride," replied Adam Beg.

"The girl in the room I was sent to is sitting so still and quiet," said Anwar Ali. "I don't know what to do. It's the first time I have ever been alone with a girl." He blushed.

"Don't worry, she's just as nervous as you are," answered Adam Beg. "Let us find Tara Bibi."

The two bridegrooms went to one of the ladies' tents. At the entrance, Adam Beg shouted, "Where is Tara Bibi?"

Several women turned, startled to see both bridegrooms standing there. One of them went off hastily to find Tara Bibi.

"What has happened?" asked Tara Bibi, hurrying toward them.

"I think we have been sent in to the wrong brides," Adam Beg replied. "The bride in the room I entered isn't wearing my ring."

"How can this be?" asked Tara Bibi.

The bridegrooms led the way from the women's tents, followed by Tara Bibi. They stopped outside the two green doors in the passage and both men turned to face her.

"This is your bride's room," Tara Bibi said to Anwar Ali, pointing to one of the doors with her right hand. "First on the right, just as I told you."

"It's the second on the left," answered Anwar Ali.

Adam Beg regarded them both in silence. Then he started

to laugh.

"That depends on how you look at it," he said.

"What do you mean?" asked Anwar Ali.

"Tara Bibi came from the women's tent at the back of the house, so that this door was the first one on the right for her. However, Anwar Ali was coming from the men's tent, so that both doors were on his left. That is why he opened the first door on his left."

Tara Bibi and Anwar Ali stared at Adam Beg in astonishment. Then, Tara Bibi's mouth twitched as she tried to stop the laughter bubbling up inside her. "I'd better go and tell both brides what has happened," she said.

The two bridegrooms waited in the passage while Tara Bibi went into each room in turn.

"I have spoken with each girl," she told Adam Beg and Anwar Ali on her return. "I am very sorry indeed that this has happened. I apologize most heartily to both of you."

Tara Bibi turned to Anwar Ali and touched the door next to her. "Go inside this room," she told him. "Your Rani is waiting for you."

Anwar Ali entered the room and bolted the door. The veiled figure on the bed held out both hands to him in welcome.

Adam Beg smiled at Tara Bibi. He had seen the laughter in her eyes. "It was a mistake," he said. "The doors look the same. The girls are unharmed."

"Go to your bride now," said Tara Bibi. "May you both have much happiness."

Tara Bibi returned to the ladies' tent. Everyone was curious to know what had happened. She told them the tale of the bride swap. Loud gales of laughter swept round the tent. A small boy appeared at the entrance.

"The men have sent me to ask what is happening" he said.

"I will come with you and explain," said Tara Bibi.

The subsequent roars of laughter from the men's tent could be heard in all the nearby houses.

As the laughter began to die down, a group of local ladies from Ghanswara in one of the ladies' tents began to discuss the weddings.

"Well, they found a husband for Sara after all," said one lady.

"She is very lucky," remarked a second lady. "He has a big house and his own business by all accounts. She will have a good life in Ujjain."

"Poor Nuri," murmured another lady. "All dressed up for her wedding and no bridegroom. Just because her father changed his mind at the last moment."

"Saeed Khan is a very proud man," said the first lady. "It is an insult for him to marry his daughter to a much older man."

"There aren't so many suitable men for her here anyway," someone else remarked. "It's going to be even more difficult for them to find a man for her now." Everyone shook their heads sadly at the truth of this.

- - - - - - - - - - - - - - - - - - - -

At Saeed Khan's house, Nuri was sitting in an upstairs room waiting for the wedding procession to arrive. With her were some of her friends and one or two older ladies including her aunt Shukri Bibi, her real mother's sister. Shukri Bibi was short and dark, a widow who lived on her small farm in the village of Munshigaon. Nuri wore her red wedding dress, a flowered *sehra* veiled her face and her head was covered. Outside they could hear the male guests talking and laughing and the sound of children playing.

Shukri Bibi's neighbor Niaz Ahmed was there with his wife and his younger brother Fayyaz Ahmed. The brothers owned a large farm that had been passed on to them by their father and they lived separately in two small houses side by side. Behind both houses was a large courtyard with an *imli* tree and a *neem* tree growing there. Fayyaz was of medium height and build, his brown skin darkened by the outdoor life he led. He enjoyed striding along the jungle tracks round Munshigaon and climbing trees, hence his nickname *Machhanddar* (monkey). Shukri Bibi had asked Fayyaz to bring his pet monkey on a leash for a *bandar tamasha* or monkey show to entertain the guests in the back yard. Nuri and the other ladies watched the show from an upstairs window.

The men and children stood in a circle while Fayyaz's monkey, Lakhoo, got up on two legs and lifted his hand several times offering *Salam* to everyone as he walked past them. Then Lakhoo danced with Fayyaz.

"Lakhoo! Eh Lakhoo!" shouted Fayyaz.

"Khoo! Khoo!" shouted the children.

"Khoo! Khoo!" answered the monkey, jumping up and down and tugging at his leash.

Everyone clapped at the end of the show.

The women in the room above heard the front door opening and footsteps coming up the stairs. Everyone moved away from the window and looked at the door.

The next moment, Saeed Khan and his wife burst into the room. "There will be no wedding," said Saeed Khan hoarsely. "The bridegroom is not suitable."

"What is this?" asked Shukri Bibi.

"He is not right for our Nuri. He is much too old for her; he is 34, and he is a widower."

Nuri gasped. Tears began to stream down her cheeks

behind the wedding garlands. She put her hands up over her face. Her shoulders shook with sobs.

Shukri Bibi put her arm round Nuri. "We will find someone for you," she said. "You can still get married."

"When will that be?" asked Nuri sadly, thinking of the months and years of waiting while her father had searched for a man willing to marry her, a man who, in his eyes, would be a suitable match for his daughter. "What use are all these wedding preparations?" In her mind's eye, she saw the wedding clothes and presents in the room downstairs, carefully laid out on a white sheet, now only fit to be stored in chests and forgotten.

Shukri Bibi rose. "Come with me," she said to Saeed Khan and Latifa Bibi, and took them into the room next door.

"If you wish it, Nuri's wedding can still take place today," she told them.

"How is this possible?" asked Saeed Khan.

"My neighbor's son Fayyaz Ahmed is outside. His father once worked for you, a very honest and hardworking man. The son is the same."

"That lazy *Machhanddar, monkeywala,*" Saeed Khan burst out. "He spends his days in the jungle climbing trees. He has nothing and he doesn't do a stroke of work. That's why I rejected him for Nuri before."

"He has changed a lot in the last few years," replied Shukri Bibi. "His father Ayyaz Ahmed had a large farm and gave it to both him and his elder brother Niaz when he left Munshigaon and went to Gurgaon."

"I heard something about that," said Latifa Bibi. "His parents got divorced. There was quite a scandal. Do you know the full story?"

"Ayyaz Ahmed is a very domineering man and often made his wife Gulnar very unhappy," Shukri Bibi answered.

"However, she stayed with him for the sake of her sons. Then one day she ran off to Ujjain with one of the farm workers, Roshan Khan. Soon afterward, she and Ayyaz Ahmed were divorced. Later, Roshan Khan and Gulnar got married and went to live in Milkipura, Ujjain."

"And how is Fayyaz now, since he and his brother took over their father's farm?" asked Latifa Bibi.

"Oh, he has changed a lot," replied Shukri Bibi. "At first he had problems with his elder brother Niaz. Fayyaz is very experienced in all types of farm work but Niaz wouldn't listen to his advice and, as a result, the farm made little profit. In the end, I offered Fayyaz a job on my farm. I have never regretted it"

"Is he a good worker then?" asked Saeed Khan.

"Oh yes," replied Shukri Bibi. "At first I wasn't able to pay him much, but since he came to work for me the farm has been making more profit than ever before. Now I pay him a very good wage. If my profits continue to increase, I will pay him even more. He has so many good ideas for making the farm more efficient."

"What happened to his father's farm?" enquired Saeed Khan.

"His elder brother manages it."

"Do their parents ever visit Niaz and Fayyaz?" asked Saeed Khan.

"No, they don't," answered Shukri Bibi. "They are both too ashamed to show their faces in Munshigaon."

Latifa Bibi brightened up. "I saw Fayyaz downstairs," she said. "He looks quite smart. He would be a good match for our Nuri."

"Who looks after the monkey when Fayyaz goes to work?" asked Saeed Khan.

"The monkey spends a lot of time in the trees at the back of the house. We all make sure that he has food and water. He is very tame and sometimes plays with the children. Everybody likes him."

Saeed Khan turned to Nuri's aunt, "Please ask Nuri, if she is willing to marry Fayyaz."

Shukri Bibi went and spoke first to Nuri and then to Fayyaz, taking each one aside in turn. Both agreed to marry each other.

"I have made no preparations for my wedding," said Fayyaz, "and I have no money for a *mehr* (marriage gift)."

"I will speak to Nuri and her parents," replied Shukri Bibi. "I am sure we will be able to come to some arrangement."

Shukri Bibi returned to the room where Nuri was sitting with the other ladies and asked her to come to the bridal chamber next door.

"We need to discuss your *mehr*," she told Nuri. "Fayyaz has no money."

"I'd like to have the *imli* tree in the courtyard," Nuri immediately replied. "I used to climb it every time I came to visit you. I want that *imli* tree in my *mehr*."

"Very good. I will go and speak with Fayyaz and your parents," replied Shukri Bibi.

Shukri Bibi went and asked Saeed Khan and Latifa Bibi to come and discuss the question of the *mehr*. Then she called Fayyaz and Niaz. Niaz's wife saw them all passing the open door of the women's room. She quickly rose and followed them into the bridal chamber next door, where Nuri was sitting on the bed, her head covered and her face concealed by the wedding garlands.

"Nuri wants the *imli* tree in your back courtyard for her *mehr*," said Shukri Bibi to Fayyaz.

"No," said Niaz's wife. "We also like *imlis*. She can have the *neem* tree."

"I want the *imli* tree in my *mehr*," said Nuri firmly.

"Well, Nuri can have the *imli* tree," said Niaz. His wife glared at him. "But on one condition only," he quickly added.

"What's that?" asked Shukri Bibi.

"We will all be allowed to share the fruit."

"That's a good arrangement," said Shukri Bibi.

"I agree," said Nuri.

"OK," said Saeed Khan. "The wedding guests are all here anyway. Let us say 'Bismillah' and start preparations straight away."

He then asked Shukri Bibi to call Fayyaz's friends to help him prepare for his wedding and gave Fayyaz a gold *safah* to tie round his head. A boy was quickly sent to the Qazi to ask him to call at Saeed Khan's house after performing the marriage ceremonies for Sara and Rani's weddings.

While they were waiting for the Qazi's arrival, Saeed Khan and his wedding guests completed the engagement ceremony for Fayyaz and Nuri. As soon as Fayyaz and Nuri had exchanged engagement rings, Fayyaz was led away. Later, the Qazi arrived and performed Fayyaz's and Nuri's wedding ceremony and they exchanged wedding rings.

A large part of the open ground next to Saeed Khan's house was covered with brightly striped *durries* (cotton carpets) for the male guests to sit on for the wedding feast. The women and children ate inside the house. All the guests were first served with *sharbat*. Then they ate *maandey* (large thin *chapatis*) and curry with *imli* chutney prepared in advance under Nuri's guidance. This was followed by *zardah* (sweet rice). A *mirasan* or woman singer sang songs while beating on the *dholak* (drum) to entertain the guests and a man played a *shahnai* or flute outside the house.

70

"Kites often build their nests in *imli* trees," remarked one of Fayyaz's friends when they had finished their meal.

"They are supposed to steal women's gold jewelry and keep it in their nests," said another guest. "I wonder if that's true."

"I was in the woods one day with Fayyaz and some other friends," said the first guest. "We found a kites' nest at the top of an *imli* tree. We couldn't see any kites around so the others asked Fayyaz to climb the tree. Just as he got near the nest, two kites suddenly swooped down on him. One of them took his cap in its beak and dropped it on a branch just above the nest. The other one started to peck at his arms and shoulders. Fayyaz got down that tree as fast as he could. We never did find out what those kites had in their nest." Everyone enjoyed the story.

The day after their wedding, Nuri and Fayyaz went to live in Fayyaz's house on the farm at Munshigaon. On the same day, two *tongas* driven by Akram and Jugnu Khan *tongawalas* left Bamboowala's house for Ujjain. Adam Beg with Sara and Mrs. Adiba Hassan sat in one *tonga*. Behind them was a second *tonga* carrying Anwar Ali with Rani, his mother, and Tara Bibi. Then came four bullock carts carrying the wedding guests, followed by the bicycle riders who had accompanied them there.

Adam Beg's sister greeted Sara and introduced the little girl at her side to her new mother.

"Look what I have brought for you," said Sara to the child, giving her a doll wearing village dress. "This used to be mine when I was little."

The child held out her hand, smiling shyly.

Anwar Ali's mother led the way through Elephant Gate to their home, followed by Rani and her son. "This is Arithewaley, the Lawyers' Den," she said. She went across the courtyard and opened a door. "This is our own private courtyard," she said. "I invite the other ladies from Arithewaley here from time to time. We have dances and meetings to celebrate weddings and other occasions. You and Sara can show us some of your village dances."

Then she took Rani to an outside staircase at one side of the courtyard that led to a large room above the rest of the house. The room and the bed had been decorated with flowers. "This room is for you and Anwar," she told Rani.

After dropping off their passengers at Elephant Gate, Akram and Jugnu Khan went to leave their *tongas* outside their employer's office. Hira Lal was already there, sitting on the step of his *tonga*.

"You found your way back from the village, then?" he greeted them. "Those two village girls were lucky to marry two fine men from our town."

"There were three weddings," Akram informed him.

"Tell me about it."

The three *tongawalas* started to walk toward Akram *tongawala's* house by the football ground behind the Qazi's residence, as Akram and Jugnu Khan began to relate the unusual events they had witnessed at the wedding celebrations.

Chapter 4: Time Out with the Tongawalas

The Khan brothers entertained their friend with the news from the weddings.

"What about the bride left with no husband?" asked Hira Lal.

"Oh, they found someone else for her, a *Machhanddar*, *monkeywala*, and held her wedding on the same day," Jugnu Khan smiled. "There were three weddings for the price of two."

The friends reached Akram *tongawala's* house at one corner of the football ground and sat down on a tatty old multi-colored carpet that had come from the graveyard adjacent to his house. Then they began to smoke *charas*, as they usually did at the end of each day's work.

Akram *tongawala* was of medium height, slim, unshaven, and dark skinned, his black hair streaked with white. He wore grubby white *pajamas*, as was common among the tongawalas, with an old striped shirt and a well-worn black hat. Jugnu Khan *tongawala* was short, fat, and strongly built, with long, straight black hair. He was equally shabbily dressed.

Everyone in Ujjain knew Hira Lal *tongawala*. He lived in one of the houses behind the football ground, along with other lower caste, working-class Hindus. Hira Lal was of medium height, thin, and unshaven, with cropped white hair and dark brown skin. He always wore a dirty colored shirt over an equally grubby white *dhoti* with *chappals* on his feet. He was happy-go-lucky and had a loud, clear voice.

Occasionally, the three friends also met in the mornings to smoke hashish. Afterward, Hira Lal would drive his *tonga* at top speed through the streets of Ujjain, shouting, "My name is Hira Lal!"

Passers-by stopped, shouted "Hira Lal! How are you?" and waved as he drove past.

Hira Lal whipped his horse hard to make him run faster. "*Bhag rey ghorey bhag* – Run, horse, run!" he cried.

"Look at my horse! Just look at him!" he exclaimed. "No other horse in this world runs like him!"

Everyone smiled and some people laughed at Hira Lal's *charsi* talk.

"This is the best *tonga* in Ujjain," declared Hira Lal. "Everyone should enjoy a ride in this *tonga* once in a lifetime. You can stand and watch and it is free. You may also wish for a free ride. Some day, you might just get what you wish for."

"Hira Lal, *Charas piya hai?* -- Did you smoke *charas*?" called some of the onlookers.

"No, no, never, I never smoke," answered Hira Lal.

Akram *tongawala* rented a two-room house from Qazi Sahib, where he lived with his wife Qulfi and their 17 year old son Nazir. Qulfi did domestic work in the houses of the ladies in the Lawyers' Den across the road from the Qazi mosque. Nazir was slim and dark with curly black hair and generally wore a sulky expression on his face. He worked as a laborer in a cloth mill. Nazir was bored with his job and bored with his life. Sometimes he tried to talk to his mother about his future, but when she was home, she was generally too tired and too occupied with her household duties to really listen. Most of the time, she was out doing her domestic work, in the houses of the ladies in the Lawyers' Den nearby. Nazir really didn't want to end up like his father, driving a *tonga* around Ujjain and smoking hashish with his friends.

- - - - - - - - - - - - - - - - - - - -

Hira Lal's *tonga* could seat four people, one next to the driver in front and three in the back. One day he picked up four well-dressed Hindus wearing spotless white *dhotis*. They were prosperous businessmen, regular clients of his, and habitual punters, who went in for *satta*, a form of gambling. Bets were made on cotton prices in Bombay, using numbers from 0 to 10. Most people just played the numbers without any clear idea of whether they would come up or not. Before getting down, the businessman seated next to Hira Lal murmured a number in his ear.

"Put your bet on this number," he told Hira Lal. "It's the latest tip from our source."

Hira Lal went straight to the betting shop and placed his day's takings on that number. The following day, he found that his number had come up and immediately went to collect his winnings.

Some weeks later, Hira Lal picked up the same four businessmen. Once again the same businessman gave Hira Lal another hot tip. Having successfully followed his advice on the previous occasion, Hira Lal decided the time had come to make his fortune once and for all and stop driving a *tonga* for somebody else.

After dropping the businessmen off, Hira Lal drove to his usual betting shop. "I've got this number and I want to place a bet," he told the bookie.

"How much do you want to bet?"

"How much will I get if I win?"

"If you bet one rupee on that number, then you will get seven rupees if you win," replied the bookie.

"I want to bet my *tonga* on this number," said Hira Lal.

"This is not your *tonga*," the bookie told him. "I cannot accept your bet."

"I am in charge of this *tonga*," Hira Lal answered, "I can do what I like with it. You must accept my bet."

The bookie knew Hira Lal well and could see that he was high on *charas* as usual. He also knew the *tonga* owner.

"OK, you can leave your *tonga* here," he told Hira Lal.

When Hira Lal had gone, the bookie sent a message to the owner of the *tonga*. "Hira Lal has left one of your *tongas* outside my shop. He's used it to place a bet with me. Please let me know what action I should take."

Shortly afterward, the *tonga* owner showed up at the betting shop. "Did you accept the bet from Hira Lal?" he asked the bookie.

"He insisted on placing it. What shall I do now?"

"Cancel Hira Lal's bet," replied the *tonga* owner angrily. "He is an old man, a *charsi*, a hashish smoker. He has no authority over my *tonga*."

"OK," answered the bookie, smiling to himself, and did so.

The owner collected his *tonga* and went home.

Hira Lal hitched a ride from a passing *tonga* to Akram *tongawala's* house. Akram was sitting outside with Jugnu Khan.

"I have just placed the biggest bet of my life," Hira Lal announced. "If I win, I will get seven *tongas*. If I win you will each drive your own *tonga* instead of working for somebody else."

Jugnu Khan silently passed Hira Lal some *charas*. Thick

clouds of hashish smoke blew over the nearby graves as the three friends reflected on the endless possibilities open to them as *tonga* owner/drivers rather than ordinary *tongawalas*.

The next day, Hira Lal learned that his number had come up and he had won his bet. Jubilant, he went to the betting shop together with Akram and Jugnu Khan, with an uncharacteristic spring in his step. "My number came up today," he cried. "Where are my seven *tongas*?"

"What do you mean? What seven *tongas*?" asked the bookie.

"When I placed my bet with my *tonga* you told me I would get seven *tongas* if I win. I have won, so you now owe me seven *tongas*. You wrote my name and my *tonga* bet in your Black Book"

"Your bet has been canceled," said the bookie matter of factly. He pointed to the entry in his Black Book. It had been crossed out.

Hira Lal's face fell. "Why has it been canceled?" he shouted.

"After you left my betting shop, I sent a message to your employer. He came here, canceled the bet, and collected his *tonga*. There is now no bet, so there are no winnings."

The three friends spent the day driving Akram's *tonga* at top speed all over Ujjain. "My employer is a *chore*, a thief, a robber of honest *tongawalas*," shouted Hira Lal. "He has taken all my winnings."

People stopped and smiled at them in a puzzled way as they drove past.

Finally, they went to the office of Hira Lal's employer. Hira Lal jumped down from the *tonga* and burst through the door. Someone was in the office with his employer.

"One minute please," said his employer to Hira Lal.

"One minute! One minute!" shouted Hira Lal angrily. "I have waited many years for this. I will wait no longer!"

Hira Lal's employer quickly showed the other man out of the office. "What's the matter?" he asked Hira Lal.

"You canceled my bet. Today I should have won seven *tongas*. Now you can drive your *tonga* yourself! I will never again drive a *tonga* for you as long as I live!"

With that, Hira Lal stormed out of the office, slamming the door behind him.

Later, the three friends sat in front of Akram *tongawala's* house, blowing clouds of hashish over the graveyard as usual. They smoked in silence, their vision of a golden life blurred in a haze of half-formed hashish dreams. Hira Lal felt a sense of loss. His *tonga* and his horse had been so much a part of his life.

"Bhagu! Bhagu!" he called to his horse. "Bhagu, where are you? I don't want to be Hira Lal any more. I want to become Bhagu and you can be Hira Lal."

In his dream, he seemed to hear his horse saying, "OK, Hira Lal. You can be Bhagu and I will be Hira Lal."

"Jugnu! Akram!" shouted Hira Lal. "Let me see how it is to be a horse. Let me live the life of Bhagu. Put reins on me and whip me like I whipped Bhagu day and night. Let me feel how it is to have the life of a *tonga* horse."

"OK," said Akram and Jugnu. In their hashish-induced haze, this sounded like fun. They tied a long piece of rope round Hira Lal. Jugnu found a whip and seized both ends of the rope in one hand.

Bhag! Bhag! Run! Run! Faster! Faster!" he shouted and started to whip Hira Lal.

When he felt the pain of the whip across his back Hira Lal, cried out, "*Bas! Bas!* Stop! Stop! No more! I don't want to be a horse any more."

Jugnu Khan put down the whip and he and Akram untied Hira Lal.

When Qulfi came home, the three friends were high on hashish and sitting in silence.

"What's the matter with you?" she asked with concern. Akram told her what had happened, that Hira Lal had placed a winning bet with his *tonga* and should have been given seven *tongas*.

"Can you do anything about it?" she asked.

"No," came the reply. "His employer canceled the bet."

"I meant his job! What are we going to do for money now?" Unable to hold back the tears, she left the room.

- - - - - - - - - - - - - - - - - - - -

The next day, Qulfi went to work in the house of Mrs. Adiba Hassan, a solicitor's wife and related the story of Hira Lal's bet.

"Come back here when you've finished working in the other houses and we will see what can be done," said Mrs. Adiba Hassan.

When Qulfi returned to Mrs. Adiba Hassan's house, she was greeted by her employer and her employer's mother, Mrs. Waheeda Begum.

"My brother Shakil Sahib the lawyer will be home soon," said Mrs. Adiba Hassan. "Wait here with my mother and I'll go and ask him if he knows someone who can give you free advice."

Shakil Sahib listened carefully to his sister's story. Then he said, "Tell Qulfi to ask Hira Lal to go and see Yousuf Ali Sahib and say that I sent him. He is a retired lawyer and he might be able to help in this matter."

Yousuf Ali Sahib was tall, slim, and very fair skinned with

a neatly trimmed beard. He lived near the Qazi mosque in Mirzawari. In his heyday, he had won nearly all his cases in court. He would start off by speaking against his own client in such a way that the prosecutor was unable to make use of these statements in his own arguments, thus making his side of the case appear less convincing. Yousuf Ali Sahib would then present his client's defense, justifying his client's actions, and turning the case in favor of his client.

- - - - - - - - - - - - - - - - - - - -

Hira Lal stood at the front door of Yousuf Ali Sahib's residence wearing, for the first time in a long time, a clean shirt and a smart white *dhoti*. He raised the door knocker and let it fall gently three times. A servant opened the door, asked his name, and told him to wait. Then he led Hira Lal into the courtyard, where some chairs were grouped around a table under a shady pomegranate tree. A large bird cage with a parrot inside it hung from a beam just beneath the verandah.

"*Kon hai, kon hai?* Who is there, who is there?" squawked the parrot.

"*Chup chaap*, be quiet, Parrot," said the servant, "*Khamosh!* Silence! This is our guest."

Yousuf Ali Sahib was sitting on one of the chairs beneath the tree. He rose and greeted Hira Lal. "Hello Hira Lal, how are you?"

"Shakil Sahib said that you might be able to help me," replied Hira Lal.

"Sit down. I will ask the servant to bring tea. How can I help you?"

Hira Lal related how he had staked his *tonga* on a number that had come up and the bookie had refused to pay him his winnings of seven *tongas*.

The tea arrived. Yousuf Ali Sahib looked across at Hira

Lal. "Betting is illegal, so it will be difficult to take the bookie to the court," he said. "Have you got any proof of the bet, such as a betting slip?"

"No Sahib," said Hira Lal. "The bookie at the betting shop takes bets and writes the details in his Black Book."

"Ah!" The lawyer smiled. "Did he write your betting details in his Black Book?"

"Yes Sahib, he did," answered Hira Lal.

"How do you know that he canceled your bet?"

"The bookie told me that the *tonga* owner canceled my bet."

"Did you see with your own eyes that your bet had been canceled?"

"Yes, Sahib! The bookie showed me the entry in his Black Book and it had been crossed out."

"Did the bookie ask your permission to cancel the bet?" asked Yousuf Ali Sahib.

"No, Sahib!"

"Good," said the lawyer. "Then you can take both the bookie and the *tonga* owner to court. It will be difficult to prove this case in court, though, as betting is illegal and it will also be difficult to get hold of the bookie's Black Book. You won't get seven *tongas* but I can get you some compensation. If you wish, I will take your case."

"Thank you Sahib," said Hira Lal.

Yousuf Ali Sahib fetched paper and a pen from his study. Then he wrote a letter to the bookie on some headed notepaper as follows:

"My client, Hira Lal, informs me that you have canceled

his bet of one *tonga* by order of the *tonga* owner and without my client's consent. You are a well-known bookmaker in this town so it will not be difficult to get evidence against you. Hira Lal is entitled to compensation. In order to avoid the case going to court, I suggest that you and the *tonga* owner come and see me at my residence to resolve this matter."

Yousuf Ali Sahib signed the letter, sealed it and gave it to Hira Lal. "Go to the bookie and hand him this letter," he said. "Tell him that it is from me and don't argue with him. I will contact you in a few days' time."

Hira Lal immediately went to the betting shop and gave the bookie the letter from Yusuf Ali Sahib. The bookie was furious that Hira Lal had managed to get a famous lawyer on his side. He was also worried about his reputation and that of his friend, the *tonga* owner. He sent a messenger to his friend's house with a copy of Yousuf Ali Sahib's letter. That evening, they spoke together and decided to visit Yousuf Ali Sahib at his residence the following day.

When the bookie and the *tonga* owner arrived at Yousuf Ali Sahib's residence, the servant showed them into the courtyard and indicated the chairs beneath the tree.

"Sahib will be here in a minute," he told them.

As they went to sit down the parrot flapped his wings and started squawking loudly, "*Chore! Chore!* Thief! Thief!"

"Don't take any notice of the parrot," said the servant to both men.

"*Chup, chaap!* Be quiet!" he told the parrot.

When Yousuf Ali Sahib entered the courtyard, the bookie and the *tonga* owner rose, each clasping the palms of his hands together beneath his chin.

"*Namaste, Vakil Sahib,*" they said.

"*Namaste,*" replied the lawyer.

"Bring tea," he told the servant.

"Hira Lal has asked me to represent him in court," Yousuf Ali Sahib told the bookie and the *tonga* owner. "He claims that both of you canceled his bet without his consent. Is this true?"

"Yes, Vakil Sahib, it is true," answered the bookie, rising to his feet defensively.

"Please sit," said Yousuf Ali Sahib.

"Sahib, Hira Lal should not have used my *tonga* as a bet without my permission," said the *tonga* owner.

Yousuf Ali Sahib welcomed any opportunity to use his extensive legal experience to help people resolve their differences out of court by mediation. "I have a suggestion," he said. "If you agree, it will save both of you from appearing in a court of law." Yousuf Ali Sahib spoke in a clear and authoritative voice.

"What shall we do, Sahib?" asked the bookie and the *tonga* owner.

"I won't ask you to give Hira Lal seven *tongas*," the lawyer answered. "However, you must both offer him some compensation."

"Hira Lal regularly brings four businessmen to my betting shop," the bookie said. "They always place high bets and they always win, so I am losing a lot of money."

"Hira Lal refuses to work for me any longer," complained the *tonga* owner. "He is a good worker and always hands over all his earnings. Not many *tongawalas* are honest like him."

Yousuf Ali Sahib thought for a moment. "Pay Hira Lal four months' wages as compensation from both of you," he said at last.

"Sahib, it is too much. We can't afford so much money," said the bookie and the *tonga* owner worriedly.

"Do you want to sort it out now or do you want to go to a court of law?" asked Yousuf Ali Sahib. "Think about it. One more thing," he added turning to the *tonga* owner, "If you settle it now, I will ask Hira Lal to go back to work for you. He will listen to me. I will tell him to start work tomorrow."

Yousuf Ali Sahib rose. "I am sending my servant now to fetch Hira Lal. If you do not decide now, I will see you in court."

When the servant returned with Hira Lal, the lawyer asked him to show Hira Lal into his study.

"I have been discussing your case with the bookmaker and the *tonga* owner," he told Hira Lal. "They are deciding what action to take. However, you must drop your claim for seven *tongas* from the betting shop owner and return to work as a *tongawala*. I will make sure that you get some compensation. After I have settled this case, you must accept whatever compensation I agree with them on your behalf. You must also agree to work for the *tonga* owner for the same money as before."

"Yes, Sahib," Hira Lal replied gratefully. "I will agree to whatever you say."

Yousuf Ali Sahib returned to the courtyard, asking his servant to stand by at the ready, on the verandah.

"What have you decided?" he asked the bookie and the *tonga* owner.

"Sahib, we can only afford to pay one month's wages each to Hira Lal and your mediation fee," they replied.

"Very well, then. You will both pay Hira Lal one month's wages each in cash now. Tomorrow Hira Lal will come back to work."

The bookie and the *tonga* owner each took out a bag from their waistcoats, counted the money on to the table, and separated it into two piles.

"These are two months' wages for Hira Lal and this is your

mediation fee," they said. "Thank you, *Vakil Sahib*, for sorting out this problem."

Yousuf Ali Sahib sent the servant to fetch Hira Lal from his study. "These two gentlemen are paying you two months' wages as compensation," he told Hira Lal. "Tomorrow you will go back to work for the *tonga* owner."

"Yes, Sahib," said Hira Lal.

Everyone was satisfied at the outcome of the mediation.

Hira Lal went to Ram Das, a well-known sweet merchant, and bought two very large boxes of sweets. He took one box to Yousuf Ali Sahib's residence and presented the other box to Qulfi as thanks for all her help and support. That evening, the three friends had a smoking session in front of Akram's house to celebrate. The following day, Hira Lal was once again reunited with his *tonga* and his horse Bhagu.

When Qulfi went to work the next morning, she told the ladies in the Lawyers' Den about the successful mediation by Yousuf Ali Sahib and shared her relief and her sweets with them.

- - - - - - - - - - - - - - - - - - - -

The house next door to the Qazi belonged to his brother. It was a two-story residence standing on a gentle slope. The household waste water flowed down to street level through a pipe to a gutter by the main road, which was covered with stone slabs up to the street corner where the slabs had been removed. A young man, Anwar Ali, rented a grocery shop on the ground floor of the residence. Business had been going well since his recent marriage to Rani, and she had settled in well to life with his mother in the Lawyers' Den. The shop counter faced the street and a rich aroma of spices and mango pickle wafted outside from the room behind. Anwar Ali also sold lentils, basmati rice, *ghee*, and vegetable oil as well as tea and biscuits. A small group of ladies living locally supplied him with homemade mango and *imli* chutney. The pavement in front of the shop was a favorite meeting place for local residents.

One day, Qulfi stopped off as usual at Anwar Ali's shop after finishing work, to buy some food. She was just paying for her purchases when she heard a child's voice. *"Ammi! Ammi!* Look! Look! What are those two men carrying in that big box?"

Qulfi took her change and turned quickly to see a small girl pointing at a passing sedan chair and pulling at her mother's sleeve. The woman was in her twenties and wore village dress with fitted white cotton trousers beneath a long-sleeved *kameez* reaching below her knees and a *dupatta* draped over her shoulders.

The woman looked lost and confused. Qulfi went up to her. "You're new here, aren't you?" she asked.

"Yes, we have just moved to Ujjain from a village called Khajurpur," replied the woman.

"Where are you staying?"

"We have rented a small dwelling in Mirzawari."

"My name is Qulfi. We live behind the Qazi's house at one side of the football ground."

"I am Chandni and this is my little daughter Meena."

Meena broke in. *"Ammi!* Those men have put the box down. Look! Look! There's a lady getting out of the box."

"That is a sedan chair," said Qulfi, smiling at the little girl. "The rich ladies from the Lawyers' Den and Mirzawari travel in sedan chairs when they go and visit their friends."

Qulfi turned to Chandni. "Are you settling down here OK?"

"My husband has found a job in the cloth mill," came the reply. "We stayed with relatives at first, but it was too crowded and we had to find a place of our own. Things are expensive in Ujjain and the wages of my husband, Fazal, are very low. I wish I could also find a job."

Qulfi's main employer in the Lawyers' Den was Mrs. Adiba Hassan, a solicitor's wife. The other ladies there had asked her to work for them in their houses as well, as she was reliable, honest, and hardworking. Qulfi now had as much work as she wanted and had even been forced to turn down work.

Feeling sorry for Chandni, Qulfi said, "I might be able to help you. I will talk to my employer. Let's meet here again tomorrow at the same time."

The following day, Qulfi spoke to Mrs. Adiba Hassan about Chandni before starting her chores. "I will talk to the other ladies and see what they say," answered Mrs. Adiba Hassan.

That afternoon, Mrs. Adiba Hassan invited some of the other ladies from the Lawyers' Den to come to tea. "Qulfi has met a woman who is looking for work," she told them. "Her name is Chandni. She has just moved to Mirzawari from Khajurpur village. Qulfi thinks she will be a good worker."

"When the woman who works for me washes my dishes, I often find that there are spoons or cups missing," said one lady.

"The woman I have is lazy and dirty," another lady put in.

"Qulfi works for me," said Mrs. Farida Begum, Shakil Sahib's wife. "She is very hard-working and does a good job."

"She is also very honest and reliable," Mrs. Adiba Hassan added. "When Qulfi has finished her work, I will speak to her and ask her to bring Chandni along to my house tomorrow."

The following day Qulfi brought Chandni and Meena to Mrs. Adiba Hassan's house to assess her. After seeing the way in which Chandni worked, Mrs. Adiba Hassan agreed to recommend her to the other ladies in the Lawyers' Den. At first, Qulfi and Chandni washed dishes and did the cleaning only for Qulfi's employers. However, word of Chandni's excellent work quickly spread, and soon she was being regularly employed by two other families in the Lawyers' Den.

One evening after finishing work, Qulfi was surprised to see her son, Nazir, waiting for her outside the Elephant Gate, leading to the Lawyers' Den. Like those of his fellow workers in Mirzawari who did not have bicycles, he walked to and from his work each day, at the cloth mill, a distance of about three miles.

"Has something happened at work?" asked Qulfi.

"No, no," Nazir replied. "It's nothing like that. I want to make plans for my future. Let's go somewhere quiet where we can talk in private."

He and his mother set off for home. They walked by the football ground toward a well opposite their house and stood there in the semi-darkness.

"What sort of plans do you have for your future?" asked Qulfi.

"I want to get married and I need your help," answered Nazir. "Will you find a bride for me?"

"There are no suitable girls living here," Qulfi murmured reluctantly.

"There are girls living in the small houses next door," Nazir pointed out.

"No, no," answered his mother. "They are Untouchables. You can't marry one of them. Your father is a good Muslim, he won't agree to such a marriage."

"What?" retorted Nazir. "That hashish smoker, a good Muslim? I have never seen him going to our local mosque."

"Once every year your father takes our Qazi in his *tonga* to Eidgah, the mosque just outside Ujjain, to lead the prayers at *Eid-ul-Fitr*," Qulfi replied calmly. "Then he joins the service and offers prayers with his heart and mind. He never smokes hashish before he takes our Qazi to Eidgah. After *Eid* prayers are finished he brings him home again. He won't take money from our Qazi for these rides in his *tonga*."

"If you don't arrange a girl for me, I will leave home. I have no life here."

"Let me think a moment," said Qulfi, upset at his response. Suddenly her face lit up. "I know someone who might be able to help me to arrange a marriage for you."

"Who?" asked Nazir.

"Chandni, Meena's mother. She and I work together for the ladies in the Lawyers' Den. She has recently come here from the village of Khajurpur outside Ujjain. She told me that it is very difficult for the girls there to find a suitable husband. The boys in the village generally move away to the towns to find work and marry there. Chandni's husband, Fazal, tried to start a cycle business in Khajurpur. Now he works in a textile mill like you and he goes there by bicycle every day. He knows everything about bicycles. In Khajurpur he was known as Fazal *cyclewala*."

"I would like to learn to ride and have my own bicycle, and learn all about bicycle repairs," said Nazir.

"I will speak to Chandni," replied Qulfi. "She will know if there are any suitable girls for you in her village. I will also tell her that you want to learn how to ride a bicycle."

"Thank you, *Amma*," said Nazir. "Now I will have a future here."

Nazir and his mother walked home slowly. Akram was sitting outside their house with his *charsi* friends Jugnu Khan and Hira Lal. A cloud of smoke hung over them.

"We all saw you both standing by the well," Akram called loudly. "What have you been talking about?"

"Oh, nothing that would interest you, *Abba*," answered Nazir.

"I'll decide that. Tell us what you said," answered Akram

brusquely.

"I have a right to talk to my own son in privacy," shouted Qulfi. "It's none of your business. We are going to eat now. Come, Nazir." She rushed past Akram, closely followed by her son.

The next day after work, Qulfi went to Anwar Ali's shop as usual, to buy food.

"Oh, look, *Ammi,* there's Qulfi," called a familiar voice behind her. Turning, she saw Meena, pulling at her mother's hand.

"Hello Chandni," said Qulfi. "I am pleased to see you. How are you?"

"Very well, thank you," replied Chandni. "Thanks to you, I now have regular work. The ladies in the Lawyers' Den are very kind. They give Meena sweets and one of them even gave me some clothes for her."

"That's good," said Qulfi. "Now I need your help."

"Of course, I'll help you in any way I can," answered Chandni.

"It's my son, Nazir. He is 17 years old. He works in a cloth mill and he wants to get married. However, I can't find him a girl in this locality. Perhaps you might know of someone in your village?"

"There are girls in the village who aren't married," Chandni replied thoughtfully. "One of them may be suitable for Nazir."

One day, soon after her talk with Qulfi, Chandni was working in the Lawyers' Den when a boy came to speak to her.

"Your brother Jawwad is waiting to see you by the Elephant Gate," he announced. "He says he is from Khajurpur."

"I will come and see what he wants," said Chandni. She informed her employer that her elder brother wished to see her and went quickly with Meena to the Elephant Gate.

"How did you get here?" asked Chandni when she saw her brother.

"I got a lift in a bullock cart delivering dates in Ujjain," he replied.

"How is everyone in Khajurpur?"

Jawwad told her all the family news. Then he said, "How about you? How's your life in Ujjain?"

"I like it," replied Chandni. "I have found a good friend here. Her name is Qulfi. She helped me to get a job. We both work in the houses of families living in the Lawyers' Den."

"Do you have any messages for the people at home in Khajurpur?" asked Jawwad.

"Yes," Chandni replied. "Tell our sister Roshni that I would like to bring my friend Qulfi to our village for a visit. She has a son called Nazir and she is looking for a wife for him. He is 17 years old and works in a cloth mill."

"I will pass this on," said Jawwad. "The village ladies will be very pleased to see you again and meet your friend -- and her son."

Jawwad took his leave of Chandni and Meena and went to Anwar Ali's grocery shop to wait for the bullock cart to take him back to Khajurpur. On his return, the news quickly spread around the village that Chandni was coming for a visit together with a friend who was seeking a wife for her son.

Two days later, when Chandni came to work in the Rent Collector's house in the Lawyers' Den, his wife took her to one side and said, "Your sister Roshni has sent a message to you through my husband. She says that they have found two girls who may be suitable for Qulfi's son Nazir. Since you and Qulfi will only be able to visit them for a short time, she suggests that you bring Nazir with you and arrive in Khajurpur as early as possible in the day so that you can meet both girls. Then, if everything goes well, you can arrange a quick engagement ceremony after lunch and get back to Ujjain before it gets dark."

"That sounds like a good idea," said Chandni. "I will speak with Qulfi. When can I send an answer to my sister?"

"My husband will be traveling through Khajurpur again in two days' time," replied the Rent Collector's wife.

When she heard the news, Qulfi said, "I will ask Mrs. Adiba Hassan if she can make arrangements with the other ladies, so that we can both have a day off to visit your village. I am sure that they will agree to this."

- - - - - - - - - - - - - - - - - - - -

A few days later, Akram drove to Khajurpur in his *tonga*, wearing a new black cap with a clean shirt and *pajama* trousers. Next to him was Nazir in a new striped shirt, white cotton *pajama* trousers, and new Bata shoes. In the back were Qulfi, Chandni, and Meena wearing their best clothes.

Khajurpur was some distance from Ujjain and was famous for its date palm trees, which produced top quality *khajurein* (dates). The road to Khajurpur led through thick jungle where robbers often hid and attacked travelers, particularly in the evening. Meena slept during the journey. They had presents for the engagement ceremony with them --a *dupatta*, a *chadar*, and an engagement ring, as well as a large box of sweets from Ram Das, the sweet merchant, and *gur* (raw sugar), which Akram had collected in his *tonga* the previous day. Qulfi also had a woven basket containing a bunch of large, top quality bananas with black spots on them from Jalgaon.

When the *tonga* from Ujjain reached Khajurpur, several of the men and women from the village crowded around as Akram pulled up next to the house of Chandni's sister, Roshni. Everyone got down from the *tonga*. Roshni's husband showed Akram where to leave his horse and *tonga* and then took him and Nazir into the front room, where they sat together drinking tea and chatting.

On the verandah, the women sat drinking tea. "How do you like life in Ujjain?" one of them asked Chandni.

"Oh, it is fine," replied Chandni. "People are very friendly. This is Qulfi. She helped me to find a job. Now she is looking for a wife for her son, Nazir."

"Was that him sitting next to the driver?" asked one of the other women.

"Yes, that's him," said Chandni.

The younger women looked at each other and started to giggle.

"He is very handsome" said one of them.

"He has curly black hair just like you," said another woman, looking across at Qulfi.

There was more giggling. Qulfi smiled at the women.

Discussion followed concerning the two unmarried girls who had been chosen as possible brides for Nazir.

"Iffat and Jannat are the right age," said Chandni's sister-in-law. "Iffat is 18 and Jannat is 17 years old."

"Iffat's family lives in a bungalow and her father is a government official," remarked Roshni. "She is also educated, so it would not be a good match."

"What about the other girl?" asked Qulfi.

"Jannat? Her father is a farm laborer. Her mother died some years ago, and she lives with her aunt."

"Does she live nearby?" asked Qulfi.

"Yes," replied Roshni. "I'll take you to see her if you like."

A little later, Roshni took Qulfi, Chandni, and Meena to call on Jannat's aunt.

"Chandni, how nice to see you," said Jannat's aunt when she opened the door to them. Turning to the other lady, she smiled warmly and added, "And you must be Qulfi. I'm so pleased to meet you. Do come in."

They sat on the verandah while Jannat's aunt went through to the back where Jannat was sitting with one of her friends.

"We have visitors," Jannat's aunt told her. "Please change your clothes and make tea for them." She then sent a boy playing outside to fetch Jannat's father, who was working in a nearby field.

Jannat's aunt returned to her guests. "What is your son like?" she asked Qulfi.

Qulfi described Nazir and said that he worked in a cloth mill.

Jannat brought in tea for the guests, smiling shyly. Qulfi looked at her with interest. Jannat was 17 years old, of medium height, slim, and elegant with dark skin.

When Jannat had left the room, Qulfi said, "She looks like a nice girl."

"Where is your son?" asked Jannat's aunt. "I would like to see him."

"I will bring Nazir and his father. They are sitting with my husband in our front room." said Roshni.

She went to her house and asked the men to come with her to Jannat's aunt's house.

Jannat's father came home and went to wash quickly and change his clothes. Just then, Roshni returned with Nazir, his father Akram, and her husband. She introduced Nazir and

Akram to Jannat's aunt and father.

After a while, Roshni took Jannat's aunt to one side. "How do you like the boy?" she asked.

"Her father and I think that he seems very suitable for our Jannat," came the reply. "I will go and ask Jannat what she thinks." She left the room and returned shortly afterward, smiling. "Jannat has agreed to marry Nazir."

Qulfi asked Nazir to step outside the door and have a quiet word with her. "I have seen Jannat," she said. "She seems to be a nice girl and would be suitable for you. If Jannat agrees, would you be ready to marry her?"

"Yes," said Nazir, smiling with pleasure.

"We have to go back to Ujjain this afternoon," said Chandni.

"If you like, we can have the engagement ceremony today," replied Jannat's aunt.

Before the *mangni* (engagement ceremony) started, Qulfi took Jannat's aunt to one side. "There is no time for us to buy Jannat new clothes for her engagement," she said, handing her money. "Please buy clothes for her on our behalf."

Jannat's aunt took the money and smiled her thanks. She then brought her visitors into the front room. Jannat and Nazir, her bridegroom-to be, sat opposite each other and were both covered with the *chadar* Qulfi had brought with her from Ujjain. As soon as they had exchanged rings, Nazir removed the sheet from his head and everyone clapped. Jannat sat, still veiled with bowed head, and her aunt raised Jannat's hand to display the fine engagement ring to everyone in the room. They agreed to hold the wedding in Khajurpur and a date was set for the following month.

The party from Ujjain went home laden with village delicacies, *laddus* (sweet balls), and *gaunkris*, round cakes cooked in the ashes of cow dung fires, which had been prepared by Jannat and her friends that afternoon. Their basket was filled with *khajurein* (dates) from the village.

- - - - - - - - - - - - - - - - - - - -

Fazal found an old bike dumped in the graveyard. He cleaned off the rust, oiled the moving parts, and repainted it. He also bought new tires, repaired the brakes, and replaced the worn down brake blocks and the missing wheel spokes. He and Chandni presented it to Nazir as a wedding gift.

Qulfi asked her employer if she and Chandni could have a day off to attend Nazir's wedding.

"Yes, of course. I am pleased that you have found a suitable wife for your son," said Mrs. Adiba Hassan.

"I have one more big favor to ask of you, Begum Sahiba," Qulfi said. "Can you please lend me some jewelry? I have none of my own."

"Yes, of course," said Mrs. Adiba Hassan. "She went out of the room and returned with a small cloth bag (*batwa*). Pulling open the strings on the *batwa*, she took out a gold necklace, and some matching gold earrings. "You may borrow these," she told Qulfi. "Please don't tell anyone except your husband that I am lending you this jewelry." She gave the bag and its contents to Qulfi.

"Thank you, Begum Sahiba, for letting me borrow this fine jewelry," Qulfi replied, clutching the bag tightly and shaking slightly, aware of its worth.

It was a hot, sunny summer day when the wedding procession assembled early in the morning in the street behind the graveyard. First came Akram's *tonga* with Qazi Sahib sitting in the back. As the only Muslim priest in Ujjain, the Qazi traveled over a wide area to perform his duties. Behind him was Hira Lal's *tonga* carrying Nazir's friend Mehboob and his wife Hasina. Nazir and Fazal were sitting in Jugnu Khan's *tonga*. Last of all were

96

Qulfi, Chandni, and Meena riding in a hired bullock cart. The horses, *tongas*, bullock, and bullock cart had all been decorated with garlands the night before.

Akram raised his hand and shouted, "*Chalo bhai chalo --* let's be off!"

"*Chal rey ghorey chal --* come on horse go!" shouted Hira Lal to his horse.

The wedding procession proceeded toward the outskirts of Ujjain and along the road to Khajurpur.

The Qazi performed the wedding ceremony. Afterward, he issued a marriage certificate. Chandni's relatives and several other villagers attended the feast for the wedding of Nazir and Jannat in a field near Jannat's house. Cold, home-made *chhachh* (buttermilk) was served to all the wedding guests. Young men and women in village costumes performed dances to the sound of the *dholak* (drum) and sang folk songs, to the guests enjoyment.

Later, the guests sat on white sheets on the ground around large *thaals* or round metal dishes on which the wedding feast was served. There were *rotis* (thick *chapatis*) with *imli* chutney, mango pickle from Anwar Ali's shop, meat curry and lentils, followed by *kheer* (rice pudding). Fresh drinking water was supplied from a nearby well. Two young men scooped the cold water from the bottom of the well in a metal bucket and emptied it into large clay jars placed near where the guests were sitting. The water was then ladled into clay bowls for the guests to drink.

- - - - - - - - - - - - - - - - - - - -

It was early evening by the time the wedding feast finished. Jannat's and Chandni's relatives invited the party from Ujjain to stay overnight in Khajurpur. "It's not safe to travel through the jungle in the evening," said Jannat's aunt.

"There are robbers in the jungle," Roshni's husband added. "No one travels through the jungle at this time."

"Let's go! There is still daylight," shouted Jugnu Khan, raising his right hand. "I will fight with any robbers." He looked at Akram for approval.

"We will fight any robbers," Hira Lal chimed in. "We won't let them get away."

"We'll be OK," said Akram. He wanted to join his friends in rounding off their wedding celebrations with an extra special hashish-smoking session.

Reluctantly, the villagers helped the party from Ujjain to load the bride's dowry into the bullock cart. Then Jannat, wearing her gold bridal jewelry, got into the bullock cart together with Qulfi wearing her borrowed jewelry, followed by Chandni and Meena. Once again, Fazal and Nazir traveled in Jugnu Khan's *tonga*, Mehboob and Hasina went in Hira Lal's *tonga*, and Akram drove in front with Qazi Sahib sitting behind him.

Darkness suddenly fell soon after they entered the jungle. The small procession stopped, lit the lanterns on the *tongas*, and the bullock cart and set off once again. The shadows by the trees on either side of the track appeared even deeper in the light of the lanterns. Two of the shadows suddenly moved and materialized into two men mounted on horses and carrying guns, one in front of the wedding procession and one at the back. They were tall and strong, their faces half covered by the ends of the *safahs* they wore on their heads.

"That is Qazi Sahib sitting in the front *tonga*," said one of the robbers quietly to his friend. "Show him respect, don't use abusive language, and leave the *tongas* alone."

His friend fired his gun into the air. "Stop and hand over all your jewelry!" he shouted in a hoarse voice.

The small procession stopped. Both men went straight to the bullock cart behind the three *tongas* where the bride was sitting. Jugnu Khan *tongawala* made a run for it. One of the robbers fired at him. The bullet grazed Jugnu Khan's ear. He froze in his tracks. Jannat and Qulfi were then forced to hand over all their gold jewelry to the robbers. They even took Chandni's silver jewelry. Then they disappeared swiftly and silently into the darkness of the jungle.

It was still dark when the sad, bedraggled wedding procession arrived at Akram's house near the graveyard, after leaving Qazi Sahib at his house. The driver of the bullock cart dropped his passengers off and left. Qulfi made tea and took it to the ladies in one room and Nazir brought tea to Mehboob, Fazal, and Akram in the other room. No one said much. The three *tongawalas* sat outside the house and smoked hashish, boasting to each other of their bravery in not panicking while they were being robbed.

The next morning, the three *tongawalas* reported the robbery of their wedding party to the police. Qulfi went in to work as usual.

"How was your son's wedding, Qulfi?" asked Mrs. Adiba Hassan.

Qulfi burst into tears and covered her face with her *dupatta*.

"What happened?" asked her employer.

"Yesterday evening our wedding procession was robbed on the way back to Ujjain. The robbers took all our jewelry. Please forgive me, Begum Sahiba." Qulfi burst into fresh sobs. "You can take money from my wages every week for the rest of my life and I will work for you as usual."

"Don't cry, Qulfi," said Mrs. Adiba Hassan. "It's not your fault. You must also keep quiet about losing my jewelry," she added firmly. "Now go and call my mother, Mrs. Waheeda Begum Sahiba."

When they were alone, Mrs. Adiba Hassan told her mother that she had lent her jewelry to Qulfi for Nazir's wedding and it had all been taken by robbers. "What shall I do?" she asked. "I must keep quiet about it."

"I will get you a gold necklace and a pair of earrings from Nagina jewelers," her mother replied. "No one will ever know that your jewelry was stolen."

They also agreed to pay Qulfi her wages as usual.

- - - - - - - - - - - - - - - - - - - -

Fazal had been one of the few men in Khajurpur who owned a bicycle. He always carried his bicycle repair kit everywhere with him and did minor repairs for the few other cycle owners free of charge. He was known as Fazal *cyclewala* and his great ambition was to have a cycle shop of his own again.

After his marriage to Jannat, Nazir continued to share his parents' home. He took his bicycle to the football ground after work and practised riding on it. Nazir started meeting Fazal before work so that they could ride their bicycles together to the mill. After work, Fazal began to teach Nazir how to look after and repair bicycles. Nazir's friends started calling him Nazir *cyclewala,* to his great pleasure.

Fazal eventually opened his own cycle shop in Mussadipura. The sign outside read "Fazal Cycle Shop -- bicycles bought, sold and repaired." Nazir started to help in the shop after work. Business quickly built up. Fazal asked Nazir to work in the shop full-time and later offered him a business partnership.

- - - - - - - - - - - - - - - - - - - -

Mrs. Adiba Hassan told her husband Waqar Hassan how the wedding party of Qulfi's son Nazir had been robbed in the jungle on their way back to Ujjain after dark. "All the ladies lost their jewelry," she said. "Everyone is most upset."

"I will ask my brother Afaq Hassan, the police inspector, to investigate this matter," her husband replied.

Chapter 5: Elephant Gate

"Nazir's wedding party was traveling through the jungle from Khajurpur after dark when it happened," said Waqar Hassan.

He and his wife, Mrs. Adiba Hassan, were sitting with his younger brother, Police Inspector Afaq Hassan, in their house in the Lawyers' Den. They had finished their evening meal and were drinking tea.

"There are bands of robbers in the jungle all round Ujjain," Police Inspector Afaq Hassan said. "They hold up people traveling in the night through the jungle in *victorias*, even government officials. Just before you asked me here, I had a message from the Governor of Ujjain, Prabhakar Sahib, informing me that the Maharajah of Gwalior has set a high reward for the capture of these robbers. He asked me to take a team of crack marksmen into the jungle to seek them out and capture them, dead or alive."

During the next few days, Afaq Hassan placed plainclothesmen in the surrounding villages to gather information on the robbers' movements. However, they learned nothing, as the villagers were afraid to talk to outsiders in case the robbers found out and took revenge on them.

Some days later, toward evening, a wedding procession set off through the jungle. It was led by the Governor of Ujjain's official carriage, which was richly garlanded with flowers. Blinds at the windows concealed the occupants. Behind the carriage came two *tongas*, each carrying three wedding guests in festive clothes, followed by two bullock carts piled high with colorful cloth covered bundles. The procession was guarded by a couple of men on horses. From time to time, one or another of them would ride out in front or drop behind to glance into the undergrowth on either side of the path.

Suddenly, a group of heavily armed robbers surrounded the wedding procession. The doors of the carriage burst open on both sides. Afaq Hassan and three other armed police officers jumped down and opened fire. They were joined by the *tonga* drivers and their passengers, who were also carrying weapons. The brightly colored bundles revealed more armed police officers. The robbers were outnumbered. They quickly took cover and returned the fire.

Three robbers and two police officers were killed. Afaq Hassan and two other police officers were taken to hospital. One police officer died a few days later. The leader of the robbers was captured alive with minor injuries, together with two of his accomplices. The police discovered the robbers' jungle hideout, a cave concealed by bushes that led into a hill. Inside it was a large cache of money, jewelry, and other items, including much of the jewelry stolen from the wedding procession of Akram *tongawala's* son Nazir.

The robbers were tried in court in Ujjain and found guilty. The leader was hanged and his accomplices were given long jail sentences.

The Governor held a feast for Afaq Hassan and his team in Governor House and gave each of them a large cash reward. Afaq Hassan was also presented with a large area of land near the village of Bhairugarh, about six miles from Ujjain, which had two wells on it.

- - - - - - - - - - - - - - - - - - - -

Gul Bhai lived with his wife and three sons on the ground floor of a two-story house in the Lawyers' Den, which was also called Arithewaley. He was plump and of medium height and was also known as Patwari Sahib. He worked as an estate manager for a rich landlord, and looked after land far away from Ujjain, so he was often away from home. An outside staircase next to the kitchen led to the first floor, where Gul Bhai's widowed sister Kausar lived with her two sons.

One afternoon, Gul Bhai came home early to be greeted by his youngest son Tiddi. True to his nickname of "locust," Tiddi would swoop down on saucers with leftover snacks, particularly sweetmeats, and leave them bare. Despite this, Tiddi was very thin and small for his 4 years. He had thick black curly hair, big brown eyes, and a cheeky grin. "I want to explore all the paths and passages around Arithewaley," he told his father. "*Ammi* won't let me go by myself. Will you take me?"

"I need some food from the shops," said Gul Bhai's wife. "Perhaps you could go there with Tiddi."

"I want to go down the passage between our house and Faiz Khan's house," said Tiddi. At the end of the passage was a wall with a small door that was bolted from the inside. Gul Bhai lifted Tiddi up so that he could open the door. It led to a stretch of ground with a wall along the left and an abandoned house close by, facing the door. Another little door on the right led to the Criminals' Den. The rest of the ground was bounded by the backs of houses separated by narrow alleys.

"This is Camel Courtyard," said Gul Bhai. "People leave their camels there when they come to see the Rent Collector."

They started to walk down one of the narrow streets leading off Camel Courtyard.

Tiddi began to slow down.

"Are you tired?" asked his father. "I'll carry you."

He lifted the boy easily onto his shoulders. Then he went onto the main road, visited Anwar Ali's shop, returned home through the main Elephant Gate, and dropped off his groceries. Suddenly, Gul Bhai noticed that Tiddi was no longer walking by his side. He quietly left the house and went through the Elephant Gate to search for his son. First, he visited Anwar Ali's shop. Some boys were standing outside. "Have you seen my little boy, Tiddi?" he asked them.

The boys saw Tiddi sitting quietly on Gul Bhai's shoulders, with a big grin on his face.

"No, we haven't seen him," said one of the older boys. "We'll help you find him." Gul Bhai moved off and they followed him, laughing quietly.

"There are some boys playing near Camel Courtyard," said one boy. "They might have seen him."

"Thank you," said Gul Bhai. He started to walk past the shops along the main road toward Camel Courtyard. One of the boys quickly ran ahead to the first shop, which belonged to a barber.

"Patwari Sahib is coming," he told the people there. "He's looking for his son Tiddi, who is sitting on his shoulders." Everyone laughed.

When Gul Bhai came to the barber's shop, one of the customers called out, "Hello Patwari Sahib, how are you?"

"I can't find my little Tiddi," came the reply.

The customers glanced at the small boy sitting on Gul Bhai's shoulders and grinning, they shook their heads. "We haven't seen him," they said.

It was the same story at the other shop that Gul Bhai visited. Forewarned by one of the boys "helping" him with his inquiries, the people in the shop joined in the joke. Meanwhile, an older boy cut through to Camel Courtyard to ask the boys playing there to tell Patwari Sahib that they had seen Tiddi going back to the house.

When Gul Bhai asked the boys playing in Camel Courtyard where his son was, one of them answered, "I saw him going through the little back door into Arithewaley."

Gul Bhai was overwhelmed with relief. He rushed toward the back door, flung it open, and was about to go through it when he felt something stopping him and heard a loud shriek.

"Is that you, Tiddi?" asked Gul Bhai in astonishment.

The boys all ran away laughing. Gul Bhai pulled Tiddi down from his shoulders and smacked him. Then he took him quickly into the house.

"That serves you right for keeping quiet all the time I was looking for you," he shouted angrily. "You little *Shaitan ka Bachcha*, everyone was laughing at me because of you."

Tiddi's mother came quickly. "Have you gone mad?" she shouted at Gul Bhai, grabbing Tiddi, "calling your own son 'son of Satan.'"

Tiddi's aunt Kausar joined them when she heard the shouting. She seized the boy's hand and took him upstairs with her.

"He's only a child," she told Gul Bhai. "You shouldn't be so hard on him."

"Why did you say nothing when your father was searching for you?" asked Kausar when Tiddi was sitting on the floor with a saucer of sweets in front of him.

"*Abba* always tells me, 'be quiet, don't interrupt when I am talking to others,'" answered Tiddi. "So I kept quiet."

- - - - - - - - - - - - - - - - - - - -

Arithewaley, the Lawyers' Den, was a separate world of its own with the Elephant Gate standing majestically on guard before it. People providing goods and services entered the Lawyers' Den through the Elephant Gate. Sirju *dhoban* collected the dirty washing from the families there. She was in her twenties with a *bindi* or brightly colored dot on her forehead and long black hair. She always wore a clean white sari with a blue border and was always smiling. She lived with her family next to the football ground. The ladies liked her, so they overlooked it when some of their sons' clothes in her children's sizes occasionally came back later than usual.

Sirju *dhoban* and her husband the *dhobi* took the dirty clothes in a donkey cart down to the river Shipra, where they joined the other *dhobis* and *dhobans* in washing the clothes by pounding them on stones by the river. The crocodiles in the river kept their distance while the *dhobis* were working.

A single water tap near the entrance to the courtyard provided fresh drinking water for everyone in Arithewaley. Two of the houses also had an inside water tap each. In summer, the water supply was sometimes cut off for a time and water carriers brought water to Arithewaley. People collected water in buckets for drinking, bathing, and washing dishes. Small drains took water from each house to a gutter in the middle of the courtyard, which was covered with stone slabs, one of which could be lifted to insert a rod to clear it when necessary or to rinse spittoons. There were two spittoons in each house, one in the bedroom and one outside the reception room for use when chewing *paan*. A *paandan*, a box containing betel leaves and the condiments chewed with it, stood on a table in one corner inside the reception room.

Singharey or water chestnut plants grew in abundance on the surface of a lake opposite Eidgah, the mosque where Muslims offered prayers at *Eid-ul-Fitr*. When the water chestnuts were ripe, some Hindu women went out by boat to harvest them. Later, one of them came to Arithewaley with a wickerwork basket of *singharey* for sale.

On Fridays, a lower caste Hindu woman wearing a grubby

white sari came through the Elephant Gate to sell freshly caught fish from a large, round, cloth-lined wickerwork basket covered with a dirty cloth, which she carried on her head. Fish was a popular dish in the Lawyers' Den, as fishing was prohibited, so fish was not sold in any shop.

There were two sets of outside toilets in Arithewaley. A four-seater toilet, enclosed by a high wall without a roof, stood next to a large open sewer about six feet deep and four feet in circumference, which was beneath the *aritha* tree that gave Arithewaley its name. The entrance to this toilet was in one corner facing away from the courtyard and was completely open. Men approaching the toilet and seeing nobody outside cleared their throats loudly before rounding the corner. The sound of throat-clearing in reply was the signal to stand and wait. Ladies generally visited the toilet in twos and one of them stood guard outside.

Beneath two of the seats were large, square, metal buckets and an open drain under the remaining two seats. After using the toilet, people washed themselves over one of the seats opening on to the drain, using water from a *lota*, a water pot with a narrow spout that they brought with them. The water flowed into the open sewer just outside the toilet. There was a similar, smaller, two seater toilet by the wall at the other end of the courtyard near the Rent Collector's house. It also had no door, but the opening was covered by a thick, dirty curtain made of sacking.

A lower-caste Hindu man came each day to change the buckets beneath the toilets. As a man coming from outside, he would enter through the Elephant Gate, suitably chaperoned by his wife, and take away the full buckets on a bullock cart to be emptied in a designated area for sewage outside Ujjain.

- - - - - - - - - - - - - - - - - - - -

About two months before *Eid*, Tara Bibi, a well respected widow and go-between, came to see the ladies in Arithewaley. "Yesterday, I saw the Blue Silk Lady," she told them. "She and her husband will be visiting you next week so that you can choose material for your *Eid* clothes."

"We also need to think about arranging weddings then," said Mrs. Waheeda Begum.

"What news did the Blue Silk Lady bring?" asked Mrs. Adiba Hassan. She was the daughter of Mrs. Waheeda Begum. Tara Bibi needed no further invitation. She loved relating what was happening in other localities -- who was getting married, who was getting engaged, who was looking for a suitable match for eligible family members, and other news of interest.

Tea was served in cups belonging to a bone china tea set recently imported from England. Silver spoons were used to serve sugar and stir the tea. Biscuits were set out on a silver tray. The ladies enjoyed the tea and chat.

"Come here again the day after the Blue Silk Lady has been to show us her cloth," said Mrs. Waheeda Begum. "We will have much for you to do then."

The Blue Silk Lady was always immaculately dressed in a top quality, light blue silk *kameez* and a blue silk *shalwar* with a two-tone light blue and white scarf and blue sandals. She and her husband brought cloth to villages outside Ujjain and also to Muslim localities all over Ujjain. Muslim ladies were able to view a wide range of materials, such as cotton, chiffon, and calico in the comfort of their own homes. There were also several types of silk from all over India and even silk from China.

The Blue Silk Lady's husband would bring the bundles of cloth into the Rent Collector's reception room by Elephant Gate and remain there keeping an eye on his donkey cart in the road outside. The Blue Silk Lady then took cloth samples to show the Arithewaley ladies, who later had tea and biscuits sent to her husband.

- - - - - - - - - - - - - - - - - - - -

The morning after the Blue Silk Lady's visit, Tara Bibi entered Arithewaley through Elephant Gate. "Tara Bibi! Come over here!" called a woman's voice. She saw Mrs. Farah Begum waving to her from the basement of Shakil Sahib's house, which, like all the houses in Ujjain, had been built well above ground level to prevent the house from flooding during the monsoon. The basement opened directly on to the courtyard and gave a good view of everything that went on there. Inside, Tara Bibi found Mrs. Waheeda Begum, Mrs. Adiba Hassan, and Kausar sitting on an oak bed in the basement.

Tara Bibi joined the other ladies on the oak bed. Mrs. Farah Begum poured her a cup of tea and passed her the biscuits.

"My daughter, Mrs. Adiba Hassan, and I are looking for a suitable bride for my son Halim Nawaz," said Mrs. Waheeda Begum. "He obtained his law degree but decided to become a teacher instead, as some of our relatives are already practising as lawyers in Mirzawari and he did not wish to have to stand up in court and fight against them."

"I do not know of any suitably qualified girl for him at the moment," replied Tara Bibi. However, I will look out for one."

"My brother Faiz Khan is also still looking for a bride who will be prepared to live with him in Neemuch after marriage," said Kausar. "Recently, he asked me if you had found anyone yet."

Tara Bibi shook her head slowly, "There aren't many girls ready to leave Ujjain and live in Neemuch away from all their friends and relatives."

"Faiz Khan would be a good husband for any girl," said Kausar. "He is 28 years old and was recently transferred from Ujjain to Neemuch in his job as an office manager. He is also a player/manager for his football team. He has kept on his house in Arithewaley and regularly takes the train back here."

"Where is he now?" asked Tara Bibi.

"In Ujjain," Kausar answered.

"I may know of someone suitable," said Tara Bibi thoughtfully. "When I was at a wedding recently, I saw a girl aged 22, the daughter of a businessman living in Masjidpura in Ujjain. She is slim, of medium height, and has long black hair and a dark complexion. Her name is Sitara Banu."

"Faiz Khan is at home today," said Kausar. "I will ask him if he will see you now, so that we can settle this matter straight away."

She quickly went over to Faiz Khan's house. On her return, Kausar asked Tara Bibi to come and meet Faiz Khan.

"I think I may have found a suitable girl for you to marry," Tara Bibi told Faiz Khan. "Her name is Sitara Banu." She described Sitara Banu, and listed her accomplishments. "She was captain of the ladies' hockey team during her school days," she added. "As you yourself are a good footballer, she will be a good match for you."

"Please find out if this girl or her parents have any objection to her going to live with me in Neemuch," said Faiz Khan.

"Yes, we will," said Kausar. "Sitara Banu is single because of her dark color."

"She is like a diamond not yet discovered," said Tara Bibi smiling.

"Please go tomorrow and see this girl on my behalf," said Faiz Khan. "If you both think that she will be a good wife for me and if she and her parents are in agreement, then I will not hesitate to marry her. I will ask for a *tonga* to be sent around for you in the morning."

The two ladies left Faiz Khan's house and made their way toward Elephant Gate.

"Haider Khan the Rent Collector wishes to speak to you privately regarding his son Diwan," Kausar told Tara Bibi.

"Is he still looking for a bride for the boy?" asked Tara Bibi.

"Yes, he is."

"Last year I found someone for him, but the girl's family did not want the match because he was unemployed."

"Things have changed," replied Kausar. "He is working now."

"When shall I call around?" asked Tara Bibi.

"Please come to his house in three days' time."

The next morning, Tara Bibi joined Kausar outside Elephant Gate. Nearby was the *tonga* Faiz Khan had ordered for them. Hira Lal sat in the driver's seat, high on *charas*. "Take us to house number 16 near the *masjid*, the mosque in Masjidpura," said Tara Bibi.

"Yes, Sahiba, at once Sahiba, I will take you there immediately. I know the mosque," Hira Lal replied.

The two ladies climbed into the *tonga* and Hira Lal set off fast as usual, hitting the horse with his whip.

"*Chal rey ghorey chal* -- let's go, horsey," called Hira Lal to his horse.

"Don't hit the poor horse! Drive it gently!" shouted Tara Bibi.

At last, Hira Lal drew up outside a house.

"This is house number 16," he told his passengers. The two ladies climbed down.

"Thank you," said Tara Bibi. "Come back after two hours and wait for us here."

Hira Lal immediately drove away at top speed.

Tara Bibi and Kausar went and knocked at the door of the house. An old lady opened it. "We have come to see the mother of Sitara Banu," said Tara Bibi.

"There is no Sitara Banu living here," came the reply.

"Is this the house of the businessman Mansur Sahib?" asked Tara Bibi.

"No, this is my house and I live here."

"This is house number 16 near the *masjid* in Masjidpura, isn't it?"

"No, you are in Milkipura. Masjidpura is on the other side of Ujjain."

"What shall we do, then?" asked Tara Bibi. "We will have to wait two hours for our *tonga* to return."

"Come in and have a cup of tea," said the old lady. She took Tara Bibi and Kausar into her sitting room. Another lady was already there.

"I am Aunt Moomani and this is my sister," said their hostess. "We are looking for a match for my niece, her daughter. She is from Jawra, and she and her daughter are here on a visit. Please sit." She left the room and they heard her speaking to someone in the kitchen. Shortly afterward she returned, followed by a young girl carrying a tray with tea and biscuits.

"This is my niece Nafisa Begum," said Aunt Moomani. Nafisa Begum was tall and slim with a fair skin. Tara Bibi and Kausar exchanged glances.

"Please bring me a glass of water," said Tara Bibi to the girl.

Nafisa Begum went out quietly. As soon as she had gone, Tara Bibi and Kausar introduced themselves to Aunt Moomani and her sister.

"We are from Mirzawari," said Tara Bibi. "We were going to visit the house of Mansur Sahib in Masjidpura. His daughter Sitara Banu is a possible match for a young man in Mirzawari. We are also looking for a suitable girl for the younger brother of Shakil Sahib."

Aunt Moomani's eyes lit up. "I've heard of him. You mean that famous lawyer from the Lawyers' Den?"

"Yes," said Tara Bibi. "His brother's name is Halim Nawaz. He is 27 years old, tall, and slim with a fair complexion. He has a law degree from Indore University, and is now a teacher in a local school."

"My sister came from Jawra with Nafisa Begum to find a husband for her in Ujjain," said Aunt Moomani.

"Tell us about Nafisa Begum."

"She is 23 years old and is an excellent cook with good dress sense, as you can see. Her father is a school teacher in the village of Jawra. She is also well educated."

"She would be most suitable for Halim Nawaz," said Tara Bibi. Kausar nodded enthusiastically.

Nafisa Begum came in holding a glass of water in both hands, politely bent down, and offered it to Tara Bibi.

Aunt Moomani rose. "Come with me," she said to Nafisa Begum. In the next room, she informed her that Tara Bibi and Kausar had brought news of a suitable marriage prospect. "I would like to make the arrangements now with these ladies," she added. "Please go to your room, change into new clothes, and wait until I call you."

Nafisa Begum nodded nervously and went to do her aunt's bidding. Shortly afterward, Aunt Moomani presented Nafisa Begum before the ladies once again. The girl wore a peach colored top in a flowered pattern, which had been hand printed in Bhairugarh village, over a white silk *gharara* with a light brown *dupatta* covering her head.

Hira Lal eventually brought the *tonga* to take Tara Bibi and Kausar back to Mirzawari. "I will come again tomorrow with Halim's mother," said Tara Bibi to Aunt Moomani as they took their leave. "Then we can confirm the details of the marriage."

On their return, Tara Bibi and Kausar informed Mrs. Waheeda Begum that they had found a suitable match for Halim Nawaz. She immediately agreed to visit Aunt Moomani the following day to see Nafisa Begum.

The next morning, Akram *tongawala* brought Tara Bibi and Mrs. Waheeda Begum to Aunt Moomani's house in Milkipura. Shakil Sahib's family had agreed to the wedding of Halim Nawaz and Nafisa Begum. After some discussion, it was agreed that Nafisa Begum would remain in Milkipura with her mother for the present. The rest of her close relatives would come to Ujjain from Jawra to attend her wedding to Halim Nawaz.

Afterward, Akram *tongawala* brought Tara Bibi and Mrs. Waheeda Begum back to Arithewaley. "Please meet me here after lunch at 2.30 p.m.," Tara Bibi told Akram *tongawala*. "Kausar and I would like to go to Masjidpura, house number16, near the *masjid*. Mansur Sahib, a businessman, lives there with his family."

"Yes, Tara Bibi Sahiba, I will be here," replied Akram *tongawala*.

After taking lunch with Mrs. Adiba Hassan and Mrs. Waheeda Begum, Tara Bibi joined Kausar outside Patwari Sahib's verandah and both ladies went through Elephant Gate to where Akram *tongawala* was already waiting for them in his *tonga*. Akram *tongawala* found the house in Masjidpura without difficulty. Mansur Sahib's wife Maimuna opened the door.

"Come in, come in," she said. "We met recently at a wedding at the house of one of my neighbors, didn't we?" she added, turning to Tara Bibi. She showed both ladies into the sitting room and sent her daughter Sitara Banu into the kitchen to make tea.

"When we met, you told me that you had not yet found a suitable match for your daughter," said Tara Bibi. "Is that still the case?"

"Yes, it is."

"I think I have found someone for her. This is Kausar, who has come with me on his behalf."

"His name is Faiz Khan," said Kausar. "He is an office manager and a well-known footballer and has recently been transferred to Neemuch because of his job. He still has his house here and comes back to Ujjain from time to time. However, he is looking for a girl who would be prepared to live with him in Neemuch."

"We have relatives in Neemuch," said Maimuna immediately. "Sitara Banu would not be alone there. I will go and speak to her. If she agrees to this proposal, we can discuss it with my husband when he gets back from the office."

Soon afterward Maimuna returned, smiling, together with Sitara Banu bringing tea and biscuits. When Mansur Sahib came home from the office, he was delighted to hear of the marriage proposal for his daughter on behalf of Faiz Khan. Tara Bibi explained that the wedding of another man in Arithewaley was also taking place, and they would try to arrange both weddings close together, to share the expenses. Family members in full time work could take fewer days off, and celebrate together.

"That's fine with us," said Mansur Sahib.

- - - - - - - - - - - - - - - - - - - -

Meanwhile, Haider Khan the Rent Collector was preparing to set off on his rounds. He worked for a large landowner visiting tenants in the villages around Ujjain and further afield and was usually away from home for three or four days at a time, changing horses two or three times in the villages he visited. His house was on the main road by Elephant Gate and he lived there with his second wife Kismet, an outsider from a distant village. He had married her 19 years ago, a year after the death of his first wife, so that she could care for his nine year old son Diwan, and they now had children of their own.

"Tara Bibi is finding suitable girls for Halim Nawaz and Faiz Khan," he informed Kismet. "I have asked Kausar to invite her to our house so that we can ask her to look for a wife for Diwan."

"Oh yes, she did mention it to me," answered Kismet. "Will you be seeing Diwan next time you go to collect the rents?"

"Yes, I will need to set off again early tomorrow morning. Please prepare *samosey* and *pakorey* for him. Diwan works hard in the jungle."

The following day, Haider Khan set off on horseback, taking a gun as protection against wild animals and a tiffin carrier containing savory snacks for his son. He was over six feet tall, deeply tanned, and wore khaki jodhpurs with a thick cotton full-sleeved shirt under a waistcoat, a colorful *safah* on his head, and thick, highly polished ankle boots on his feet.

After following the bus route through the jungle for several miles, Haider Khan took a well marked track leading off it on the left toward a village. Soon he spotted a plume of smoke rising through the bushes on one side. It came from a fire outside a hut. Diwan was sitting nearby with a notebook and a pen.

Haider Khan dismounted and handed the tiffin carrier to his son. Diwan opened it and eagerly sniffed the contents.

"Have you eaten?" asked his father.

"No, not yet. I just have to finish calculating the total number of grass bales sent to the village."

While Diwan was enjoying his snack, Haider Khan told him the reason for his visit. "I have asked Kausar to inform Tara Bibi that we are seeking a bride for you."

"Yes, I can support a wife," said Diwan eagerly. "I am

earning good money."

"How is life in the jungle with so many wild animals?" asked his father.

"There are lions, bears, and many poisonous snakes, but they don't come near our hut because of this fire," replied Diwan. "We keep it going day and night."

"Your hut is opposite a small hill," said Haider Khan.

"There is also a brook not far away where the animals come to drink," Diwan told him. "We go regularly to the village to collect water and fresh milk in metal buckets."

"The snakes and wild animals are dangerous," said his father.

"The contractor told us not to attack an animal. If attacked, do not run; defend yourself with a stick and poke at the eyes of an animal that is attacking you. One man carries a large axe with him all the time. I have a well oiled stick to ward off snakes. None of us carry guns."

"Have you been in the jungle?" asked Haider Khan.

Diwan's eyes lit up. "Yes, occasionally. There are lions and deer in the jungle on the other side of the hill opposite our hut." He pointed with his finger. "There is also a big black bear. He comes down the hill every day to drink water from the brook at the bottom. Then he sits under the tree halfway up the hill. He always chooses the same spot, which he keeps very clean. One day the sun was setting behind the hills. The black bear came out from under the tree and descended the hill very slowly toward the brook, stopping from time to time and looking around. It was the greatest moment of my life to see a bear drinking water in the wild."

Haider Khan returned home, pleased that his son had settled down well in his work. Shortly afterward Tara Bibi came to visit Kausar and both ladies went to Haider Khan's house.

"We are still looking for a girl for our son Diwan," Haider Khan told them. His wife had brought tea and was now sitting silently next to him.

"I haven't seen any suitable girl recently," answered Tara Bibi.

"What happened to that girl Karima Bibi whom you visited last year for Diwan?" Haider Khan enquired.

"Well, her parents want someone who works and can support her. Diwan wasn't working at that time," replied Tara Bibi.

Haider Khan drew himself up. "Diwan is now working," he proudly announced.

"What job does he have?"

"He works for a big grass contractor counting grass bales and noting down the numbers. The grassland is near the jungle, so he and the other men stay in a hut in the jungle for one month at a time."

"Karima Bibi's family is no longer living in Ujjain," said Tara Bibi.

"Why is that?" asked Haider Khan.

"Her father lost his job and was unable to find work elsewhere, so they returned to their village. He is now working in the fields and his wife is once again helping another village woman to dye cloth to sell to the ladies in Ujjain."

"Which village is that?" asked Kismet.

"Nunga Sadhu Gaon (Naked Sadhu Village). It is about three hours by *tonga* from Ujjain near Bhairugarh village. The women there know some special ways of dyeing cloth."

"We also know many ways of coloring cloth in our village," Kismet remarked.

"Is this family still looking for a boy for their daughter?" asked Haider Khan.

"As far as I know, Karima Bibi is not married yet," answered Tara Bibi. "If you are interested in her for your son, I can visit them with Kausar and find out for certain."

Kismet thought back to her own marriage. She was the eldest in a family with four girls living in a small village. As they got older, the village boys left home to find work. Some of them later married village girls, but many girls remained single, an unspoken financial burden to their families. One day, the Rent Collector visited their house to collect the rent. "It is a year now since my wife died," he told Kismet's father. "I need a woman to look after my house and be a mother to my son."

Kismet's family welcomed the chance of making such a good match for her. Later, she found that his nine-year-old son Diwan was a slow learner. Kismet's marriage had later paved the way for the weddings of her three sisters.

"What sort of girl is Karima Bibi?" Kismet asked Tara Bibi.

Tara Bibi had met the girl the previous year and was able to describe her in detail.

"She is now 26 years old. Her complexion is very dark. She is short, strong, and well able to do all the household chores."

"*Achha,* OK, go to Nunga Sadhu Gaon tomorrow and fix Diwan's marriage to Karima Bibi on our behalf," said Haider Khan to Tara Bibi and Kausar. "She sounds like a most suitable girl for our Diwan." He looked across at Kismet and she nodded, smiling.

The following day, Akram *tongawala* brought both ladies to Nunga Sadhu Gaon. An old woman was sitting outside one of the houses.

"We are looking for the house of Karima Bibi's family," Tara Bibi called to her. "We wish to see her parents."

"They aren't at home," the old woman answered. "Come, I will show you where her mother is working."

She took them around the back of a house further down the street. Two women were standing over a large cauldron in the back yard dipping cloth into it. Lengths of cloth in shades ranging from pink to deep scarlet hung over wire lines.

"This cloth is beautiful!" Kausar exclaimed. "What dye are you using?"

"The recipe for this dye is a closely guarded secret," answered one of the ladies.

"We are from Ujjain," said Tara Bibi and turned to Karima Bibi's mother. "We wish to speak with you regarding your daughter."

"I remember you," said Karima Bibi's mother to her. "You came to my house in Ujjain last year about my daughter."

"We have more business to discuss with you concerning her," replied Tara Bibi.

"Take these ladies to your house," said the other woman.

On the way to the house of Karima Bibi's parents, her mother stopped a small boy and asked him to call her husband, as they had visitors from Ujjain regarding their daughter.

Over tea and biscuits, Tara Bibi and Kausar put forward the Rent Collector's proposal on behalf of his son. "Diwan is 28 years old, tall, slim, and fair skinned," said Tara Bibi.

"You came to us last year regarding this boy," Karima Bibi's father remarked. "At that time he was unemployed."

"He is working now," replied Tara Bibi. She described Diwan's work.

"He sounds like a good match for Karima Bibi," said her father.

Her mother left the room. On her return, both parents confirmed that they accepted Haider Khan's proposal on behalf of his son Diwan. Soon afterward, Karima Bibi came in, greeted their guests, and cleared away the tea things.

Tara Bibi told the family that two other weddings were being arranged in Arithewaley at around the same time and she and Kausar would let them have the wedding dates later. Karima Bibi's mother offered the ladies a supper of *gaunkris* and *toor daal* or yellow lentils. They sat on the ground to eat this popular village specialty. Each person was served with *toor daal* cooked with fried garlic in pure *ghee*. A large metal *thaal* containing *gaunkris* over which *ghee* had been poured was placed before them. Then Karima Bibi's mother brought a metal jug and poured warm *ghee* over everyone's *toor daal*. Each person took a *gaunkri*, broke it, and used the pieces to scoop the yellow lentils from the dish.

"This tastes good," said Tara Bibi. "How do you prepare the *gaunkris*?"

"We make a fire with dried cow dung and bake balls of dough in the hot ashes of the fire," answered Karima Bibi's mother."

"How do you pick up the *gaunkris* from the hot ashes?"

"With tongs. Then we dust the ashes off the *gaunkris* before putting them on a dish and pouring hot *ghee* over them."

- -

Three weddings for three men in the Lawyers' Den had now been agreed on. As soon as the wedding dates had been fixed, the ladies in the Lawyers' Den started celebrating. They put on bright clothes and danced with Anwar Ali's mother and his wife Rani in the enclosed courtyard in front of their house. Background music was provided by a woman playing a *dholak*, a drum, and a *mirasan* singing girl. The dancing and singing were resumed at intervals during the three-day wedding celebrations.

It was decided to hold all three engagements and weddings over a three-day period, allowing one day for the engagement and wedding ceremonies for each couple. The relaxed restrictions on food rationing enabled about 30 people -- including family members, friends, and relatives -- to celebrate each wedding. The wedding feasts would be held in the Lawyers' Den, with the men seated in the courtyard and the women and children in the surrounding houses. The food for each feast would be cooked on the Qazi football ground.

Close friends and relatives helped the brides-to-be to prepare for their weddings. Faiz Khan's bride Sitara Banu lived in Masjidpura, Ujjain, with her family. Nafisa Begum and her mother had remained in Milkipura in Aunt Moomani's house and were being joined in Ujjain by her close relatives from Jawra, who were staying nearby. Karima Bibi's family traveled from Nunga Sadhu Gaon to Ujjain, where her father's friend and a neighbor invited them to stay in their houses in Mirzawari for the wedding.

On the morning of her wedding day, each bride came to the Lawyers' Den together with her friends and relatives. The engagement and marriage ceremonies for each wedding were held in the reception room of the house of Haider Khan the Rent Collector, which had been specially prepared for this purpose. After the engagement ceremony, *laddus* (sweet balls) were distributed to friends and relatives.

The first wedding was that of Faiz Khan and Sitara Banu. The following day, Halim Nawaz and Nafisa Begum got married and Faiz Khan left Ujjain for Neemuch with his new bride. The third wedding celebration was for the marriage of Diwan Khan and Karima Bibi.

Sweets for the engagement ceremonies and wedding feasts were prepared by Ram Das, the well-known local sweet maker who had six people working for him. Two men called regularly at his shop to collect the freshly made sweets and vegetarian snacks for the guests. Sometimes the sweets were not quite ready, so they waited and watched the men making them in a large, poorly-lit room. The six workers were neatly dressed in white *dhotis* and cream colored Bengali full sleeve shirts, their heads covered by white caps.

Several cooks had brought provisions to the football ground for the engagement and wedding feasts. Covered pots containing uncooked meat stood near sacks of rice, onions, garlic, spices, and ginger. Nearby were large cauldrons that were placed in turn on a semi-circular brick furnace in which a wood fire was kept burning. There was a sack of flour for preparing *maandey*. Two men were seated before a large *tawa*, a heavy rimless iron pan with a rounded base and no handle, tossing a constant succession of *maandey* -- large thin round *chapattis* -- into the air with their hands and widening them at the same time before dropping them on to the heated *tawa* Afterward, the *maandey* were stacked in large baskets between two cotton cloths and taken to be served hot to the guests. While preparing meat curry or meat *pulao* for each day's feasting, the cooks were closely watched by an audience of small boys.

Before each wedding feast, two large, white sheets containing dried dates were distributed to the men and women guests. Two men took one sheet and held it open while a third man flung fistfuls of dates at the male guests sitting in the courtyard. The boys rushed forward to gather up the dates in the fronts of their long shirts. During the wedding feast the *mirasan* sang farewell songs. The bride's mother cried with joy that her daughter would be starting a new life.

After the wedding feast, a procession illuminated by lanterns left the Lawyers' Den to go round Mirzawari. It was led by the bridegroom on horseback, this time followed by the bride in a beautifully decorated sedan chair carried by two strong men. On arriving back at Elephant Gate the procession came to a halt. The bridegroom dismounted and opened the curtain of the sedan chair. The bride was squatting on the floor inside holding her legs with both hands. The bridegroom gently turned her and, putting his arms round her from the back, clasped her around her legs and carefully lifted her from the sedan chair. Then he began to carry her toward the bridal chamber as quickly as he could.

As the bridegroom entered the courtyard in the Lawyers' Den, some young girls ran toward him, forcing him to stop. They were the bride's relatives. Supporting his bride on his knee with one hand, the bridegroom plunged his other hand into a pocket and pulled out money for them.

"Not enough! Not enough!" came the cries. The bridegroom expected this and took out more money from a second pocket and handed it over. Eventually, the girls let him pass.

Things were not quite so simple for Diwan Khan. Karima Bibi was short, squat, and heavily built. He lifted her from the sedan chair and staggered under the unexpected weight. Then he started to haul her toward Elephant Gate where the women were waiting to welcome them. Just inside Elephant Gate, his arms gave way and he dropped her on the ground. A gasp went up from the small crowd in the passage and someone laughed. One of the women quickly stepped forward and helped Karima Bibi to her feet. "I think you'd better walk," she said, and escorted her to the bridal chamber holding her hand, with Diwan following them. Outside the bridal chamber, he duly handed over money to Karima Bibi's young relatives before entering.

News of the three weddings had spread around Ujjain. *Hijras* (professional male dancers in women's clothes) began to gather uninvited outside Elephant Gate during the day to dance and sing. A professional flute player also took up his station outside the Lawyers' Den and played music almost continuously throughout the wedding celebrations. All of them were given money.

The aroma of curry, *pulao* rice, and sweet rice permeated the courtyard and the surrounding houses of the Lawyers' Den. The male and female relatives of each bridegroom served his wedding feast.

After each wedding feast the guests went to view the wedding gifts to the bride. These were displayed in the reception room of the bridegroom's house on *charpoys* and on white sheets covering the floor. The guests filed round the room to inspect them. They included cloth for making suits of *shalwar kameez* in silk and chiffon and also *dupattas* in different colors and designs. There were also plain and hand printed cotton clothes and many pairs of tight cotton *pajamas* and tops. Silk saris in various shades printed in gold were displayed with several pairs of sandals nearby. All the ladies were particularly impressed by the unusual colors and designs of the clothes for Diwan Khan's bride Karima Bibi from the village of Nunga Sadhu Gaon. After they had seen the gifts, all the relatives and guests were served a sweet red farewell drink of *sherbat*.

Four teenagers from the Lawyers' Den who belonged to the local football team volunteered to help out at all three weddings, serving food and water to the guests during the whole three days of celebrations. Their names were Zaheer, Gitta, Tinka, and Kana. They worked continuously with only short breaks for rest. On the evening of the third day after they had finished work, they made a bet to see who could sleep the longest without getting up. They told Anwar Ali and he invited them to come and sleep on the verandah by the front yard of his mother's house. He put out four mattresses and covers and told the boys that they could sleep there as long as they liked. Betting was not allowed, so the four boys and Anwar Ali kept it secret.

All four boys slept soundly during that night and the following day and night. During the morning of the second day, one or two of the boys began to stir. Tinka was the first to wake. He sat up slowly, rubbing his eyes. Then he lay down again quietly. He heard Kana starting to stir.

"So you are awake at last," said Tinka.

"What?" asked Kana, yawning loudly. He stretched and lay back again on the mattress.

Both boys began to doze. Some time later they heard a sudden sound like a donkey braying. It came from Gitta.

Zaheer won the continuous sleeping contest. When he finally woke up, the boys went to buy vegetarian savories, *katchoris* and *samosey* and two sweet *gulab jamuns* each, with the other three paying for the winner.

"Let's go and see my friend Bihari Lal," said Gitta. "His father has just opened a new sweet shop near the football ground."

"I believe that Ram Das is his relative and supplies sweets to this shop," said Tinka. "We can buy the sweets and snacks from Bihari Lal's father, then walk to the football ground, sit on the stone walls of the well, and eat there," suggested Gitta.

Everyone agreed. They went to the shop and told Bihari Lal about the weddings and their secret bet. Bihari Lal's father gave them each an extra *gulab jamon* and snacks on the house. Then they went to the football ground to celebrate the end of the three weddings.

- - - - - - - - - - - - - - - - - - - -

Faiz Khan and Sitara Banu settled down well in Neemuch. Sitara Banu enjoyed polishing Faiz Khan's collection of football trophies, which he had won from the British Army and other Central Indian football teams.

Mrs. Nafisa Begum joined her new husband Halim Nawaz in the family house that they shared with his widowed mother Mrs. Waheeda Begum and elder brother Shakil Sahib and his family. It faced onto an inner courtyard together with the five other houses in the Lawyers' Den.

A few days later, Mrs. Nafisa Begum looked out from the verandah on the ground floor and recognized the short, dark-skinned figure of Karima Bibi walking toward the water tap near the entrance carrying a large clay pitcher. She called to her and rushed down the stairs to the courtyard. Karima Bibi greeted her with a smile.

"How do you like life in the Lawyers' Den?" asked Mrs. Nafisa Begum.

"Very much," answered Karima Bibi. She looked admiringly at Mrs. Nafisa Begum. "You look very elegant. Did you sew your clothes yourself?"

"No," answered Mrs. Nafisa Begum. "I told the seamstress how I wanted them done. I chose the cloth and coordinated the colors of each outfit. Your clothes are beautifully colored. Did you dye them yourself?"

"Yes, I did."

"My sister-in-law Mrs. Farah Begum has been telling me that the ladies here come to our house some evenings to have discussions on all sorts of things," said Mrs. Nafisa Begum.

Just then Mrs. Farah Begum joined the new brides. "We are having a discussion group tomorrow evening," she told them. Turning to Karima Bibi, she added, "Perhaps you and Kismet would also like to come along."

Chapter 6: Life in the Lawyers' Den

When Karima Bibi and Kismet joined the discussion group the
following evening, Mrs. Farah Begum poured tea for them and
they smiled in greeting at Mrs. Adiba Hassan, Mrs. Waheeda
Begum, Mrs. Nafisa Begum, and Kausar. The ladies were seated
on the base of a large wooden oak bed resting on thick legs in the
basement overlooking the courtyard. It was covered with a white
sheet, on which were trays with tea and biscuits. Mrs. Nafisa
Begum saw Karima Bibi looking curiously at the bed. "This bed
was specially made to order for Shakil Sahib," she said. "We eat
all our meals on it."

"I heard that you come from a village outside Ujjain near
Bhairugarh," said Mrs. Farah Begum to Karima Bibi.

"Yes, it is called Nunga Sadhu Gaon or Naked Sadhu
Village." Karima Bibi responded, looking down and blushing.

"What a fascinating name," exclaimed Mrs. Waheeda
Begum. "What's the history behind it?" "Just outside our village
is a cave, a very sacred *gupa* beneath a hill," replied Karima Bibi.
"A naked sadhu lived there once many, many years ago. Inside
the cave is a large flat stone that he used as a bed. On the hill there

are many different herbs and plants, which do not grow anywhere else in Central India. The sadhu brought the roots and seeds with him when he first came to the cave. He made preparations from these plants and rubbed them all over his naked body to stay cool in summer and warm in winter. He also made dyes from the plants and painted his body with them. Sadhus from all over India came to visit him and pay their respects. The herbs and plants still remain."

"Do the people in your village still use these herbs and plants?" asked Mrs. Adiba Hassan.

"Yes, we make our own skin products from them, among other things."

"What sort of skin products?" asked Mrs. Nafisa Begum with interest.

"Mainly face cream and skin lotions, also creams for use as rouge and lipstick."

The other ladies noticed the subtle make-up and smooth softness of Karima Bibi's skin and the radiance of her complexion.

"Did you make your skin products yourself?" asked Kausar.

"Yes, I did. I brought a large quantity with me to Ujjain."

"The *kajal* you are wearing on your eyes is of very fine quality," said Mrs. Adiba Hassan.

"I made the *kajal* myself from soot in the usual way," answered Karima Bibi. "Then I added a preparation made from certain plants to give it extra smoothness and make it effective in protecting one's eyes and treating eye ailments."

"Perhaps you could bring along some of your skin products to our next discussion group," suggested Mrs. Farah Begum.

Word went around about the planned beauty session and

the next discussion group in Mrs. Farah Begum's house was very well attended.

Karima Bibi had brought along a large pot of face cream, along with several smaller pots of skin lotions and make-up.

"Would you like to show these ladies which products would best suit them?" she asked Mrs. Nafisa Begum.

Mrs. Nafisa Begum smiled. "I will be delighted to do so."

"I wonder what sort of beauty treatment you can give older ladies," said Mrs. Waheeda Begum. Age and hot weather had lined and darkened her skin.

"I think we can do something for you," answered Karima Bibi. The other ladies watched with interest as Mrs. Waheeda Begum seated herself on a chair. Karima Bibi looked closely at Mrs. Waheeda Begum's face. Then she set out some pots on a small table nearby.

"I think these lotions would be best for your skin," she said. "Mrs. Nafisa Begum, perhaps you would care to apply them to her face."

Mrs. Nafisa Begum stepped forward and began to smooth some lotion on to Mrs. Waheeda Begum's face. Karima Bibi handed her various lotions in turn and she gently massaged them over Mrs. Waheeda Begum's cheeks, jaws, and neck. Mrs. Waheeda Begum sighed and leaned back, her body visibly relaxing. Finally, Mrs. Nafisa Begum added just a touch of make-up and held out a hand mirror to Mrs. Waheeda Begum.

"Would you like to have a look at yourself?" she asked.

Mrs. Waheeda Begum took the mirror from her. "My goodness, you have made me look younger!" she exclaimed. "I can hardly see the lines on my face now and my skin feels much smoother! Thank you very much!"

The other ladies were equally impressed and eager to see how they too, could have their appearance transformed.

Afterward, Kismet carefully placed samples of Karima Bibi's cosmetics into the small pots that each lady had been asked to bring along to the meeting for this purpose. From then on, Karima Bibi and Mrs. Nafisa Begum became part of the group, and started offering beauty treatments to the ladies in the Lawyers' Den for special occasions.

As the ladies were leaving, Mrs. Adiba Hassan stopped Karima Bibi. "Do you make dyes in your village?" she asked. "I am very interested in different ways of dyeing clothes."

Karima Bibi's face lit up. "Yes, we do," she replied.

"Could you please join us next time we have a dyeing session here," said Mrs. Adiba Hassan. Then you can show us the methods you use in your village."

- - - - - - - - - - - - - - - - - - - -

Three little girls were listlessly playing catch with an old football in the courtyard, when Meena came to the Lawyers' Den with her mother, and Qulfi. Meena joined them, as Chandni and Qulfi hurried off towards Mrs. Adiba Hassan's house. "Would you like to play some other game?" Meena asked the girls.

"Hopscotch would be nice," said one of them with a sigh.

"The squares are all faded," remarked another girl sadly. "What shall we do?"

Meena looked round. Her mother and Qulfi were bringing bricks from beneath the *aritha* tree into the courtyard.

"What are you doing, *Ammi?*" she called, running over to her.

"We are building a *chulha*, a semi-circular hearth," answered Chandni. "The ladies are preparing dyes. They want to find out how to color clothes, especially *dupattas* and *kameezen*. Would you four girls like to help us to bring over some logs to build a fire?"

When the *chulha* had been built and filled with logs, Chandni went back into the house. She returned soon afterward along with Qulfi and another lady, all staggering under the weight of a large, two-handled iron cauldron. They were followed by more ladies carrying pitchers of water. The girls gathered around, watching with interest.

"Why have you brought out that heavy iron *karah*?" asked one of the girls.

"We are going to heat water in it for dyeing clothes" answered Qulfi.

"Would you girls also like to dye some cloth?" Mrs. Adiba Hassan asked.

"Ooh, yes please!" came the enthusiastic reply.

Mrs. Adiba Hassan had invited Azizah, the wife of a well-known dyer from Bhairugarh, to come and stay with her for a couple of days to show Kismet, Karima Bibi, and some of the other ladies in the Lawyers' Den how to color clothes. Azizah's husband supplied hand printed garments to different parts of India and she was equally expert at hand printing. Mrs. Adiba Hassan preferred to use dyes from the English manufacturer, ICI.

Azizah showed everyone how to tie knots in the cloth to get a variety of beautiful shades on it when it was dipped into various dye solutions. Kismet and Karima Bibi used their experience in cloth dyeing to introduce some interesting variations to Azizah's methods of tie-dyeing. ICI dye was added to water heated in a *karah*, a two-handled cauldron, in the open air in the courtyard of the Lawyers' Den. This made the strong chemical odor of the dye less noticeable. Everyone was amused and intrigued by the patterns produced on their cloths, and the girls were delighted when they were each presented with their own multi-colored pleated cotton *dupatta*.

- - - - - - - - - - - - - - - - - - -

Mrs. Adiba Hassan and the other ladies from the Lawyers'

Den always bought English Parker Royal Blue fountain pen ink for their families.

"This ink is really good, but it's so expensive," said one lady.

"You're right," replied Mrs. Adiba Hassan, "but we haven't really got a choice." Suddenly she caught her breath sharply. "I've just had a brilliant idea. Let's make our own fountain pen ink."

Everyone wanted to have a go. Word was sent to Azizah, and a few days later the ladies were once again gathered around the *bara karahi* or cauldron in the courtyard, watching the blue dye solution boiling in it. When Halim Nawaz, the teacher, came home, he was surprised to see them all grouped together in the courtyard.

"What's going on?" he asked the ladies.

"We are making our own Royal Blue fountain pen ink," Mrs. Adiba Hassan replied. "Could you please put this sample into your Parker fountain pen and see if the color is right?"

Halim Nawaz immediately emptied his Parker fountain pen on to the ground and filled it up with the sample ink. His wife, Mrs. Nafisa Begum, quickly produced a notepad for him to write on.

"This ink is too light. Make it a little darker," he said.

Some time later, Mrs. Nafisa Begum came into the dining room. "We have managed to produce a darker ink," she said to her husband, who was checking his students' school work. "Would you like to come and try it?"

Halim Nawaz went out with her and filled his pen with the fresh sample. "This is very good," he said after writing on the notepad. "When you have produced enough ink, please fill my ink pot. I will pay you cash for it. I don't need to buy any more ink from the shop."

Soon Mrs. Adiba Hassan, Mrs. Nafisa Begum, Kismet, and Karima Bibi were regularly producing their own fountain pen ink and selling it locally, more cheaply than the English Parker Royal Blue fountain pen ink. They also started to supply a local fountain pen retailer through Halim Nawaz and shared the profits with him.

- - - - - - - - - - - - - - - - - - - -

One day Kismet, the Rent Collector's wife, was in a room upstairs when she heard the pattering of feet on the roof above. She rushed outside onto the open roof, looked up, and saw two monkeys, each clasping a *laddu*. When they spotted her, they jumped across to the roof of Shakil Sahib's house next door and then on to the *aritha* tree.

Small Rhesus Macaque monkeys, crows, sparrows, Indian cuckoos, and mynah birds often visited the *aritha* tree, and one or two peacocks would perch on the top branches. Some of the old ladies used the seeds from the *aritha* tree for washing clothes, but most people preferred English Lifebuoy soap.

Kismet quickly took four freshly prepared *chapatis* from the kitchen, folded some carrot halva between two of them to make two *do-purti rotis*, and put them onto a large metal plate. She went out to the *aritha* tree holding the plate, raised it, and looked up at the monkeys, pointing at the *chapatis* with carrot halva. Then, placing the plate on the ground, she opened her *dupatta* and pointed at the *laddus* in their hands.

"Give me the *laddus* and you can have this food," she said to the monkeys.

"*Khon, Khon*, Thank you! Thank you!" said the larger male monkey. He took the *laddu* from the female's hand and dropped it. Kismet quickly darted forward and caught it in her *dupatta*.

The *laddu* was about the size of a tennis ball. Kismet broke off a small piece and put it into her mouth. It was sweet and slightly crunchy and tasted of nuts. "Thank you, give me another one," said Kismet to the monkey, pointing at the second *laddu*.

The monkey immediately dropped it right onto Kismet's *dupatta*. She drew the ends together. Then she pointed at the plate and moved away. "Eat, eat," she told the monkeys.

Both monkeys quickly came down the tree, seized the stuffed *chapatis*, and went off to eat them.

The women of Mirzawari knew that *laddus* made by monkeys contained various nuts and roots and gave a lot of energy. Kismet put the monkey *laddus* into a dish to share with her neighbors. Cries of "*Khon! Khon!*" came to her ears as the monkeys jumped from the tree onto the roofs of two nearby houses and disappeared.

- - - - - - - - - - - - - - - - - - - -

One day, Umer was playing in the courtyard of the Lawyers' Den with his cousin, Shakil Sahib's son Hashim, when Afaq Hassan's wife called them from the verandah.

"There are rats in our bedroom," she said. "Can you boys get rid of them for me?"

"Yes, we'll sort them out for you," the boys replied. "We'll just get some sticks."

Afaq Hassan and his wife occupied a large bedroom on the ground floor of the house they shared with his elder brother Waqar Hassan and his family. When they were staying in Ujjain, they slept there on a *charpoy*. However, they spent most of their time in Bhairugarh, so the room mostly remained empty. It was just behind the verandah, had a bare earth floor, and was dimly lit by a small window.

The boys came back with sticks and Afaq Hassan's wife let them into the bedroom. The boys went inside and stood waiting silently in one corner of the room with raised sticks. Suddenly they heard the scrabbling of claws. Large rats appeared and started to run all over the floor. The boys hit out at them. Most of the rats disappeared down holes in the floor, but some of them got stuck trying to squeeze down small mouse holes. Each boy seized a rat by the tail, swung it round his head, and flung it out of the window. When the room had been cleared of rats, they waited quietly until more rats appeared and then repeated the same process. At last the rats stopped coming, so the boys collected some small stones from Camel Courtyard and filled in the holes. Afaq Hassan's wife thanked them both and gave them money. They bought *rajgareh kay laddus* (sweets) and shared them with their friends.

Umer's family lived in the upper part of the house they shared with his uncle and aunt, Afaq Hassan and his wife. Umer was able to touch a branch of the *aritha* tree from his bedroom window. His parents, Waqar Hassan and Mrs. Adiba Hassan, had another son who went to school. At 4 years old, Umer was too young to attend school. He watched in fascination when his elder brother opened a book and read aloud in Urdu.

One day, Umer took an elementary reading book from his brother's room, while he was at school, and crossed the courtyard to the house opposite to see his aunt Mrs. Farah Begum, Shakil Sahib's wife.

"Please teach me how to read," he said, showing her the book.

"Whose is that book?" she asked.

"My brother's."

"Did he let you take it?"

"No, I am not allowed to touch his books," answered Umer.

"All right, I will teach you to read," said Mrs. Farah Begum after a pause. "I will teach you for half an hour, every morning. I will also ask your mother if she will help you as well. Don't tell anyone else about this. You must also look after this book very carefully. Now come and sit on the oak bed in here with me."

Mrs. Farah Begum went back to her work in the kitchen, recited the first three letters of the Urdu alphabet, and asked Umer to read them to her from the book. She then asked him to repeat them to her until he knew them by heart. In this way, Umer gradually learned how to read and recognize the whole Urdu alphabet and soon started reading simple sentences.

One day Mrs. Farah Begum asked Umer to bring his slate and some chalk with him to the next reading session. To his delight, she started showing him how to form each letter. Umer was very proud of himself when he eventually managed to write simple words. At last he came to the end of his brother's book. He triumphantly copied the last two words from the book onto his slate - "The End" - and proudly showed it to Mrs. Farah Begum and his mother.

Boys generally started pre-school at the age of five before going on to Urdu Middle School. Umer, however, was eager to start. "I know the Urdu alphabet and I can read and write as well," he told his parents.

"I think Umer would benefit from attending pre-school, even though he is still only four," Mrs. Farah Begum said to them.

The new school year had just started when Umer's father took him along to pre-school. The teacher showed Umer an elementary book. "First you will learn the Urdu alphabet and then you will do some reading," he said.

"I already know the alphabet," replied Umer and began to recite it. The teacher and his father listened to him, amused.

"Can you read the book as well?" asked the teacher with a laugh.

"Yes, of course I can," answered Umer.

The teacher opened the book in the middle and asked him to read out from it. Umer quickly read through a couple of pages.

Then the teacher asked him to read the last two pages of the book. Umer did so and looked up in triumph when he had finished.

"Where did you learn all this?" asked the teacher, surprised.

"I borrowed my brother's elementary book and my aunt taught me how to read," Umer explained. "I can write as well," he added.

"It is no use for Umer to attend this class," said the teacher to Umer's father. "He might as well go to the Urdu Middle School now instead of next year."

Umer and his father left the building and went to the Urdu Middle School. After the teacher there had tested Umer, the headmaster allowed him to join a class straight away. At break time the other boys crowded round the new arrival, who was much younger than any of them, and looked curiously at him.

"What are you doing here?" came a familiar voice.

Umer looked up and saw his elder brother at the back of the crowd. He explained how he had come to join the school. That evening, Umer's elder brother told him off for taking his book without asking and then said, "You have done very well. However, do not take any more of my books without my permission, understand?!"

- - - - - - - - - - - - - - - - - - - -

When they were not at school, the children spent a lot of time playing in the courtyard of the Lawyers' Den. One day, Karima Bibi called them over to her house.

"One of the hens has had some chickens," she told them. She took them to a small room beneath the house next to an outside toilet, where she and her husband Diwan Khan kept a few hens and a cockerel.

"Can I hold them? Can I have one? Let me hold one!" cried the children, clustering around her and holding out their cupped hands.

"Careful now! Gently! Gently!" said Karima Bibi and gave each child in turn a chick to hold.

"What is that beautiful perfume coming from your house?" asked Meena.

"That is *agarbatti* and *loban*," replied Karima Bibi. "Yesterday was Thursday, so I offered *fatiha* praying for the souls of the dead and burned *agarbattis*. Today I read the Quran and burned *loban* in the room."

- - - - - - - - - - - - - - - - - - - -

One family in the Lawyers' Den kept a couple of nanny goats, to supply them with milk and sometimes left them for an hour or so in the Qazi football ground to graze. The boys playing there would then seize a nanny goat, hold it by the head, and grasp its back legs tightly. Then each boy in turn would hold the goat's teat in one hand and squeeze the warm, fresh, smelly milk directly into his open mouth, spitting out the goat hairs as he did so. Other families bought buffalo milk from a farmer, who brought it to Mirzawari by bullock cart and then sold it on the street outside the Lawyers' Den.

Most of the Rent Collector's visitors came by bullock cart or camel. The camels and bullock carts were left in the Camel Courtyard behind the Lawyers' Den. People also sometimes left a bullock in the courtyard near the Rent Collector's house.

One day a man led a bullock into the courtyard of the Lawyers' Den, tied it to a post by the Rent Collector's house, and brought a bundle of hay that he flung into one corner of the courtyard before going to see the Rent Collector on business. Tiddi spotted them and rushed over to Camel Courtyard where Umer and another boy were playing football.

"There's a bullock in our courtyard!" he called.

The boys immediately followed him into the Lawyers'

Den. They took it in turn to feed hay to the bullock and make friends with him. Afterward, the boys went behind the bullock one by one to pull his tail. Unable to move, the bullock lashed out with his hind legs while the boy darted away.

A few days later, the boys spotted a man bringing a camel into Camel Courtyard. After tying the camel's reins to a post, the man went to see the Rent Collector. The boys stood watching the camel from a distance. Then, Umer crept up behind the camel, pulled his tail, and ran away. The camel turned his long neck and tried to bite down on Umer's head. When Tiddi went to pull the camel's tail, he was a little too slow in getting away. The camel seized the thick Afghan fur hat he was wearing, shook it between his teeth, and dropped it on the ground. Tiddi jumped back. Umer darted forward to pick up Tiddi's hat and pushed it into his hand, and the boys ran away laughing.

- - - - - - - - - - - - - - - - - - - -

From spring time onward, fireflies began to appear on the Qazi football ground and in the Lawyers' Den during the evenings, giving off a cold, pale, yellowish or greenish light. They often flew so low that the children were able to catch one of them and watch its light glowing through their fingers, before releasing it. On hot summer evenings, one or two bats even came to the verandah, to feed on the insects flying there.

When darkness fell, silence settled over the Lawyers' Den. People lit storm lanterns in their houses. The children lit candles so that they could see to do their school homework. The girls tied back their hair with a scarf while they studied, but the boys refused to wear a hat in the house, so they often singed their hair in the candle flame.

- - - - - - - - - - - - - - - - - - - -

One hot summer evening, Shakil Sahib had a message through one of his sons that the Qazi wanted to speak to him. Shakil Sahib immediately went to the Qazi's house. The two men exchanged greetings and the Qazi thanked Shakil Sahib for coming so quickly. "The Qazi of Bhopal has informed me that the

Nawab of Bhopal's uncle is coming to Ujjain shortly and will be staying overnight," he said. "He has asked me to arrange suitable accommodation for *Nawab* Sahib's uncle. I have been told that *Nawab* Sahib's uncle is very large and is unable to climb stairs. This means that my own guest house will not be suitable. Is your bungalow available?"

"It will be my pleasure to offer *Nawab* Sahib's uncle my bungalow for his stay," Shakil Sahib told the Qazi. His bungalow had a spacious reception room on the ground floor and three sets of servants' quarters on one side.

The *Nawab* of Bhopal's uncle arrived by train, in a special carriage accompanied by three uniformed servants. At the station he was welcomed by Qazi Sahib, Shakil Sahib, and Mr D'Silva, secretary to the Governor of Ujjain and a personal friend of Shakil Sahib. They accompanied him to Shakil Sahib's bungalow in an official dark blue *victoria,* with the coat of arms of the Maharajah of Gwalior state painted in gold on its sides. His servants followed by *tonga* and were accommodated in the servants' quarters of the bungalow.

Nawab Sahib's uncle was in his late fifties, well built, more than six feet tall, and dark skinned. He wore a *kameez* with a pattern in gold and blue on the collar and white cotton pajamas. Shakil Sahib showed him into the reception room of the bungalow, which was large and lavishly furnished. A *durrie* or carpet covered the whole floor. A large, thick mattress with a white sheet over it lay next to the wall. On the mattress against the wall were two bolsters covered with white silk with a Chinese pattern on it, together with several colorful cushions nearby. There were small rugs just inside the doors to the room. A large *pankha* hung from the ceiling.

Umer and three other small boys from the Lawyers' Den ran to the courtyard of the bungalow, to catch a glimpse of royalty. The *Nawab's* uncle was lounging on the mattress in the reception room with one arm resting on a bolster, reading a book. Next to him was a low table holding a metal tray, on which was a glass of water scented with rose petals. Another table stood in one corner of the room. On it were a jug of cold water, a jug of *sharbat*, and a couple of glasses. Sandalwood matting with *khas* or sweet scented grass over it covered the large doors on both sides of the reception room, which were open to let in fresh air. One servant stood on a chair by one door. From time to time he poured cold water from a *lota* over the matting. On the ground next to him was a bucket of cold water. Two servants, one at each end of the room, took turns pulling the *pankha* so that fresh air, scented with *khas* and sandalwood, blew over *Nawab* Sahib's uncle.

The boys were awed at the sight of a real live *Nawab* and quickly moved to one side, hoping that he hadn't seen them.

"I'm not scared," said Umer, "I'll go and speak to him."

The other boys ran away. Umer stood at the door of the reception room watching silently. The *Nawab's* uncle was reading a book. Suddenly he put it down and looked straight at Umer.

"*Assalam-o-Alaikum, Nawab* Sahib," Umer greeted him, raising his hand.

"*Walaikum assalam,*" replied *Nawab* Sahib's uncle. "Come in boy, sit down." He beckoned to the servant at the door.

"Bring the boy a glass of *sharbat,*" he said and turned to Umer. "What is your name?"

"*Nawab* Sahib, my name is Umer."

The servant poured *sharbat*. Umer sat in silence holding the glass.

"Drink your *sharbat,* Umer," said the *Nawab* of Bhopal's uncle.

Umer gulped the *sharbat* down and put the glass on the table.

"Thank you, *Nawab* Sahib," he said and got up, sweating with nervousness.

"What are you boys doing?" asked *Nawab* Sahib's uncle.

"We are going to play on Qazi Sahib's football ground," replied Umer.

"*Achha jao.* OK, go and play."

"*Khuda Hafiz, Nawab* Sahib," said Umer, raising his hand in farewell. He left and joined the other boys. *Nawab* Sahib's uncle continued reading his book.

That evening, Qazi Sahib, Shakil Sahib, and Mr. D'Silva joined *Nawab* Sahib's uncle for an elaborate feast served with *sharbat*, which they ate beneath the fruit trees in the courtyard. Afterward Mr. D'Silva left and the other three stayed on, sitting beneath the trees and chatting. The following day, the *Nawab* of Bhopal's uncle returned to Bhopal.

- - - - - - - - - - - - - - - - - - - -

Waqar Hassan often met other solicitors and lawyers at the Chand Hotel in the Chowk Bazar in Ujjain. They would stand by the *paanwala's* shop opposite the hotel, chewing *paan* and spitting on the open ground next to the shop, while discussing court cases. They were well known in Ujjain and people would often come up to them and ask for legal advice.

Shakil Sahib and Waqar Hassan frequently worked together on court cases. One such case involved two brothers. They and their families lived together with their father in his large house until he died. Forty days after his death, the elder brother Qutub claimed sole possession of the house. "You and your family must now leave the house and find somewhere else to live," he told his younger brother Raunak. "This is my house. I looked after father all my life. I paid for his food and I also paid for all his medical treatment."

"No, that's not true. You didn't pay a single *paisa* from your own pocket," Raunak cried. "You took all the money from father's metal trunk in his room. I saw a lot of 100 rupee notes there with my own eyes. Where is all that money now? I want my share."

"I have already seen a lawyer and I will kick you and your family out of this house legally," said Qutub calmly. "Then you will have to pay the legal costs as well."

Raunak went straight to Shakil Sahib's office and spoke to the solicitor, Waqar Hassan. "I want my share of our father's property and also my share of our father's money that he kept in his trunk, which my brother stole for his own use."

"Would you and your brother consider mediation?" asked Waqar Hassan. "This will save both of you spending a lot of money on this case, if it goes to court."

"Please come and talk to my brother yourself," Raunak requested. "He might listen to you. I only want my half share of the property and the money."

Waqar Hassan went to the house where the two brothers lived with their families and knocked on the door. Qutub opened it. His little son was sitting on his shoulders. As soon as he recognized Waqar Hassan, Qutub quickly put the boy in the room behind him, closed the door, and came outside.

"I believe you are taking legal action against your brother," said Waqar Hassan. "I have come to ask you to consider mediation. It will be much cheaper than going to court."

"I have spent a lot of money on my father and have always given him the best possible care," answered Qutub. "My brother never spent a single *paisa* on him. I am ready for mediation if he agrees to get out of the house. This will save him legal costs." With that, Qutub went back into the house.

Waqar Hassan climbed the outside stairs to speak to the younger brother. "Your brother will only accept mediation if you and your family leave this house," he told Raunak.

"I cannot do this," replied Raunak. "Would you please arrange a defense lawyer for me?"

This was the start of a very expensive court case. After a few months, Waqar Hassan advised both brothers to come to an agreement. "This case is becoming more and more costly day by day," he said to them.

His words fell on deaf ears. Now both brothers had become sworn enemies, and neither would back down. Several more months passed. Once again, Waqar Hassan warned the brothers of the consequences of continuing to fight their case in court. "Both of you will lose your only property," he warned them. "Think clearly about yourselves and your families. The lawyers' fees are mounting up. Neither of you will be able to pay them. In the end, the lawyers will have to sell this house and take the money from it for their fees and other expenses. This is your last chance to agree to mediation. I will not come and advise you again."

Both brothers gave the same reply. "No, my family and I will go and live in a hut, rather than let my brother have any share in this house."

The case dragged on for years. In the end, the house was sold and the money was distributed among the lawyers. Both brothers went to live in separate huts in different localities.

- - - - - - - - - - - - - - - - - - - -

Many Muslims were unable to obtain justice in disputes due to lack of knowledge about the law and the fear of being asked to pay fees that they were unable to afford, if they approached a lawyer for help. As a retired lawyer, Yousuf Ali Sahib was well aware of this and felt that something should be done to break down these barriers. He spoke to the Qazi, who agreed to arrange an informal meeting to discuss ways in which legal advice and help could be made more readily available to Muslims who were too poor to pay.

Next, Yousuf Ali Sahib sent his servant with messages to several people in Arithewaley, inviting them to attend the meeting. He wrote to Shakil Sahib the lawyer, Waqar Hassan the solicitor, Halim Nawaz the teacher, and Moon Khan, the brother of Faiz Khan the footballer, who had gone to Neemutch after his marriage. Moon Khan now lived alone in the house and was a solicitor working in a law practice that specialized in cases of domestic violence. Police Inspector Afaq Hassan was also invited to attend.

The meeting was presided over by the Qazi and was held beneath a tree in an open courtyard next to the Qazi's house. Everyone was seated in chairs before a round table and was served with tea and water. Local people passing by could pause and listen to what was going on.

Everyone agreed that Qazi Sahib's mediation was helpful in settling minor family disputes. Afaq Hassan was asked to instruct the policemen under his command to bring any such disputes in poor families to the attention of the Qazi. Waqar Hassan and Moon Khan volunteered to offer free legal advice to poor families.

Then Shakil Sahib spoke. "The go-between Tara Bibi informs me that there has recently been a rise in the amount of domestic violence affecting women, especially those in Gharib Colony, where there are many poor people."

"Qazi Sahib, may I speak?" Everyone turned to see Fazal *tongawala* standing nearby.

"Yes, Fazal, speak," said the Qazi.

"I heard you discussing the problems in Gharib Colony, Qazi Sahib. Tara Bibi's good friend Khatoon Bibi, a retired nurse, often helps people there to sort out their domestic problems. She also gives them simple medical treatment free of charge. Her medical supplies are provided by a charity paid for by local businessmen. She would be able to inform you of any women and children there needing your help."

"Thank you, Fazal, for mentioning this," said Qazi Sahib.

"I propose that we offer support through Tara Bibi to Khatoon Bibi in her work, by giving free legal advice and mediation to the women of Gharib Colony, whenever necessary," said Shakil Sahib. Everyone agreed.

"I will take Tara Bibi there in my *tonga* free of charge," said Fazal *tongawala.*

Everybody clapped. Qazi Sahib closed the meeting.

The following day, Yousuf Ali Sahib informed Tara Bibi that some lawyers from the Lawyers' Den were prepared to offer their services free of charge to the men and women of Gharib Colony. Later that morning, Fazal *tongawala* took Tara Bibi to visit Khatoon Bibi. When she arrived at Khatoon Bibi's house, Tara Bibi was surprised to find Shakuri and her mother there. Both women were weeping.

"What's going on?" Tara Bibi asked her friend. "Isn't this one of the girls whose wedding was arranged by Mirza Sahib when his daughter Shabnum got married?"

"Yes, that's right," answered Khatoon Bibi. "Shakuri and her husband Murad live with his mother and his two younger brothers and a sister. Murad always used to be very nice to Shakuri. Since their marriage, however, he has started to treat her badly."

"In what way?" asked Tara Bibi.

"He beats Shakuri because she is slow in preparing the food. Murad's mother buys the firewood they use for the *chulha* to cook curry and *roti* or thick *chapati* and pays for it by weight. When it's Shakuri's turn to cook the meal, Murad's mother saves money by buying cheaper wood from a supplier who sprinkles water on it so that it is heavier and also more difficult to burn. Then Shakuri is late with the meal and Murad beats her with a stick."

"How often does this happen?"

"About two or three times a week. Also, Shakuri never gets money to buy anything for herself. Once a week, Murad and the others go out shopping and leave Shakuri alone, at home, to do the cooking. Afterward, they buy *samosey* from Samosa Khan and eat them there. They bring none for Shakuri and always say loudly how delicious Samosa Khan's *samosey* taste. They all know how much Shakuri used to love eating those *samosey* before marriage."

"Poor girl, she doesn't have much of a life," said Tara Bibi.

"Last time Shakuri went home for a visit, her mother gave her some money," Khatoon Bibi went on. "Yesterday, she bought a couple of *samosey* and brought them home to eat. This morning, her mother-in-law told Murad that Samosa Khan had given Shakuri free *samosey* the previous day. Murad did not believe Shakuri when she said that she had bought them with the money her mother had given her. He beat her very badly and told her never to go outside the hut again. Then Shakuri took the *chimta* tongs and hit him on the head so hard that he fell to the ground and she ran home to her mother. She is not going back there to live with Murad again."

"That's really bad," said Tara Bibi sympathetically.

"I have often seen and treated wounds on Shakuri's body," said Khatoon Bibi. Now we don't know what to do."

"I think I can help you to seek justice," Tara Bibi replied. "Let us go and see Qazi Sahib. He can arrange for Shakuri to have free legal advice from a lawyer in Arithewaley."

Hira Lal was bringing Murad back from the hospital with a bandaged head when he was surprised to see Fazal standing with his *tonga* outside Khatoon Bibi's hut.

"Wait, Fazal, I'll be back in a moment," said Hira Lal.

When Hira Lal heard Shakuri's story, he offered a free ride to two of the ladies.

Moon Khan was sitting on his verandah in the Lawyers' Den, preparing for an important case, when the four ladies came to visit him. He listened to Shakuri's account of Murad's behavior and advised the ladies to go to Qazi Sahib and seek a divorce for Shakuri, as Murad was unlikely to change. They accordingly went on to see Qazi Sahib.

"Come back tomorrow with Murad," he told them.

Tara Bibi offered Shakuri a bed for the night. Fazal *tongawala* took Khatoon Bibi and Shakuri's mother back to Gharib Colony. Murad refused to accompany Khatoon Bibi and Shakuri's mother to Qazi Sahib's court the following day. Qazi Sahib granted Shakuri a divorce and Khatoon Bibi asked Gulzar Khan, a retired security guard, to keep an eye on Shakuri and her mother. Whilst grateful for the divorce, the loss of her marital status and the knowledge that she would never be able to marry again was too great a loss for Shakuri to face. So she buried the pain deep in her heart, wondering briefly if she would ever be strong enough to face it. The necessities of life were screaming for her attention and, almost welcoming the distraction, she set about the task of finding a job, gritting her teeth to face her friends and family and her new reality.

- - - - - - - - - - - - - - - - - - - -

One evening, Yousuf Ali Sahib and his wife invited Halim Nawaz and his wife, Mrs. Nafisa Begum, to their bungalow for an evening meal. Afterward the talk turned to poetry. Yousuf Ali Sahib quoted some verses by Omar Khayyam, a Persian poet. Then his wife left the room and returned with a notebook.

"Perhaps you might like to hear these poems," she said shyly.

"Yes, please read them to us," her guests replied.

The poems described simple events in simple language that echoed the experiences of family life, women in the kitchen, and children at play.

Mrs. Nafisa Begum was struck by the vividness of the images. "I like your poetry," she said.

"I enjoy listening to poetry, it's really relaxing," Halim Nawaz sighed contentedly.

"Perhaps we could invite some people to our bungalow regularly for a social gathering to listen to poetry," suggested Yousuf Ali Sahib.

"It would be a lot of work for you," said Mrs. Nafisa Begum. "I am sure people would be very happy to contribute toward the refreshments from their own kitchens and also offer to help, if you do decide to organize something like this."

A couple of weeks later, Yousuf Ali Sahib invited some people living in the Lawyers' Den and nearby, to come to his bungalow and recite poetry by well-known authors or read out their own compositions to the gathering. The meeting was a great success. Halim Nawaz, Mrs. Adiba Hassan and Tara Bibi recited some of their favorite poetry, while Yousuf Ali Sahib's wife, Mrs. Nafisa Begum, and Anwar Ali's wife, Rani, favored the audience with their own original work. After the session, the ladies served light refreshments. It was decided to hold similar social gatherings each month. Later, a chess club for men was set up in a separate part of the bungalow.

- - - - - - - - - - - - - - - - - - - -

Umer's great-aunt Mrs. Firdaus Begum was 99 years old and very independent. She lived in Bhairugarh with Afaq Hassan and his wife and went each day to fetch water from a nearby well, walking unaided with her back slightly bent. Mrs. Firdaus Begum was a graceful lady with a very fair complexion and light brown hair, of slim build, and about five feet seven inches tall. She visited the Lawyers' Den occasionally on the weekend with Afaq Hassan and his wife. One time she was feeling unwell on her arrival, so Mrs. Adiba Hassan asked her to stay on, when Afaq Hassan and his wife returned to Bhairu Garh. Each morning Mrs. Firdaus Begum would stand outside the house and gaze intently at the green *aritha* tree for five minutes. She said that this helped her to see well, so that she did not need spectacles. A few months later, she died of natural causes.

- -

One day, Umer came home from the nearby football ground and found no one in the courtyard of the Lawyers' Den. He opened the door in the wall enclosing the small courtyard, in front of the house where Anwar Ali lived with his wife Rani and his widowed mother, to see if some celebration was taking place. Across the courtyard, he saw Anwar Ali's mother standing in front of the high wall bordering it. Umer greeted her as usual and she smiled back at him. An aura of happiness surrounded her. Then he noticed Rani, together with several other ladies, beneath the verandah on the right. They were all grouped around a bed and some of them were weeping.

"What's the matter, why is everyone crying?" asked Umer.

"Your aunt has died," answered an old lady.

"No, that can't be true," said Umer. "When I entered the courtyard, just now, I saw her standing by the wall."

The old lady came over to Umer and took his hand. "Show me where you saw your aunt," she said gently.

Umer took her to the spot. "She has disappeared," he said.

"Come with me," answered the old lady. She took Umer back to the verandah, lifted him up by the bed, and showed him Anwar Ali's mother, lying there in peace.

"Now go to the playground and come back later," she told him.

- -

People having problems with their teeth went to the government hospital, where treatment was free of charge. A male *compowder* there dispensed medicines and also gave simple medical and dental treatment. One day, three teenagers from the Lawyers' Den were on their way to the football ground when they spotted Izhar, Patwari Sahib's son, crouched by the open gutter, near Anwar Ali's shop. He held both hands to his face and was groaning loudly.

"What's the matter with you?" one of the boys asked him.

Izhar looked up. His face was swollen. "I have very bad toothache," he told them.

"How long have you been in pain?" asked the eldest boy.

"About a week now," replied Izhar.

"Why don't you go to the hospital?"

"I don't trust him, that *compowder* in the hospital. Once I went there with toothache and he pushed a sharp needle right into my gum," answered Izhar.

"OK, we will take out the tooth for you," said the boy. "We'll be very gentle. You won't even notice when it comes out."

The three boys took Izhar to Camel Courtyard. When they got there, the eldest boy took one of the others aside.

"Go to my room and get my pliers," he said quietly. "Pour boiling hot water over them, then rinse them with cold water and bring them back to me. Don't let Izhar see them. Then we will take out his tooth."

When the boy returned, he quietly slipped the pliers into his friend's hand.

"Open your mouth, Izhar!" said the eldest boy. He held Izhar's jaw and quickly seized the loose tooth with the pliers.

"No! No! No!" shouted Izhar.

"Don't worry, it won't take long," the boy reassured him.

He gave the tooth a sharp pull. It didn't come out. Izhar shouted with pain, firmly pushed the boy away, and quickly closed his mouth.

"Take Izhar and hold him tightly," the eldest boy

instructed the others. "Your tooth is nearly out," he reassured Izhar. "It'll only take a few seconds now. Let me finish, otherwise you will have to go to the hospital."

Despite Izhar's protests, the two other boys grasped him firmly, while the eldest boy forced his mouth open, grasped the tooth firmly with the pliers, twisted it, and then pulled with all his strength until it came out -- together with a stream of blood. Izhar shrieked loudly and started crying.

"See! I told you it wouldn't take long," said the eldest boy. "Now go back to the gutter outside the shop and sit there for a few minutes. Then the pain will disappear forever."

"Why did you send him back to the open gutter?" asked one of the other boys.

"He'll feel happier sitting at the same spot where we found him," came the reply. "The smell from the gutter will quickly cure him."

- - - - - - - - - - - - - - - - - - - -

Gul Bhai, the estate manager, also known as Patwari Sahib, lived in a house next to the boundary wall between the Lawyers' Den and the Criminals' Den next door. His widowed sister, Kausar, and her two sons also lived there. Gul Bhai's two older sons, Lalu and Izhar, worked in the local cloth mill.

One evening, on his way home from work, Gul Bhai met Siddique Bhai, who was a foreman at the cloth mill where Lalu and Izhar worked.

"*Salam alaikum,* Patwari Sahib. How is Lalu?" asked Siddique Bhai. "Has he recovered from his illness?"

"What illness?" Gul Bhai was puzzled. "He and Izhar have been going in to work every day."

"Lalu hasn't been coming to work for the last few weeks," replied Siddique Bhai. "Izhar told me that he was ill."

"Thank you for letting me know," said Gul Bhai. "I will find out what's been going on and see that he comes in to work tomorrow."

When Lalu and Izhar returned later that evening, Gul Bhai greeted them on their arrival.

"Go into your bedroom, both of you," he said and followed them into the room carrying a cane. Then he bolted the door behind him.

"Now, what's been going on?" he demanded.

"What do you mean?" asked Lalu.

"What do I mean?" answered Gul Bhai. "What do you mean by not going to work for the last few weeks and then getting Izhar to tell lies for you? What have you two been up to?"

"I wasn't feeling well," Lalu replied.

"What have you got to say for yourself?" asked Gul Bhai turning to Izhar. "Why did you lie to Siddique Bhai?"

"Lalu said he would beat me if I didn't do as he asked," answered Izhar.

"You should have told me that Lalu wasn't going to work," said his father and hit him with the cane. "Tell me where he went, you *pilla*, you puppy."

"Lalu went fishing and he also played chess sometimes," answered Izhar in a small voice.

Gul Bhai began to beat Lalu with the cane. *"Kaam chore haram khor"* - you idle work-shy good-for-nothing," he shouted. "You will go back to work tomorrow. Go to work every day, or I will break your legs, *Mein teri khaal utaar doonga* - I will take your skin off. *Suar ka bachcha* - you piglet."

The boys' mother and Kausar heard Lalu shouting with pain and quickly rushed to the bedroom door.

"What is wrong with you, calling your son a piglet? Open the door!" screamed Gul Bhai's wife.

The bedroom door suddenly opened and both boys rushed out sobbing loudly. Both boys went to work together the next day, still sore from the beating. After that, even if Lal did occasionally genuinely feel unwell, he went to work regardless.

Chapter 7: Next Door Neighbors

"I wonder what's going on over the wall in the Lawyers' Den," remarked Bhura. He and his friend Arif were in the small upstairs room that Arif shared with his elder brother Aftab, carefully examining a large selection of top quality, thick fur Afghan hats in the dim light coming through the half open door.

"That shouting is coming from Gul Bhai's house," said Arif. "He must have found out that Lalu is a *kaam chore* who prefers to go fishing rather than work." They laughed then paused, listening to the door banging, cries, and shouts. "Never mind that now. Which hat do you think suits me best for *Eid* prayer?"

Arif and Aftab lived in one of the little houses in the Criminals' Den with their grandmother, who had a room downstairs and was slightly deaf. These houses surrounded a courtyard similar to but smaller than the one in the Lawyers' Den. Each courtyard had its own back door to Camel Courtyard, which was surrounded by a maze of narrow lanes into which petty criminals could easily escape. When people from the Lawyers' Den and the Criminals' Den attended the Qazi Mosque, they stood side by side for prayers.

The Afghan hats now heaped on the floor in front of Arif and Bhura were new and of top quality and had been obtained after careful planning some weeks previously.

"Those boys from the Lawyers' Den always wear new, top quality Afghan hats for *Eid*," Arif had remarked to Bhura.

"We could also have hats like that," his friend replied. "Do you know where they buy them from?"

"They go to Fida Hussain Bhai *topeewala* in Ujjain Chowk Bazaar in the town center." "He is a *Bohri* businessman and sells only the best quality hats."

"You should pay him a visit yourself, then," said Bhura. "Find out when he will be getting his next delivery of Afghan hats for *Eid*."

Some days later, Arif visited the shop of Fida Hussain Bhai *topeewala* wearing one of his brother's smart business suits. When he entered the shop, the owner moved forward to greet him.

"I am looking for top quality hats for my father and brother," Arif told Fida Hussain Bhai. "They have asked me to find out when your new stock of Afghan hats will be delivered for *Eid*."

"Bring me the register," Fida Hussain Bhai called to his assistant. He opened the book and ran his finger down the page.

"They will be coming on Tuesday afternoon in two weeks' time," he told Arif. "I look forward to seeing you all in our shop then."

That Tuesday afternoon found Arif on the footpath opposite the shop of Fida Hussain Bhai *topeewala*, waiting for the delivery van to arrive. Bhura was stationed nearby with his bike, ready for a quick getaway. When the van came, the driver got out, went around to the back of the van, opened the door, took out some hats, and went inside to deliver them and drink tea, leaving the van door open. Arif touched his forehead to Bhura as though offering *"Salam,"* climbed inside the van, and swiftly stuffed a large sack with Afghan hats. When he jumped out, Bhura was there with his bicycle. Arif got on the back of the bicycle with his sack and both friends made their getaway through a maze of back streets to Arif's home in the Criminals' Den. Leaving Bhura's bicycle outside, they took the sack upstairs to Arif's room, fully satisfied with the result of their morning's work. Arif hid two hats for himself and Bhura took away the rest of them to sell.

A month later, Arif and Bhura attended *Eid* prayers at Eidgah, a mosque some distance outside Ujjain where the Ujjain Muslims assembled for prayers on *Eid* Day. Aftab was away on business, having left the house some days earlier, smartly dressed, to take the overnight train to Bombay on one of his regular business trips.

Two policemen also attended *Eid* prayers. They recognized Arif from the Criminals' Den and spotted that he and his friend were wearing new Afghan hats. After *Eid Namaz,* they waited for the boys outside the mosque. "You are both wearing fine top quality hats," said one of the policemen.

Arif and Bhura smiled and nodded.

"They look very much like the expensive Afghan hats that recently disappeared from a van outside the shop of Fida Hussain Bhai *topeewala,*" remarked the second policeman.

"Come with us and tell us where you got those hats," said the first policeman.

At the police station, the policemen questioned Arif and Bhura. They refused to believe that the hats were a present from Bhura's relative who had had a win on *satta.*

"You told the shop owner that you were looking for hats for your father and brother," said one of the policemen to Arif. "Your father is in heaven with your mother. Is he coming back to Earth for *Eid*?"

The policemen took off their belts and gave both friends a

good beating. "This is your *Eidi* from us for this year," said one policeman when they had finished. "Like the present we gave you last year, when you stole the new shoes of the people attending Friday prayers at Qazi mosque, just before *Eid*."

Aftab and Arif were orphans. Their mother had died when Arif was small. Their father's mother, a widow, had then moved into the house to look after them. Their father had worked as a skilled weaver in the cloth mill, but was killed in an industrial accident just before Aftab was due to take the Urdu Middle School examination. The owners of the cloth mill never admitted liability, but they paid some compensation to the bereaved family. Aftab became the main breadwinner. His neighbor, Siddique Bhai, was a foreman at the cloth mill and found Aftab a job there. However, Aftab soon left this job after discovering more profitable ways of making money.

Arif found it difficult to learn reading and writing and avoided attending school whenever possible. Instead, he began to mix with petty criminals. They operated mainly at the bus and railway stations and also in the town center, stealing money and goods from villagers and businessmen. The police often caught them and took them along to the police station, where they were sometimes beaten and afterwards sent home with a stern warning. Occasionally, Aftab came to the police station to fetch Arif, so he knew some of Arif's associates and tried to dissuade him from mixing with them. When Arif was 12, Aftab spoke to Siddique Bhai, who found Arif a job in the cloth mill.

Later that *Eid* evening, Aftab returned home from Bombay. He went to his bedroom and dropped a thick roll of rupee notes inside his trunk. While he was changing into his everyday clothes, he noticed Arif lying on his bed.

"What's the matter with you?" he asked.

"I'm not feeling well," answered Arif in a subdued voice.

"Did you go for *Eid Namaz*?" asked Aftab.

"Yes, I did."

"I will go out and get some nice food for all of us," said Aftab.

As Aftab approached Anwar Ali's grocery shop, some boys greeted him. "How is Arif? Is he back from the police station yet?" asked one of them.

"What are you talking about? He's at home," Aftab replied.

"We saw him today with Bhura at *Eid Namaz*," said another boy. "They were both wearing fine Afghan hats. They left with two policemen."

"Bhura, that bicycle thief!" exclaimed Aftab. "I will punish him for going with that cycle *chore*."

Aftab bought food for *Eid* dinner for his granny and brother, including sweets from Ram Das sweet merchants. On returning home, he went upstairs to speak to Arif.

"Why were you with that cycle *chore* Bhura?" he asked his brother angrily.

"I told Bhura I wanted a top quality Afghan hat for *Eid,* so we stole some from Fida Hussain Bhai *topeewala*. The policemen at *Eid Namaz* recognized the hats, took us to the police station, and punished us." Arif was crying, fearing more punishment from his elder brother. "Please don't beat me. I have never stolen anything in Mirzawari."

"Today we are celebrating *Eid*," answered Aftab. "You have been punished enough, so I will not punish you again. However, you must promise *Qasam khaa*, word of honor, that you will never ever again go with Bhura, that cycle *chore*."

"*Mein qasam khaata hoon* -- I hereby solemnly swear that I will not see Bhura again," answered Arif.

"Have you been taking many days off work?" asked Aftab.

Arif hung his head and did not reply.

"My business does not bring in a regular income," Aftab pointed out sharply. "You also have family responsibilities. It is not good that our old granny should have to go out and do housework to help support us. She isn't strong and she can earn very little."

"You are right," replied Arif. "I feel ashamed that I do not share the burden of supporting our family. I promise that I will go to work regularly at the cloth mill from now on."

The brothers embraced each other and wept with joy. Then they and their granny celebrated *Eid* in style, with fine food and sweets.

The following day, Aftab took his brother to visit Siddique Bhai in his home. Arif told Siddique Bhai that he would return to work after the three days of *Eid* celebrations and come to the cloth mill every day.

- - - - - - - - - - - - - - - - - - - -

Aftab was tall and handsome with a fair skin and a prominent scar on his face. This only added to his good looks. On his business trips to Bombay, Aftab always wore a very expensive three-piece suit with a white shirt and tie and highly polished black shoes. He also had a heavy gold watch on his wrist and a gold chain round his neck over his tie. Expensive gold cufflinks glinted beneath the sleeves of his jacket.

Aftab was away from home for about a week on his next business trip. As always, he took an express train and traveled first class for the three-day journey to Bombay. His fellow passengers were rich businessmen, clutching cloth bags containing large amounts of cash. At night they dropped off to sleep at times, their bags clasped to their chests. Aftab also leaned back in his seat with his eyes closed. Sometimes a businessman recognized Aftab from descriptions given by other regular travelers on the night train to Bombay, who had shared a compartment with him and woken to find him gone along with their cash. The businessman would then call Aftab into the corridor, hand him about two hundred rupees, and quietly request him to move to another compartment.

On his return from Bombay, Aftab found that Arif had not come home from work. He asked the boys outside Anwar Ali's shop if they had seen Arif.

Mehboob, the messenger, saw Aftab talking to them. "Are you looking for Arif?" he asked.

"Yes, have you seen him?"

Mehboob drew Aftab to one side. "He is at the police station," he told him quietly.

"Oh no, what has he done now?" asked Aftab groaning.

"He and Bhura stole a bicycle belonging to Ghaffar *dabbawala* together with some tiffin carriers."

"How did they do it?"

"Ghaffar had left his bicycle with the tiffin carriers to collect a cooked lunch from Judge Sahib's home. When he came back, he saw that Bhura was cycling away at top speed on his bicycle with Arif sitting in front. Ghaffar shouted at them, but they didn't stop. Ghaffar then informed the police and they caught Arif later. Arif admitted that he and Bhura had gone to a park and eaten the tiffins, which Ghaffar was to have delivered to the law court for the lawyers' lunches. A police officer later went to the park and found two empty tiffin carriers in the bushes."

At the police station, Aftab found that Arif had already been taken to court and fined by the judge for his part in the theft. Aftab paid the fine in order to save their grandmother from shame, and also to avoid bringing unwanted attention to his regular business activities on trains to Bombay. Then he brought his brother home in a *tonga*.

"You broke your promise and went with Bhura again," Aftab shouted angrily and gave his brother a beating.

- - - - - - - - - - - - - - - - - - - -

Some days later, the court judge invited the lawyer, Shakil Sahib, to come to his office. "Both my court and the police are wasting a lot of unnecessary time dealing with petty criminals," he told Shakil Sahib.

"Several of them live near my residence," said Shakil Sahib. "I will see if I can find a solution to this problem."

Shakil Sahib informed Yousuf Ali Sahib, a retired lawyer, that the court judge was trying to find an effective way of dealing with petty criminals. "I am sure we can help these people to develop skills that will enable them to earn an honest living," he added.

Yousuf Ali Sahib's bungalow was next to the Qazi Mosque. He told the Qazi what Shakil Sahib had said, and they agreed to arrange a meeting, to discuss how to help the petty criminals among their neighbors to lead honest lives.

The meeting was held around a table beneath a tree in the courtyard next to the Qazi's house. The Qazi presided over it. Shakil Sahib was present, along with Yousuf Ali Sahib, Police Inspector Afaq Hassan, his brother Waqar Hassan the solicitor, a retired Major, Halim Nawaz the teacher, and one of Halim Nawaz's colleagues. Tara Bibi the go-between was also there, as she would be liaising with the women in the families of the petty criminals. After some delay, the Qazi made an announcement.

"I apologize for the delay," he said. "We are waiting for Siddique Bhai, the foreman at the cloth factory. He appears to have been unexpectedly detained elsewhere."

The meeting began. It was agreed that Police Inspector Afaq Hassan would ask the policemen to hand over petty criminals to Yousuf Ali Sahib, who would send them on to Major Sahib.

"I'll teach those boys the meaning of discipline," Major Sahib told the meeting. "They will learn to work regular hours at my bungalow, during the day, by doing simple domestic tasks, gardening, and other odd jobs. My servants will keep an eye on them and see that they stick to the routine that they are given."

"We will teach them to read and write in the evening after school," said Halim Nawaz.

"I will inform the women in the families of the petty criminals how we are trying to help them to lead decent lives," said Tara Bibi.

"Once these boys have shown that they know how to conduct themselves, I will inform Siddique Bhai that they are ready to work in the cloth mill," said Major Sahib. "He has promised to help by offering them work there."

Siddique Bhai was short and stocky. He lived with his wife in the Criminals' Den. Every morning, he would rub coconut oil into his hair, put on his hat and walk the three miles from his home to the cloth mill. The black Afghan hat had been given to him by his in-laws on his wedding day 22 years previously. He wore it each day, even in the heat of summer. Sweat and coconut oil would pour from under the hat onto his large round head down his forehead and face and onto his thick neck. From time to time, he would wipe his face with his sleeve. The Afghan hat had not been washed since his wedding day and was heavily stained inside with sweat and coconut oil.

Siddique Bhai was well known to everyone who saw him on his daily walk to and from the cloth mill.

"I don't think Siddique Bhai has been parted from that hat for a single moment since he got married," one old man observed idly to his friends, as they stood near the Qazi Mosque watching him come home from work.

"I wonder why he never washes his hat?" another man mused.

"Perhaps he does not wish to wash out the golden memories of his wedding day," answered the first man drily.

"Or he is hiding something beneath it," joked a third man.

When the children playing in the street saw Siddique Bhai, they would pause and greet him respectfully, saying, "*Salam, Siddique Bhai.*" He would nod and smile in acknowledgment. Occasionally, he slid one fat finger beneath his hat to squash a bug or two on his head, giving a glimpse of his short black hair.

"I wonder why Siddique Bhai isn't here," remarked Shakil Sahib. "He said he would come to our meeting."

"I saw him this morning when I went shopping," said Halim Nawaz. "He told me he was going fishing before coming here."

Just then, the meeting was interrupted by Hira Lal *tongawala*, who came rushing breathlessly into the courtyard.

"What's the matter, Hira Lal?" asked Shakil Sahib.

"It's Siddique Bhai," answered Hira Lal. "He's been mauled by a lion. I've just taken him to the hospital in my *tonga*."

"What happened?" asked the Qazi.

"I had dropped off a passenger, when I saw a bullock cart coming toward me with Siddique Bhai sitting in it supported by a villager. His clothes were bloodstained and he was covered in bandages. The driver told me they had come from a village near the jungle.

"Five villagers had been walking along the top of a hill when they looked down and saw him on the path below, carrying a gun. Suddenly, a lion leaped out of the bushes and attacked him. The gun fell and he had to fight the lion with his bare hands, jabbing at the lion's eyes with his fingers. The lion started to maul him. The villagers rushed toward them, shouting and brandishing their axes. As they approached, the lion lunged for his head and disappeared into the jungle together with his hat."

"That man was badly mauled," the driver told me. "We have done our best to bandage him with cloths and we are now taking him to a hospital in Ujjain."

"The two villagers helped me to lift Siddique Bhai into my *tonga* and I quickly took him to the hospital," Hira Lal went on. "He told me he was supposed to be at a meeting with you, so I came straight here to tell you what had happened."

After staying in hospital for a month, Siddique Bhai became aware that something was missing. "Where's my hat?" he asked one of the nurses.

"What hat? There was no hat with you when you arrived here."

Siddique Bhai spoke sadly of his hat to his wife, the next time she came to visit him.

"That filthy old Afghan hat, you mean?" she asked. "Good riddance to it."

"That hat was part of our marriage," said Siddique Bhai. "I received it on my wedding day." He sighed. "It was part of my life."

"That hat saved your life," his wife told him. "The lion took it in his teeth when he went for your head."

A few days later, Siddique Bhai's wife came to see him carrying a shapeless, black fur object with tooth marks on it.

"Hira Lal brought this to me yesterday," she said to her husband. "One of the villagers found it, near the bushes where the lion attacked you. It was really smelly, so I washed it thoroughly."

- -

Aftab was very friendly with the boys on both sides of the wall separating the Lawyers' Den from the houses of the petty criminals. One day, he came upon two small boys from the Lawyers' den, in the Chowk Bazaar at the town center. One boy had several rupee notes stuffed into the front pocket of his *kameez*.

Aftab greeted them with a smile. "What are you doing

here?" he asked.

"We have come to do some shopping," answered the older boy.

"Do you have money?" asked Aftab.

"Of course," answered the older boy. He put his hand up to his pocket. "Oh God, where is my money? It's gone. I have lost my money!" he exclaimed.

"It's here," said Aftab with a smile, handing him the rupee notes. "Always keep your money in an inside pocket."

The boy took the money from Aftab and thanked him. He never forgot the lesson Aftab had taught him and always kept his money well hidden after that.

A few days later, Aftab met the same two boys outside the local cinema. They wanted to see the film. Men and boys were milling round shouting, "Ticket, please!" and pushing their arms through the small window of the ticket office with the money clutched in their hands. The ticket clerk tickled the hand of each man beneath his fist, so that he dropped his money into the clerk's hand. The clerk then moved over to the cashier sitting behind him, gave the money to the cashier, and returned with the cinema ticket, which he then placed into the customer's empty hand.

"Are you waiting to see the film?" Aftab asked the two boys.

"Yes, we have money, but the window of the ticket office is too high for us to reach," replied one of them.

"I'll get the tickets for you," said Aftab. "You boys wait here."

The two boys held out their money to Aftab.

"No, keep your money," said Aftab with a smile. "Just watch me."

Aftab was taller than most of the other men. He went to the ticket office and pushed his closed fist through the window.

"Two tickets, please!" shouted a man, holding out his fist. The man was too short to see that the ticket clerk had just gone to collect tickets for another customer. Aftab tickled the man's fist and took his money. When the clerk returned to the window, Aftab handed over the money, collected the two tickets and gave them to the boys. The short man was left shouting for his tickets.

- - - - - - - - - - - - - - - - - - - -

Kausar and her two sons shared her brother, Gul Bhai's house. Her elder son, Ashraf, worked as a ticket inspector on the trains. Most of his fellow railway employees were Anglo-Indian, as English was essential for their work and they spoke English at home. After passing a test at the Railway Recruitment Center at Nagda Railway Junction, Ashraf had therefore been particularly pleased to be called back for an interview, together with the other successful candidates. He presented himself before the railway board with a black hat on his head, wearing a black blazer over a white shirt with a tie and trousers that he himself had carefully ironed three times. His new, black, well-polished *Bata* shoes outshone those of the other candidates. Ashraf had been delighted to be offered the job of ticket inspector on the trains running between Nagda and Bombay. He soon became known as Babu Sahib, like all the other ticket collectors.

One day, after coming home from work and taking his evening meal, Ashraf went to see Yousuf Ali Sahib, the retired lawyer.

"What can I do for you?" asked Yousuf Ali Sahib, when they had exchanged greetings.

" I just found out what kind of business takes Aftab to Bombay," announced Ashraf.

"Come to my study and tell me about it."

"His business is not in Bombay, but in the trains traveling

between Nagda and Bombay," Ashraf answered. "I check the tickets of all the passengers on the trains running between Nagda and Bombay and I am on the night shift. The rich businessmen always travel first class. Many of them carry large amounts of cash in cloth bags. When I entered one first class compartment, I was surprised to see Aftab sitting there. He was wearing an expensive suit with a shirt and tie and seemed to be half asleep. Next to him was a businessman carrying a bag. I greeted Aftab and checked both their tickets. Aftab had a first class return ticket from Nagda to Bombay and was very quiet.

"Our train stopped at a small railway station and had just started off again when the businessman who had been sitting next to Aftab came to see me. He had been asleep and had woken to find that his money bag had disappeared, along with the man sitting next to him. The train was just moving out of the station. The businessman and I looked out of the train and saw Aftab on the platform with a large leather bag in his hand walking toward the waiting room. 'That's the man who was sitting next to me!' exclaimed the businessman."

"What did you do next?"

"I immediately telegraphed the station master at the station we had just left. The railway police found a man answering Aftab's description sitting in the waiting room, with a leather bag. When they asked him to open the bag, they found it contained a cloth bag stuffed with rupee notes like the one stolen from the businessman. The railway police arrested Aftab and put him in custody to stand trial at the station court room, today. When I contacted the station master on my return journey, he informed me that the man had escaped from custody. I did not tell the station master that I knew this man."

"Thank you for letting me know," said Yousuf Ali Sahib. "I thought Aftab had stopped his criminal activities. Please ask Halim Nawaz to come and see me urgently."

Ashraf took his leave of Yousuf Ali Sahib, did as he was requested, and went home.

When Halim Nawaz arrived, Yousuf Ali Sahib led him to his study.

"Thank you for coming to see me at such short notice," he said, when both men were seated. "Arif's elder brother Aftab has been caught stealing money from businessmen while traveling on the train. He has escaped from custody and disappeared. I expect he is hiding at home now."

"That is very bad. He is a most intelligent boy," answered Halim Nawaz.

"We have to see how we can prevent him from going to jail," said Yousuf Ali Sahib. "Tomorrow I will ask Major Sahib if he can take Aftab for training."

My colleague and I will be pleased to help Aftab in the evenings, to prepare to take the Urdu Middle School Examination," said Halim Nawaz.

"How are Arif and Bhura getting on?"

"Both boys have benefited from their training and have jobs at the cloth mill. They attend work regularly and are most industrious. However, they have difficulty in learning to read and write and it will be a long time before they acquire these skills."

"I need to speak to Aftab straight away. Please, can you show my servant where he lives."

In due course, the servant returned with Aftab and showed him into Yousuf Ali Sahib's study. Yousuf Ali Sahib looked up from his papers. "Take a seat," he said. "I know the details of your activities on the trains between Nagda and Bombay."

Aftab shifted uneasily on his chair and said nothing.

"You now have a choice. Learn some skills and earn your living like your brother or go to jail."

Aftab hung his head in silence. "I don't want to go to jail," he muttered finally.

"Very well then," said Yousuf Ali Sahib. "You will work for Major Sahib for three months. In the evenings, a teacher will prepare you for the Urdu Middle School Examination. Afterward, Siddique Bhai will find you work in the cloth mill according to your abilities."

Aftab found it difficult to adjust to working for Major Sahib after being self-employed for so long. However, he enjoyed studying for the Urdu Middle School Examination and was particularly interested in learning mathematics and English. He was successful in the examination and Siddique Bhai managed to find him a job in the accounts office of the textile mill.

- - - - - - - - - - - - - - - - - - - -

Aftab, Arif, and their grandmother occupied one of the four two-bedroom houses around the Criminals' Den courtyard. Siddique Bhai and his wife lived in the second house. A young man, Zamir Khan, had the upstairs bedroom of the third house, which he shared with his mother, who slept downstairs. The engineer, a widower, lived in the fourth house together with his 11-year-old daughter, who had a bedroom downstairs and did all the housework.

The main entrance to this courtyard was bolted from inside to prevent strangers, particularly policemen, from entering. People living there generally knocked at the door and called out for someone to open it, or returned to their houses through a door leading off Camel Courtyard. Each house had one upstairs bedroom with a window and one windowless bedroom downstairs, outside of which was a verandah with a kitchen on one side.

Zamir Khan had only been four years old when his father disappeared from his life. His mother had been waiting for her husband, Sher Khan, to return home through the door from Camel Courtyard, so she had ignored the banging at the door to the Criminals' Den. Soon afterward, someone knocked at her front door and she heard Siddique Bhai calling to her. When she opened her door, she saw him standing there along with his wife and a policeman.

"What's happened?" she asked, alarmed at the sight of the policeman.

"It's bad news," answered Siddique Bhai quietly. "They've arrested your husband".

"Why? What for?"

"He's killed a man," said the policeman. "He says that it was in defense of his friend Hoshiar Gul."

Siddique Bhai's wife remained with Zamir's mother, while Siddique Bhai went down to the station with the policeman to find out more. Sher Khan asked Siddique Bhai to inform his friend, Hoshiar Gul, of his arrest. Hoshiar Gul immediately promised to support Sher Khan's family while he was in prison and arranged to make regular payments to the Qazi, to pass on to them. At the Qazi's request, Tara Bibi, the go-between, brought the money to Zamir's mother. Tara Bibi also accompanied her when she went to visit her husband, in prison.

When he was five years old, Zamir started school. He was intelligent, enjoyed reading and writing, and showed strong leadership qualities. After school, he and a group of his friends hung around aimlessly in the street, occasionally slipping into a shop to snatch a sweet or a piece of fruit from the counter. They soon became known to the local police and also to the gangsters.

Zamir was 12 years old when Hoshiar Gul offered him a job. "Your father was a good friend to me," he told Zamir, "so I would like to give you the chance to earn some money. Your friends can also stay with you if you wish and you can give them tea."

"What will I have to do?" asked Zamir.

"I would like you to work for me in a shop, near the Qazi

mosque. Someone will come from the railway station each day, to bring bales of Chinese silk and leave them in the shop. Your job is to stack them by the back wall and look after them carefully, until the same man comes back in the afternoon to take them to the warehouse."

Chinese silk was imported into Ujjain, Gwalior state, from other Indian states and sent by railway, via Nagda junction, to Ujjain railway station. A policeman there ensured that customs duty was paid on all goods entering Ujjain from other states. Hoshiar Gul collected the silk at the station and bribed the policeman to avoid paying this duty. He then sent it with one of his men to the shop. Policemen's wages were low, so they relied on the bribes as a source of extra income and welcomed the chance to work at Ujjain railway station.

Zamir was paid well and enjoyed the work. He dressed smartly and always wore a silk shirt. When he was 15 years old, Hoshiar Gul told him about his father.

"Your father killed a man in my defense and went to prison," he said to Zamir.

Zamir was stunned at this news.

"This is why I am under an obligation to him," Hoshiar Gul continued. "The silk shop is closing down soon, so I would like to offer you another job."

"What kind of job?"

"You will collect money on my behalf from my customers."

Zamir agreed to take the job.

Later, Zamir learned more about the events that had led to his father being sent to prison.

His father Sher Khan and Hoshiar Gul used to watch cockfights every weekend and place bets. Both were illegal.

Lohar *ghundah*, the local gangster leader, organized the cockfights, which were held in a specially dug pit, in Murgha Medaan, in one corner of Gharib Colony. At the bottom of the pit was a flat area with a white line drawn down the middle. A fence around the pit with two entrances on opposite sides had old rags hanging over it to conceal the activities in the pit. While the cockfights were going on, two men kept watch. When the police appeared, they gave the alarm. Two *ghundahs* then seized the cockerels and disappeared with them from the pit into the maze of mud houses of Gharib Colony. When the police eventually gained entrance to the pit, they found a game of *kabaddi* in full swing with two teams each of seven men surrounded by onlookers.

The cockerels taking part in the fights had been specially trained on a nearby farm. They were rubbed all over with herbs and fed red hot chillies. Before the fight started, both cockerels would be raised high and displayed to the audience so that their colorful feathers shone in the sun. Lohar *ghundah* then took bets. The cockerels were let loose to fight and the loser was taken away to be curried. The owner of the winning cockerel received Rs.25 ($0.45). All winnings from bets were paid on the spot.

"I think there is money to be made in cockfighting," Hoshiar Gul said one day to Sher Khan. "Would you like to organize it with me?"

Sher Khan agreed and they set up the cockfights in another part of Gharib Colony. Hoshiar Gul soon became popular because he gave Rs.45 ($0.80) to the owner of the winning cockerel.

Lohar *ghundah* was very angry when he found out about the rival enterprise. He sent along two *ghundahs* to put a stop to it. In the ensuing brawl, Sher Khan knifed one gangster to death and the other one fled. Sher Khan and Hoshiar Gul were defended by Yousuf Ali Sahib, the lawyer. Hoshiar Gul had not taken part in the fight, so he was released without charge. Sher Khan was jailed for 15 years. Zamir was four years old at that time.

Lohar *ghundah* and the other gang member were caught.

No one was prepared to testify against Lohar so he was released and his accomplice was jailed for five years for instigating violence. Both cockfighting enterprises were closed down.

When Zamir started working for Hoshiar Gul, he soon found that Hoshiar Gul's clients were paying him for illegal drugs that they then sold to the end users. Zamir's work took him around Chowk Bazaar in Ujjain town center.

Lohar *ghundah* never forgot that Hoshiar Gul had been responsible for the loss of his cockfighting business and his profits from betting. When one of his *ghundahs* became lame following a gang fight, Lohar set him up in a shop dealing in drugs on Hoshiar's territory, at one corner of the busy crossroads at Chowk Bazaar, opposite the shop of Shakir *paanwala*, a betel seller popular with the local lawyers. This *ghundah* was known as "Langra" or "Lame." He wore a white silk shirt with a gold-design on it over white pajamas. His shop was always very clean. On the floor was a mattress covered with a white sheet. He would sit on the mattress chewing *paan* with one hand resting on a bolster by the wall. From time to time he would get up, limp to the entrance, and spit betel juice onto the pavement outside.

Langra regularly gave money to Ghinwa, the beggar sitting outside the Chand Hotel at one corner of the crossroads. Solicitors and lawyers often stood near the *paanwala's* shop opposite the hotel, chewing *paan* and spitting on the open ground next to the shop. Langra would greet them and exchange a few friendly words whenever they passed his shop. Langra felt safe in his shop. It was on the territory of Hoshiar Gul, the leader of a rival gang, but it was also on a busy road. Hoshiar Gul would be unable to prevent Langra from doing business there.

Ghinwa was unable to walk or talk. He was in his mid-twenties, plump, and dark-skinned with short black hair. He was always smiling and would sit with his arms on his knees and his head moving up and down nonstop. He was barefoot and wore a shirt with a torn sleeve. A widow with a bungalow in Mirzawari looked after him in her home and a man brought him by *tonga* once a day to sit outside the Chand Hotel for an hour or so, with a cloth on the pavement in front of him. Passers-by and people going in and out of the hotel would drop a few coins onto the cloth. Some men bought him tea and then helped him to drink it. Later the man who had brought him to the hotel took him back to Mirzawari by *tonga*, with the money wrapped in the cloth.

Hoshiar Gul's shop was a little away from the city center. When he found that he was losing business to his rival, he ordered Zamir to go and call on Langra. "Tell Langra he is on my territory and must close his shop or pay me protection money," he said.

It was mid-morning and the crossroads were busy as usual when Zamir came to stand by Langra's shop door.

"What do you want?" asked Langra.

"Hoshiar Gul has sent me to tell you to close your shop or pay him protection money. You are on his territory."

"Get out, you Hoshiar Gul *ka bachcha*, you son of Hoshiar Gul. Your own father is in jail and has been there for many years." Langra leaned back on to the bolster and gave a mocking laugh.

"What do you mean by that?" asked Zamir angrily.

Some passers-by stopped to see what was going on and Langra turned to them.

"See this Hoshiar Gul *ka bachcha*," he said pointing at Zamir. "He doesn't even know who his own father is."

This infuriated Zamir. He drew out the sharp knife that he always carried for protection, darted forward, and stabbed Langra viciously a few times. Langra fell to the floor bleeding.

"This will teach you not to talk to me like that," shouted Zamir and stabbed him in the throat. "You will never again call me names."

Some spectators rushed forward to pull Zamir away from Langra and one of them seized his arm.

"That's enough now," he said, forcing Zamir to drop the knife.

The sound of the struggle and the shouting penetrated the constant fog surrounding Ghinwa's mind. His head became still and he turned his face toward the noise. "*Nahi maar, nahi maar,* don't kill, don't kill," came a rusty, almost unrecognizable shriek. It was the long unused sound of Ghinwa's voice. When his benefactor later came to collect him, he found that Ghinwa had died of shock.

The onlookers handed Zamir over to the police. Later in court, several witnesses testified in his defense. Yousuf Ali Sahib the lawyer, now retired, also spoke in Zamir's defense. In view of the mitigating circumstances, the judge sentenced Zamir to eight years in prison.

A few months later, Lohar *ghundah* and two of his *ghundahs* went to Hoshiar Gul's shop. The *ghundahs* soon overpowered the two men standing on guard there and held each man with a knife at his back while Lohar went inside the shop.

"You had Langra killed. You think you can get away with that?" he shouted at Hoshiar Gul.

"It was an accident," cried Hoshiar Gul.

Suddenly Lohar leapt forward, knifed him, pushed him on to the floor, and stabbed him again and again. Blood streamed from Hoshiar's body, as his life ebbed away. Lohar cleaned his knife on Hoshiar's *kameez*, went outside, and waved it before the two guards standing outside.

"This knife has Hoshiar's blood on it," he told them. "If either of you says one word to the police, your blood will also be there."

Lohar *ghundah* and his men quickly left. Hoshiar's men went into the shop and discovered Hoshiar's bleeding body on the floor. They were left with no choice but to report it to the police.

"You will both have to appear in court as witnesses when this case comes to trial," the police inspector told them.

"If we do this, Lohar *ghundah* will have us killed," cried the men, anxiously.

"Last time Lohar *ghundah* killed a policeman and no one was prepared to come forward as a witness," answered the police inspector. "This time we want to catch him and send him and his accomplices to jail. If you help us, we will put you and your families under police protection."

Both men agreed to act as witnesses. When the case came to trial, it attracted a lot of publicity. Many people in Ujjain breathed a sigh of relief when the judge sentenced Lohar *ghundah* to jail for life and his accomplices to ten years each. A few weeks later, there were reports that Lohar *ghundah* had been shot dead while attempting to escape from jail, after bribing a prison guard to help him.

- - - - - - - - - - - - - - - - - - - -

A year later, Sher Khan was released from prison after serving 13 years due to good conduct. He walked round the neighborhood where he had once lived and found that it appeared little changed. He thought of his son Zamir, now serving a prison sentence, and tried to imagine him as a child, growing up there. He wondered what sort of games Zamir had liked to play and what sort of friends he had had. Sher Khan regretted that he would now never meet his friend, Hoshiar Gul, to thank him for providing regular financial support to his wife and son over the years. There was no money in his pocket now, no way to buy special food for his wife, to celebrate his release from prison.

Sher Khan's wanderings had brought him to the graveyard. He surveyed the rows of tombstones and then looked away over the open football ground next to the graveyard. A cockerel was flapping its wings in one corner. It must have escaped from the Qazi's backyard, where the Qazi's son kept a flock of hens and cockerels. Sher Khan touched something soft

178

with his foot and looked down. It was an old bag made of sacking. He quickly picked it up.

"God has provided me with fresh meat and the means to bring it home," he murmured to himself and raised his eyes to heaven. "Thank you, God."

Sher Khan strode over to the cockerel. It made no attempt to flee. Quickly, he reached out, seized the cockerel by the neck, and stuffed it into the sack. Then he walked back to his house, holding the sack with the struggling bird to his chest.

"*Allah mehrban hai,* God is kind," Sher Khan told his wife as he entered the house. That evening they both enjoyed a fine meal of chicken curry.

Yousuf Ali Sahib asked Siddique Bhai to find a job for Sher Khan. Shortly afterward, Sher Khan started working regularly at the cloth mill.

- - - - - - - - - - - - - - - - - - - -

Forged silver rupees were turning up in people's small change. For some months the police had been trying to find out where they were coming from. They asked the shopkeepers and stall holders in Ujjain to inform them when they found forged rupees in their takings. This was not easy as the forgeries were very good. Eventually, the police had a lead. The owner of a grocery shop in Milkipura received a forged silver rupee from a customer. This had happened before and the bank had refused to accept the forged rupee, when the shopkeeper deposited his takings there. This time he told his small son to follow the customer and find out where he lived.

The boy followed the man back to the Criminals' Den and watched as the man knocked for admission at the door to the courtyard. Then he went back to his father and told him where the man lived. The shopkeeper went to the police.

"Can you describe this man?" asked the police inspector in charge of the investigation.

"Yes," answered the shopkeeper. "He is tall and slim with short graying black hair and dark skin."

This was the breakthrough the investigators had been waiting for.

"There are only four houses in the Criminals' Den," said one of the policemen.

"That man sounds very much like the engineer," said the Police Inspector. "He lives in the house by the entrance to the Criminals' Den. Let's go and pay him a visit."

The inspector and a team of four policemen set off for the Criminals' Den. The inspector sent two policemen around to Camel Courtyard to cover the back entrance. Some children playing there ran past them into the Criminals' Den. Then the Inspector went with the other two policemen to the front entrance. A group of children and some passers-by joined them to see what was going on. From his upstairs bedroom window, the engineer saw a small crowd gathered outside his house, surrounding the inspector and two policemen. He went to the small, coal-fed furnace in the middle of his bedroom, picked up a little metal die together with some newly made silver rupees lying at the side of the furnace, and quickly wrapped them in a cloth.

There was a knock at the door to the courtyard. The engineer went into the courtyard and asked one of the children playing there to answer the door. He then called his daughter from the kitchen to come upstairs with him.

"Open the door!" called the police inspector from outside.

"I can't reach the latch," shouted the little boy from inside.

"Go and call somebody then," said the police inspector.

Meanwhile, the engineer brought his daughter into his bedroom and handed her the small cloth covered bundle containing the die and the silver rupees.

"Hide that under your *dupatta* and take it downstairs to

180

the kitchen," he told her. "Be careful, it's still warm."

Meanwhile, one of the neighbors had opened the front door to the courtyard.

"Where does the engineer live?" shouted the police inspector.

Three or four children ran past him into the engineer's house and up the stairs. They were followed by the inspector and the two policemen.

"Come on, children, everybody downstairs!" shouted the inspector. "Let us pass!"

All the children rushed down the narrow staircase, laughing with excitement. Among them was the engineer's daughter, carrying a small bundle under her *dupatta*. The inspector and the two policemen stood aside as they passed. Then they climbed the stairs and entered the engineer's bedroom. They searched the room thoroughly, opened a trunk and a suitcase, and looked through his clothes. Then they examined the furnace, lifting the lid and looking at the coal inside.

"What do you use the furnace for?" asked the Police Inspector.

"I sometimes cook my food on it, late in the evening, so that I won't have to disturb my daughter downstairs," answered the engineer.

The police were unable to find any dies or other evidence of forgery. However, they took the engineer back to the station with them for questioning. One of the children informed Siddique Bhai's wife what had happened and she went to stay with the engineer's daughter overnight.

The following day, Police Inspector Afaq Hassan went to see Yousuf Ali Sahib, the retired lawyer. "I have every reason to believe that the engineer was involved in the recent appearance of forged silver rupees in people's change," he told him.

"Have you spoken to him about it?" asked Yousuf Ali Sahib.

"We visited his house yesterday and took him in for questioning last night," the Police Inspector replied. "However, we were unable to find any evidence linking him to the forgeries - this time. Please inform the engineer that we are aware of his activities and we will catch him one day."

It was late at night when the police finished questioning the engineer about the forged silver rupees and were forced to release him, for lack of evidence. He left the police station, relieved at his narrow escape from the law. On his way home, he was surprised to see that the shop of Ram Das, the sweet merchant, was still open. He decided to buy some sweets for his daughter.

It was then that the engineer discovered evidence of the existence of other dimensions, where beings led parallel lives to people on Earth.

Chapter 8: Glimpses of the Unseen

We are generally not aware of other dimensions of time and space in the earthbound existence of our daily lives. However, the veil is occasionally raised slightly for a favored few, to reveal for a short time some of the wonders of these other worlds. Standing in an open space in the morning sunshine, on a busy street at midday, or in a quiet square as dusk falls, we may sometimes sense something that is not there. It may show as a sudden flash of light or a deepening of the shadows, as another world briefly touches our own.

Night was drawing in and street lamps lit the roads, as the engineer started to walk back to Mirzawari from the police station. It was Thursday. Most people were at home taking their evening meal or putting the children to bed. The street was still and quiet, its few shops locked and shuttered - except one.

As he approached the shop of Ram Das, the sweet merchant, the engineer was surprised to see that the door stood wide open and the shop inside was lit up. The scent of sandalwood, from *agarbattis* burning at both sides of the shop door, perfumed the street outside. Ram Das was just bringing fresh supplies of sweets into the shop from the food factory behind it. The aroma of freshly made *jalebi, imarti, gulab jamun, laddu, ghaiver, kalakand* and *sohan halwa* filled the shop.

"What sort of customers is Ram Das expecting to visit his shop at this time of night?" the engineer wondered. "Since he is open, I might as well buy some sweets for my daughter."

The engineer was a regular customer there and knew Ram Das well.

"It's the wrong time to be putting out fresh sweets," he told Ram Das after greeting him. "Everyone else has long since shut up shop. You won't get many customers at this time of night."

"That's not true," answered Ram Das quietly. "Every Thursday, I get a lot of customers coming to my shop, after midnight. They are only interested in my sweets, they don't buy savories. Please tell no one about this."

The engineer was surprised and puzzled. "I won't say anything. Who are these customers?"

"I think they are all Muslim *genies*," said Ram Das in a low voice. "They all wear Muslim dress with Afghan hats. They are very good customers and never haggle over the price."

"What sweets do they buy?"

"All of them. They have a very sweet tooth. They don't seem to like any of the savories though. They never buy any of my *puri bhaji, dahi barey* or *khasta kachori*."

"Have you ever seen their wives or children?" asked the engineer.

"They never bring their wives and rarely come with their children. They are very quiet and well-behaved and always stand patiently in a queue. They also have a leader. He has a bigger head than the rest. His hat is also different to theirs. On the front, there is a large silvery white moon with a gold star against a blue background."

"What's he like?"

"Oh, he is very pleasant," Ram Das answered. "He told me that if any of his men give me any kind of trouble, I must let him know and he will sort it out. I only had trouble once. There was a young man who was new and he started arguing about the price. I believe that one of the others reported him to the leader because I never saw him again. They are very generous and they are my best customers."

"That's interesting," said the engineer. "I should like to buy some of your savories if you have any left."

"Of course," Ram Das indicated the display. "What would you like?"

The engineer asked for *saag puri, dahi barey, pakorey* and *khasta katchoris*. He also bought his daughter's favorite sweets – *gulab jamuns* and some *ghaiver, imarti and sohan halwa*.

The next morning, the engineer thanked Siddique Bhai's wife for staying with his daughter while he was at the police station, and gave her some of the sweets he had bought from Ram Das. Then he made a point of passing Ram Das' shop once more, to see if the sweets were still there, and was surprised and pleased to find that they had all disappeared. He stopped at the shop. Ram Das' assistant appeared.

"What can I get you?" he asked.

"Do you still have any of the sweets I saw in your shop last night?" asked the engineer.

"Sorry, we don't have any sweets just now," the assistant answered. "Fresh supplies will be available this afternoon."

The engineer thought about the unusual happenings at Ram Das' shop the previous evening and the explanation he had been given. Later, he spoke to his neighbor, Siddique Bhai.

"On my way home late last night, I saw something really strange. Please keep quiet about it."

"I'll keep it to myself," Siddique Bhai replied, intrigued.

"Ram Das's shop was all lit up and he was just putting out a large batch of sweets. He told me that *genies* visit his shop after midnight on Thursdays to buy sweets. This morning I visited the shop and was told that there were no sweets left."

"The *genies* always buy sweets on Thursdays, so that they can offer *fatiha* and blessings for the souls of the dead and all their family members after Friday prayers," Siddique Bhai explained. "They can speak many languages. They can change their appearance in seconds; that is why they look just like ordinary people in normal dress. They lead ordinary lives, except that they all live in underground houses that are invisible to humans."

"Hmm," said the engineer. "That is most interesting. Thank you for explaining." He spent the rest of the day reflecting on this new revelation.

- - - - - - - - - - - - - - - - - - - -

The women in the villages near Ujjain were slim and wiry, with light brown skin and an elegant carriage. They had their own fashion in clothes. Their colorful saris were beautifully hand printed and they wore them with one end draped over a short, upright, wooden pole that they tied on top of their heads with a bunch of hair. Occasionally they were seen in various parts of Ujjain.

Late one evening, a group of boys was gathered on the open ground near the Qazi's house. Ten of them were playing volleyball watched by two others sitting on the grass. Darkness was falling, but the players wanted to finish the game. Suddenly there was a cry of "Ghost! Ghost!" The two spectators leapt to their feet and pointed toward Shakil Sahib's bungalow. The players looked. They saw the two spectators fleeing toward the Qazi's courtyard. Then they saw a tall, dark, shadowy figure about 12 feet high and four feet wide standing by Shakil Sahib's bungalow. It looked like a woman wearing her sari over her head, in the fashion of the village women. She was standing motionless, gazing fixedly at the ground. For a moment the players remained transfixed, staring at the apparition. Then they ran away as fast as they could.

The next morning, the boys returned to the playing field to look for signs of the woman they had seen the previous night. The ground was thick with mud where the ghost had stood facing them. When they looked more closely, they saw traces of two footprints that had been made by two very large bare feet. However, the heels were in front and the toes were at the back.

- - - - - - - - - - - - - - - - - - - -

Rizwan Sahib lived in a large house in the center of Bhairugarh village with his wife and two children, a boy and a girl. They often invited their Ujjain relatives to come and visit them. It was a lovely spring day when Mrs Waheeda Begum and her daughter, Mrs Adiba Hassan, decided to go and stay, bringing with them Umer and his elder brother.

Rizwan Sahib had a two-story house with two bedrooms, a kitchen, and a bathroom downstairs. Upstairs, were two more bedrooms and a small room, the door to which was always kept locked. One day, Rizwan Sahib unlocked the door of this room, went inside, and carefully closed and locked the door behind him. Umer and his brother tried to look through the keyhole but the key had been left inside it. Once they peered through the keyhole after Rizwan Sahib had left the room. They saw that the room was very clean and bare with a white sheet in one corner. The scent of sandalwood wafted through the keyhole. The boys were puzzled and told their mother. She told them to play in the orchard and not to try to get into the room.

Later, Mrs. Adiba Hassan was drinking tea in the sitting room with Rizwan Sahib's wife. "My boys wondered about the locked room in your house," she said. "They noticed the scent of sandalwood by the door."

"Every Thursday, Rizwan Sahib goes there to communicate with a *genie*," his wife answered.

"How does he do it?" Mrs. Adiba Hassan asked curiously.

"I don't know," came the reply. "He never discusses it with me. All I know is that he goes into the room each Thursday and sometimes on Fridays and speaks to people from the other world."

"Has he often met *genies*?"

"Yes, he sees them regularly. Once he met a *genie* lady by the river Shipra."

"How did he know she was a *genie*?" asked Mrs. Adiba Hassan.

"She was by herself," came the reply. "No lady from our village would walk alone by the river."

"Did they speak together?"

"Yes, the lady asked him if he had a spare room in his house where she could come and live."

"What was your husband's reply?"

"He said, 'I am sorry, I don't have a spare room. However, I know a widow in the village who may have a room you can live in. I have to go now and buy sweets from Ram Das in Ujjain. I will meet you later in Bhairugarh and take you to see the widow. Where are you staying?' The lady didn't answer. 'What sweets are you getting from Ram Das?' she asked. '*Gulab jamuns* and *jalebis*,' my husband replied.

'You don't need to go there, I can get you these sweets,' said the lady. Then she clasped her two hands loosely together, closed her eyes, and prayed. A couple of minutes later, she opened her eyes and gave two packets of sweets to my husband. He looked inside each packet and quickly realized that they were of a far superior quality to any sweets he had ever seen before.' 'Thank you for the sweets,' he said. 'Who are you and where do you live?' 'I am sorry, I cannot answer those questions.' said the lady. 'No one in the village will let you have a room unless you answer these questions,' my husband told her. Immediately, a look of great sadness came over the lady's face and she disappeared. After that day, my husband never saw the lady *genie* again."

- - - - - - - - - - - - - - - - - - - -

Rizwan Sahib taught Arabic and the *Quran* in the village of Bhairugarh. Several boys attended his lesson each day. He knew them all and knew which families they belonged to, except for one boy. This boy came each day together with a man who brought him into the classroom and then left. The boy would sit silently listening while Rizwan Sahib taught the class. After each class, the boy would come up to Rizwan Sahib and give him money and a lot of sweets. Rizwan Sahib accepted the boy's unusual behavior and asked no questions. He guessed the boy was probably the son of a *genie*. *Genies* are very fond of sweets and not short of money. However, Rizwan Sahib's wife was curious and wanted to find out more about the boy.

One day, Rizwan Sahib had to go away on business and his wife came to teach the class instead. This was the opportunity she had been waiting for. She taught the class as usual and when the lesson was over, she called the strange boy over and asked him to wait until the others had left.

"Where do you live?" she asked. "You are not from this village."

"No," replied the boy.

"Who are your parents? Where do you come from?" she went on.

"I cannot tell you," the boy answered.

Rizwan Sahib's wife had never really understood why her husband had simply accepted this boy in his class together with the money and the sweets he brought without wanting to know more. She continued asking questions.

Finally, the boy said, "All right. I will tell you, but you

will be very sorry. Please stand back!"

Rizwan Sahib's wife moved away from him and he went to the door of the classroom. Suddenly his appearance changed. He started to grow, getting bigger and bigger each moment until he towered over her. Rizwan Sahib's wife stared at him, her eyes wide with amazement. Then he disappeared and she fell to the floor in a swoon. After that, the boy never came to the class again.

- - - - - - - - - - - - - - - - - - - -

On the bank of the river Shipra is Kaliadeh Palace, a fine example of Persian architecture. Over the front door are two inscriptions in Persian recording visits made there by the Emperors Akbar and Jehangir. In 1920 it was restored by the Maharajah of Gwalior, Madhav Rao Scindia.

Afaq Hassan, the police inspector, covered the area right up to Kaliadeh Palace with a team of police officers from Ujjain. He lived in Bhairugarh and traveled everywhere on horseback with his gun.

One day the governor of Ujjain, Prabhakar Sahib, summoned Afaq Hassan.

"How many men guard Kaliadeh Palace?" the governor asked.

"There are always two *chowkidars* in civilian clothes on duty day and night, Governor Sahib," answered Afaq Hassan.

"The Maharajah of Gwalior will be visiting the palace. Two more uniformed police officers should be there when he comes."

"Sir, I can spare only one man from my force at the moment," said Afaq Hassan. "I will need to recruit an extra man to guard the palace."

"I will see that your request for a new recruit is officially approved," replied the governor.

The following day, Afaq Hassan transferred a policeman from his force to guard duty at Kaliadeh Palace and looked for a second man. He remembered a distant relative whom he had met recently at his aunt's funeral. His name was Fasiuddin and he was a trained soldier who had recently moved to Gaunkrigaon from Bhopal and was looking for work. Afaq Hassan asked Fasiuddin to come and see him at the police station and told him he was looking for someone for guard duty at Kaliadeh Palace.

"Will you take the job?" he asked.

Fasiuddin immediately accepted. "I must find accommodation in Ujjain," he added.

"My brother and I have a house in Arithewaley," answered Afaq Hassan. "You and your family can live in my part of the house, as I am mostly in Bhairugarh."

Fasiuddin and his family soon settled down in Ujjain and he took up his new duties as a palace guard. Each day he went by bicycle from Ujjain, through the jungle and across the bridge over the river Shipra, to Kaliadeh Palace to start his shifts.

The other guard also lived in Ujjain and regularly cycled through the jungle. "Sometimes I meet a ghost in the jungle," he told Fasiuddin. "He always speaks through his nose and appears by the path in the evening about one and a half miles away from the bridge."

"What shall I do if I see him?" asked Fasiuddin.

"Just read an *ayat* from the *Quran*, then blow over the ghost through your pursed lips saying, "*Chhooo!*" as some people do when they have finished their prayers. Then the ghost will disappear. He is harmless. I think he's just lonely." Fasiuddin accordingly learned an *ayat* in Arabic by heart, beginning "*Qulho walla ho ahad – he is Allah, the one.*"

Fasiuddin was strongly built, more than six feet tall, and wore khaki jodhpurs and a thick cotton shirt with a brown *safah* on his head. Every day he would polish his black boots and bind *patties*, broad strips of cotton, around his legs before setting off for work. One cold, dark night, he was riding his bicycle through the jungle toward the bridge, when a thin white figure suddenly appeared and started running by his side. Fasiuddin started to pedal faster.

"Wait, wait, I want to talk to you," came a nasal voice close to his ear. Fasiuddin pedaled faster.

"Why are you riding so fast?" shouted the ghost. "Please stop, I just want to talk to you."

Fasiuddin was terrified. Then he remembered the *ayat* he had learned from the *Quran*, started to recite "*Qulho walla ho ahad*," and found that his mind had gone completely blank. All he could say was "*Qulli, Qulli, Qulli*." Finally, he drew a deep breath, pursed his lips, and blew out "*Chhooo!*" sending a strong aroma of curry toward the ghost running by his side. The ghost duly vanished but soon reappeared running on the other side, well away from the fumes of Fasiuddin's breath.

"Why are you saying '*Qulli, Qulli, Qulli?*' asked the ghost. "Please stop, I only want to talk to you."

Sweat broke out all over Fasiuddin's body and the scent of meat curry surrounded him, causing the ghost to keep its distance.

Fasiuddin went on pedalling, muttering "*Qulli, Qulli, Qulli*" and repeating "*Chhooo!*" as the ghost ran alongside his bicycle. Just before he reached the bridge over the river Shipra, the ghost suddenly disappeared. Fasiuddin paused at the bridge. Sweat was pouring from his face and body. He wiped the sweat from his face using both shirt sleeves and then tossed a one paisa coin from each side of the bridge into the river, as thanksgiving for a safe crossing.

"I saw the ghost, but I forgot the *ayat* from the *Quran*," he told his colleague later that night. "However, I managed to tire him out."

After that, the ghost never followed Fasiuddin again.

- - - - - - - - - - - - - - - - - - - -

One day, on a hunting trip in the jungle near Ujjain, Siddique Bhai and two of his friends were following the tracks of a tiger that had been taking goats belonging to the farmers in some of the nearby villages. Eventually they found themselves deep in the jungle in a place none of them recognized, surrounded by trees and thick undergrowth. The tiger's tracks led into some bushes to one side of the path. No one wanted to follow them and risk cornering the tiger in his den.

The friends tried to retrace their footsteps and found a clearly marked path, so they started to follow it. After some time they came upon an old man in a clearing. He was surrounded by heaps of metal objects that seemed to be made of copper and brass.

Siddique Bhai picked up one of the pieces of metal and turned it over in his hands. "This looks like gold," he said at last. "Is it solid gold?" he asked the old man.

"Yes, it is," the old man replied.

"How did you make it?" asked one of Siddique Bhai's friends.

"That is a secret," came the answer, "but you may take as much of this gold as you wish, if you go away and promise never to come back here again."

"We do not want your gold, we simply want to know how to make it," said the second friend.

"Just show us how to make the gold," said Siddique Bhai.

They were so insistent that the old man finally agreed to show them how to make gold. He went to the bushes around the clearing and gathered leaves from several of them. The three men followed him and made a mental note of the appearance of the bushes he selected so that they could recognize them again. Then the old man threw the leaves into a pot and boiled them until they were liquid. Next, he distilled the liquid and at the same time heated one of the metal objects in a furnace until it was red-hot. Then he dipped it into the distilled liquid and left it to cool. When it was cold the men examined it and found that it had been turned into solid gold.

They thanked the old man, bid him farewell, and left, anxious to get home and try out this method of making gold for themselves.

They were rushing back through the jungle, when Siddique Bhai suddenly stopped.

"What's the matter?" asked his friends.

"We cannot be sure that we will recognize the bushes from which the old man picked the leaves to make gold," he replied. "They'll look different when they are growing elsewhere. We should have asked him their names."

"All right then, we'll go back and find out what they are called," they said. "We can also take some of the leaves from each of the bushes as samples."

The men quickly retraced their footsteps back to the clearing, but found no sign of the old man, or the heap of metal objects. They took a few leaves from some of the bushes surrounding the clearing and put them into a small bag.

"These look like the leaves the old man used," said Siddique Bhai somewhat uncertainly.

"These are definitely the leaves the old man took," his friends replied.

With great difficulty, the three men managed to get their bearings in the jungle and make their way home. Then they collected leaves from the same kinds of bushes as the old man had done. Next, they collected all the copper and brass pots and pans they could get hold of, much to the annoyance of their wives, who were left with nothing with which to cook. They put the pots and pans in a pile and broke them up. Following the old man's method, they distilled liquid from the leaves, heated up some pieces of copper pan, and plunged them into the liquid. However, as they cooled, the copper pieces still remained copper and the three men were left with a heap of broken copper and brass utensils and urgent requests from all three wives to buy them new pots and pans.

- - - - - - - - - - - - - - - - - - - -

During the cool summer evenings, the men in Arithewaley withdrew to a separate bungalow to play cards or chess. Meanwhile, the women sat on string beds in the enclosed courtyard for *charpoy* chatter, breathing the fresh air coming from the open sky. The children played nearby or went to sleep. Mrs. Waheeda Begum invited Tara Bibi to bring Khatoon Bibi to join the other ladies there. Tara Bibi introduced Khatoon Bibi to everyone else - Mrs. Adiba Hassan, Mrs. Farah Begum, Karima Bibi, Kausar, and Mrs. Nafisa Begum, who was fanning herself and looked rather pale.

"Mrs. Nafisa Begum is newly married," said Tara Bibi.

"Many women feel unwell in the early stages of pregnancy," Khatoon Bibi told Mrs. Nafisa Begum.

Mrs. Nafisa Begum smiled shyly.

"Khatoon Bibi is a retired nurse," said Tara Bibi. "She also used to be a midwife."

"You must have had some interesting experiences, said Mrs. Nafisa Begum.

Khatoon Bibi smiled reflectively. "I will never forget one case in particular."

"Tell us about it," said the other ladies.

"My husband was alive then and we lived here in Mirzawari," Khatoon Bibi began. We had just gone to bed.

Suddenly, there was a loud knocking at our front door. I wasn't expecting anyone at that hour. At that time I worked in the local hospital as a midwife and everything had been as usual when I finished my shift.

'I'll see who it is,' said my husband. He rose, lit a lantern and went to answer the door. I heard him asking the caller what he wanted and then the sound of a man's voice speaking upper-class Urdu. I peered around the bedroom door, careful to keep myself concealed.

"In the light of the lantern, I saw a tall young man with a moustache. He wore a military uniform with a royal coat of arms on his jacket and a shirt and tie. 'My wife is expecting her first child,' I heard him say. 'Her time has come and she needs the help of a woman who understands these things. We have been informed that Khatoon Bibi is an experienced midwife. Please ask her to come and see my wife.' 'You are not from these parts,' said my husband. 'Where are you staying?' 'Our lodgings are on the outskirts of Ujjain. I have transport outside and can take her there immediately.'

"My husband was moved by the young man's plea and came to tell me that my services were urgently required. I quickly put on my blue and white hospital uniform, picked up the bag of medical supplies that I always kept by me for such emergencies, and went to the door with my husband. Outside was a horse-drawn *victoria* with its hood pulled up. On the blue coachwork was a coat of arms engraved in gold, shining in the light of two lanterns at the front of the *victoria*. Green silk curtains hung over the sides beneath the hood. The young man opened the door.

"A maidservant climbed down to greet me. She wore a brown silk top over a white cotton *gharara* with a pale brown *dupatta* over her shoulders. She took my bag and helped me inside the *victoria*. When we were both seated, the young man went to sit in front with the driver. "The brown leather seats were very comfortable and an unfamiliar sweet, slightly heavy perfume hung in the air. The maidservant sat down opposite me and smiled. 'The Prince of Alampur is fetching you personally to attend to his princess,' she told me. 'They are staying near Ujjain for a few days. The Princess is about to have her first child and her time has come upon her sooner than expected.'

"I had never heard of these fine people. However, since you are all from Ujjain you know that the royal family of Alampur are *genies* who live underground with their own kingdom and a leader. I have since learned how they have the power to change themselves into humans and are able to speak any language, and can appear and disappear at will. However, at the time I just saw the situation as that of a mother about to bear a child who needs care and attention, and I could help. Soon I began to feel sleepy and closed my eyes. The next thing I knew, I was being gently shaken awake. 'We are nearly there,' said the maidservant.

"I saw that our *victoria* was speeding along a brightly lit passage underground. We came to a tall gate that was standing open and drove along an avenue with flowering plants and bushes on either side. I had never seen such flowers before. Some were large and brightly colored, others were small and sweetly scented, studding the bushes like rubies and sapphires in their dark green leafy setting. Eventually, we arrived at a magnificent residence, like a king's palace, and quite unlike any house I had ever seen in or around Ujjain.

"The maidservant showed me into the residence and followed me carrying my bag. Fine tapestries adorned the walls of the entrance hall. Sandalwood and *chambeli* scented the air. Two lady attendants welcomed me and led me through a magnificent arch along several passages, past doors and walls hung with more tapestries. At last we stopped by a door. One of the attendants opened it and stepped aside to let me enter.

"A large, four-poster bed stood in the center of the room. On it lay a beautiful young woman. Her face was pale and her eyes were closed. 'Thank you for coming to attend to our mistress,' said the attendant. 'How is she?' I asked.

"The young woman opened her eyes and smiled weakly at the sound of my voice.

'How long have you been in pain?' I asked her. She told me all I wished to know and allowed me to examine her. I turned to the maid and the two attendants. 'Your lady is in the final stages of labor,' I told them. 'Soon it will be time for her baby to enter the world. Bring cloths and a basin of hot water.' The two attendants swiftly went to do my bidding. Shortly afterward, I successfully delivered a healthy baby boy. I held him up, slapped him lightly, and he began to cry.

"'All is well,' I told the new mother and her attendants. They made the princess comfortable while I washed the baby and placed him in the cradle next to his mother. One of the attendants remained with the mother and baby while the other one showed me to a sitting room. Shortly afterward, the maidservant who had accompanied me in the *victoria* entered, bearing a tray with a gold beaker from which steam was rising. 'Our master wishes to thank you for your services to our mistress,' she said. 'Please have this drink before you return to your home.'

"I took the beaker and sipped the contents. It was delicious, quite unlike anything I had ever drunk before. 'What is this?' I asked the maidservant. 'It tastes very good.'

'We call it *achhwani*,' she replied. 'It is made from the milk of mountain goats and we give it to a new mother for a few days after she has given birth, to help restore her strength.' 'Please tell me how you make it,' I requested.

"The maidservant took me to the kitchen. A cook stood before a great pan of steaming liquid. I watched as she added dried dates, raisins, sultanas, ground almonds, ground pistachio nuts, herbs, and various seeds to the liquid. The maidservant listed all the ingredients and gave me details of the secret recipe for preparing the royal *achhwani*.

This recipe has been known to the royal family of Alampur for many centuries," she told me.

'Then the maidservant took me to the door of the palace. It was still night. Outside was a chariot with two men on horseback to act as escorts. 'There has been much political upheaval in the kingdom of Alampur, so the royal family cannot travel during daylight,' she explained. "They have many enemies seeking them, so they have to remain underground."

"One of the princess's attendants came to see me off. As I got into the chariot with the maidservant, she handed me my bag of medical supplies. The chariot set off and I fell into a deep sleep. The next thing I knew, the chariot had stopped and one of the horsemen had opened the door so that I could alight. 'We are on the main road near Milkipura,' he told me. I looked round the dark deserted streets. I could easily walk from where the chariot was leaving me to our house in Mirzawari. 'This is for you,' said the man and gave me a basket. 'It is a gift from the Prince of Alampur as a token of thanks for your services to his wife. We must return to the palace before dawn breaks.'

"I looked inside the basket and saw a cloth bag made of some rich material. When I looked up, the chariot and the horsemen had disappeared. I put down my bag of medical supplies and opened the cloth bag. It was filled with small dark lumps of some heavy substance. I took out one of the lumps and ran my fingers over the rough surface. It looked and felt like coal. I was disappointed and angry. 'Is this the royal reward for all my hard work during the night? Only a bag of coals?' I asked myself bitterly. 'Oh! What am I going to do with all these coals?'

"Wearily, I began to walk home, carrying my bag and the basket containing the cloth bag. I stopped, opened the cloth bag, took out one of the lumps of coal, and threw it away. I went on walking. After a while I stopped again, removed another piece of coal from the bag, and dropped it on the ground. Bit by bit I discarded the coal as I made my way along the quiet streets. It was daybreak when I entered the house. My husband greeted me. 'I let them know at the hospital that you were called out to assist at an emergency last night,' he informed me. 'They said that you can come in to work later on when you are rested.' 'Thank you,' I answered. I went to the bedroom and put my medical bag in one corner of the room with the basket next to it. Then I ate some food, went to bed, and slept.

"The sun was shining brightly when I rose fully refreshed some hours later. I took the bag from the basket and examined it more closely. The cloth was richly embroidered and quite unlike any material I had ever seen before. 'Strange that such a fine high-born prince should call me out in the middle of the night to deliver his child and then reward me with lumps of coal in such a beautiful bag,' I said to myself. Then I opened the cloth bag and looked inside. A small lump of the heavy dark substance was sticking to one corner. I took it out and examined it closely. Some gold dots on the surface shimmered in the sunlight. It did not look like coal. I rubbed it all over and saw that it was in fact a lump of gold. Then I took the basket with the bag inside and went back along the way I had come from Milkipura to my home the previous night. All the coal black lumps had disappeared without trace. I tried to find out which direction the chariot had taken to reach the underground royal palace but I was unable to do so.

"When I showed a goldsmith the dark colored lump, he told me that it was pure gold of a quality he had never seen before. He immediately offered me a very good price for that gold."

Khatoon Bibi fell silent. Her face showed a trace of sadness as she reflected on the untold riches that might have been hers, had she realized the nature of the reward offered by the genie royal family of Alampur, and been prepared to carry that heavy basket all the way home.

The other ladies were spellbound by her story. "I remember when we first learned about *achhwani*," said Mrs. Waheeda Begum. "We prepared it when Adiba gave birth to her first child."

Kismet turned to Mrs. Waheeda Begum. "You showed me how to make this drink with dried fruits, herbs, almonds, and pistachio nuts added to buffalo milk."

"In Rajasthan they use camel milk to make *achhwani*," said Mrs. Nafisa Begum.

"We don't make it with seeds," said Mrs. Waheeda Begum.

"Did you sell the gold to the goldsmith?" asked Tara Bibi.

"No, although I was very tempted to do so," Khatoon Bibi answered. "I decided to keep it. I will not get another such present from the Royal Family of Alampur."

"How much did the goldsmith offer you for the gold?" asked Mrs. Waheeda Begum.

"Please keep this price and the whole story secret," said Khatoon Bibi.

"We will," the other ladies assured her.

"The money the goldsmith offered me for that little lump of gold was equal to six months' salary from the hospital. Had I kept all the gold I received that night, I would have become the richest woman in Ujjain."

Her audience gasped and gazed at her in awe mingled with respect. To have been in contact with a real princess from the Royal Family of Alampur at such a time!

- - - - - - - - - - - - - - - - - - - -

Mrs. Adiba Hassan turned to Karima Bibi. "Do you know any interesting story from your village Nunga Sadhu Gaon, Naked Sadhu Village?" she asked.

"We do have some tales about our village," answered Karima Bibi. She hesitated a little. "There's one in particular, but I don't know if it is true or not."

"Oh, come on, let's hear it," urged the other ladies.

"Our village was once part of a large estate belonging to a rich nobleman," Karima Bibi began. "He owned a *haveli*, a mansion, which had been built in the hills just outside Nunga Sadhu Gaon, and employed the villagers to work for him on the land and in the *haveli*. No one lives in the *haveli* now. It has been empty for many years. One day, three young men from the village decided to go there and see if they could find out why it had been left deserted for so long.

"When they came to the mansion, they saw that the walls were still standing. Many of the shutters hung from the hinges and birds were nesting beneath the eaves of the roof. The front door was locked, but they managed to get into the building through the servants' back entrance. The kitchen was empty. All traces of food were long gone and there was a chill in the air. They heard scuffling and loud squeaks and saw dark shapes moving across the kitchen floor."

"Rats," said Tara Bibi with a laugh.

"That's right. They went through a narrow passage into the hall. It was completely bare. Everything of any use had long since been looted - the magnificent hangings that had once adorned the walls and all the furniture and carpets. A stone staircase led to a landing on the next floor. Several doors opened off it, leading into what must once have been the chambers belonging to the nobleman and his family. Narrow stone stairs led further up. They decided to explore the attics first and then find out what lay in the chambers. An opening at the top of the stairs brought them on to a small landing with a couple of closed doors leading off it.

"They opened one door with a loud creaking of rusty hinges and looked into an empty room. 'Let's see what's in the second room,' said one of the men. This door opened onto a much larger room. A long bench stood by one wall and there were marks on the floor as if a heavy chest had been dragged across it and out of the room. In the middle of the room were two large, heavy, steel cupboards with closed doors, standing opposite a window that looked out on the hills outside.

"The men sat down on the bench and looked around. 'I wonder why no one came up here to take the cupboards and this bench,' said one of them. 'They seem to have cleared out the rest of the house. Let's open the cupboards.'

"Suddenly, they heard the sound of banging on one of the cupboards. 'Is anyone there?' called the second man. There was more banging on the cupboard wall. 'Stop it! Come out and show yourself!' shouted the third man. The banging became even louder. The men got up to see where the noise was coming from. Suddenly there was a loud shriek. Something brightly colored streaked toward the window. Another louder shriek came from outside, as though someone was falling.

"The men rushed to the window and stood there stunned. A young girl wearing a red and gold wedding sari, with heavy gold jewelry on her neck and wrists, was falling down the gorge beneath the window. As they watched helplessly, she disappeared. The men stood there unable to move.

"Then they ran downstairs, out the back entrance of the mansion, and along the path toward the gorge beneath the attic window. An old man was coming toward them.

'What's the hurry? Why are you running like that?' he asked them. 'A young girl has just fallen from the attic window,' answered one of the men breathlessly. 'We must go and see if we can help her. It may be too late.'

'I fear that it is far too late,' answered the old man. 'That girl died many years ago. What you saw was the ghost of Princess Chamkilee. She was the only daughter of a king of Ujala Nagar. Her mother died when she was 12 years old. A year later, her father took a new wife. This woman wished to ensure that the princess did not inherit the throne from her father and searched all over the kingdom for a suitable husband for her. She eventually found a rich man with a large estate. He was fat, ugly, and over 60. The king wanted to please his new wife in every way and was deaf to his daughter's pleas not to marry her to that man. Her stepmother forced the princess to go through with the wedding. Afterward, her attendants took Princess Chamkilee to her chamber on the top floor of the mansion and prepared her for her wedding night. Then they left her alone, seated on her bed with bowed head and veiled face, to await her new bridegroom. When they had gone, the princess rose from the bed, went to the window, and jumped down into the gorge below.' The men were shocked and saddened by this tale and never entered the *haveli* again."

Everyone was silent when Karima Bibi had finished speaking. "There are a lot of sad things in Indian history," said someone at last.

"I'll go and make everyone a nice cup of tea," suggested Kausar.

"I'll give you a hand," said Mrs. Nafisa Begum.

- - - - - - - - - - - - - - - - - - - -

It was evening. Akram *tongawala* and his two friends Jugnu Khan and Hira Lal had left their *tongas* with their employer and were seated outside Akram's house, smoking *hashish*.

"Once I made a bet and my numbers came up," said Hira Lal. "However, I am still only a poor *tongawala*."

"I also once had dreams," said Akram. "I didn't follow them." He looked sad. "Who knows what I might have achieved?"

"I was once a boxer," said Jugnu Khan. "Alas, I was forced to abandon my career. The trainer saw me smoking *hashish* and made me leave the team. He used this as an excuse, because he wanted his own man to join the team."

"The paths of our lives are now set," said Akram. "We are old and we cannot change them. We must accept our fate." The three friends continued smoking in silence.

"There are some people gathering nearby under the *kabeet* tree on the football ground," remarked Jugnu Khan after a while. "Let's go and see what they are doing."

The men finished smoking, got up, and went over to investigate. Moon Khan, a solicitor from Mirzawari, was talking to some men from Arithewaley - the solicitor Waqar Hassan, the shopkeeper Anwar Ali, and the teacher Halim Nawaz. Mehboob, a lawyer's messenger, stood nearby.

"What is it you are discussing?" Akram *tongawala* asked them.

"We are talking about *Bhartari Gupa*," Moon Khan replied.

Bhartari Gupa was a well known cave near the bank of the river Shipra. It had long been abandoned and there were many legends surrounding it.

"I know *Bhartari Gupa*," said Hira Lal. "I know this cave very well. I went there many times with my grandfather when I was a young boy."

"Can you tell us about the cave?" asked Anwar Ali.

"My grandfather worked there as a guide. He would take visitors for a short tour inside the cave, which was lit by *diye* or oil lamps. Many, many years before that, my great, great, great grandfather sat outside the *Bhartari Gupa* and sold *diye* to people who wanted to walk in the dark *Gupa*."

"What is inside the cave?" asked Waqar Hassan.

"This cave goes a long, long way. No one knows how far it goes or what secrets are hidden deep inside it. Once my great, great, great grandfather sold four *diye* and one thousand gallons of oil to a very rich man and his friend who wanted to explore the cave and find out how far it went. They loaded the oil drums on to several donkeys together with food for themselves, fodder for the donkeys, and plenty of water, and went down the cave. They were away for many days. My great, great, great grandfather thought that they had died or got lost. Then one day they returned. 'Did you find out how far the cave runs?' my ancestor asked them. 'No,' answered the rich man. He and his friend were tired and dirty, their faces hollow with hunger. Only three of their donkeys had returned with them. 'We went many miles along the cave,' the rich man said. 'When half of our oil had gone we turned around and came back.'"

"Has anyone else tried to explore the *Bhartari Gupa* since then?" asked Anwar Ali.

"I have heard no more stories from my family about people trying to find out what is in this cave," answered Hira Lal. "However, I have heard that this cave was built during the Raj of Vikramaditya, the so-called Golden Age in the history of India. The king built the cave so that he and his men could travel swiftly on horseback to distant places in his kingdom without difficulty."

"I don't believe that anyone within living memory has ever found out where the *Bhartari Gupa* ends," remarked Halim Nawaz. "There have been many different stories about this *Gupa* over the centuries. I heard that the cave was given its name during the Golden Age. Bhartarihari, the stepbrother of Vikramaditya, was known as a great scholar and poet. However, he renounced the world and came to this spot to live and meditate."

"I went to the *Bhartari Gupa* a few days ago with some friends," said Moon Khan. "We wanted to explore the cave. After we entered it, the passage before us gradually became darker. Soon there was hardly any light coming in from the cave entrance. We continued walking, feeling our way along the walls of the passage, as we had no lamps with us. It was pitch black as far as we could see. We were just about to turn back when we saw a light in the distance moving slowly towards us."

His audience listened, spellbound.

"As it came closer, we were able to make out the figure of a slender old man wearing a white *dhoti* and a long-sleeved Bengali shirt with a white cotton cap on his head and old *chappals* on his feet. He was holding a *diya* in his hand. He stopped a short distance away and beckoned us toward him. We turned and fled. We stopped just inside the entrance and looked back. The old man with the *diya* was behind us. As we watched, he suddenly floated up in the air and disappeared deep inside the cave without a trace."

"The man with a *diya* you have just described was my grandfather," said Hira Lal. "He is harmless. All he wanted to do was to take you on a short guided tour of the cave, just as he used to do with the visitors when he was alive. Since he died, there have been no guides to the *Bhartari Gupa.* My father started driving *tongas* and I did the same thing. I wish I could have been there to see him." He looked sad to hear of this glimpse into his family's previous life.

"You have been privileged. Few people hear of visions from their family's past," said Akram *tongawala* to Hira Lal. "*Chilam pio, khush raho,* smoke and be happy. Come, let us go back to my house," he added, turning to his friends.

The three *tongawalas* took their leave of the group beneath the *kabeet* tree and returned to their *charas* smoking session.

"Muharram preparations will start soon" said Jugnu Khan. "I will have to start teaching the boys in Gharib Colony display stick fighting for the Muharram procession, which I do each year."

Chapter 9:

Events and Festivals during the Muslim Year

People in Ujjain started preparing for Muharram, the Islamic New Year's Day, about six weeks in advance. One evening, a group of older boys and young men from Mirzawari gathered beneath some trees on one side of the local Qazi football ground.

"I've been thinking about taking part in a Muharram procession this year," said Nazir.

"Are you going to carry a *firsha* or a *neza*, (a battleaxe or a spear)?" asked Arif.

"I wouldn't mind carrying a *chaarya*, (a round iron brazier of burning coal at the end of a long pole)," remarked one boy.

"You might drop it," said another boy.

"Aftab, you're nimble fingered, you could give a display of

juggling," said a third boy. He turned to the others, laughing. "He'd be good at that, don't you think?"

"Write down what you just said," said Aftab, passing the boy a piece of paper.

The boy reached for his shirt pocket. "My Parker fountain pen! It's gone!" he cried.

Aftab waved the pen in the air. "Just watch what you say about me in future," he warned.

"How about asking Jugnu Khan to give us lessons in stick fighting?" suggested Nazir, tactfully moving the conversation along.

"He's just a *tongawala*," said the others, dismissing the idea.

"Jugnu Khan was known as "Ustaad" because he was a champion stick fighter," replied Nazir earnestly.

"We want to learn stick fighting as well," came a small voice. The older boys looked around and saw Umer and Tiddi standing nearby.

"Father's sitting outside our house with Jugnu Khan and Hira Lal," said Nazir. "Let's go there now."

As they approached, Akram *tongawala* greeted the small group.

"Hello, boys, what can we do for you?"

Nazir turned to Jugnu Khan. "We want to learn display stick fighting so that we can take part in the procession during Muharram," he told him.

"We want to learn stick fighting as well," put in Umer and Tiddi.

Jugnu Khan smiled. "I can show you all display stick

fighting here on the Qazi football ground in the evenings. Bring your sticks with you tomorrow. Make sure you bring a slender wooden stick, well oiled, and about three feet long."

The next day, the boys met Jugnu Khan beneath the *kabeet* or wood apple tree.

"The *kabeet* tree is your opponent," he said. "Three of you stand next to it and hit it from the right and from the left in the face and on the legs. Nazir, you come and stand opposite me with your stick."

Jugnu Khan and Nazir faced each other holding their sticks.

"Hit me on the head," said Jugnu Khan.

Nazir hesitated. "I don't want to hurt you." Everyone laughed.

"Come on, do it. I want to show you how to save yourselves from an attack."

Nazir lifted his stick and struck at Jugnu Khan's head. Swiftly Jugnu Khan raised his stick in both hands and held it up in front of his head. Nazir's stick struck it with a loud thwack!

"Now, get in groups of two and practice what I have shown you," said Jugnu Khan. "However, remember, the art of display stick fighting is to avoid injuring your opponent, so take it slowly while you are learning."

The boys practiced for half an hour under Jugnu Khan's supervision. Then he went to join Akram and Hira Lal for their usual *charas* smoking session, leaving the boys to take turns practicing hitting the trunk of the *kabeet* tree.

Just before Muharram, the Hindu potters in Ujjain made small copies of Imam Hussain's *dul dul* horse. The toy *dul duls* were very popular with Muslim children. The boys from Arithewaley used to go and watch a Hindu potter in Gonde-ki-Chowki, about five minutes walk from the Lawyer's Den, making small *dul duls* from clay, which he then left to dry in the sun. Later, he wiped them with a white cotton cloth and painted them in bright colors. The boys particularly liked buying them as soon as they were dry.

Over the next few weeks, the boys learned some of the many variations of display stick fighting. Two boys, each with a stick, would slowly circle each other, gradually coming closer. Suddenly, one boy would hit out at the other one, who immediately hit back. This was repeated again and again, faster and faster, each boy taking turns to hit to the right and the left of his opponent, who would then immediately counter the blow with his own stick. Blows were aimed first at the upper part of the body, then the legs, and finally the head. The two boys would then circle each other slowly once again and repeat the display. Despite their best efforts, each had some colorful bruises to show for their newfound skill, but nobody minded as it was such fun. Even the younger ones persevered with enthusiasm.

"Would some of you also like to learn display sword fighting?" asked Jugnu Khan a couple of weeks later after an evening session.

"That sounds like a good idea," said Nazir. Mehboob, Aftab, and another older boy also expressed interest.

"Gulzar Khan might agree to teach you. He is an ex-security guard and lives in Gharib Colony," said Jugnu Khan.

Soon afterward, Gulzar Khan started to teach the four boys display sword fighting. Jugnu Khan brought him by *tonga* each day to and from Mirzawari. Gulzar Khan lent Jugnu Khan four swords from his collection for use in the lessons. Talib Sahib gave Mehboob some afternoons off since he was kind and did not want Mehboob to miss out on the chance to learn display sword fighting together with his friends.

At first, the boys used sticks to practice display sword fighting, then gradually real swords were introduced. Both Jugnu Khan and Gulzar Khan were delighted with their progress in display stick fighting and display sword fighting.

"The boys have been beating that poor *kabeet* tree on the Qazi football ground for the last few days," remarked Qulfi. It was evening and she and Chandni were bringing tea and biscuits to the ladies resting on the oak bed in Shakil Sahib's house.

"They are practicing for the Muharram procession," said Kausar. "Tiddi is really looking forward to giving a display of stick fighting with Umer." The ladies all smiled at this.

"We'll have to start dyeing the children's clothes soon," remarked Mrs. Adiba Hassan, her mind turning toward their contribution to the festivities.

In Ujjain, in accordance with local tradition, some Muslim boys wore home-dyed green shirts and girls wore a green finely pleated *chunri or dupatta* to cover their heads to celebrate the Muslim New Year.

A few days later, Mrs. Adiba Hassan asked Azizah, the wife of a well-known dyer in Bhairugarh, to come and stay with her for a couple of days to help some of the local ladies to dye the children's clothes green for Muharram. Qulfi and Chandni came with Chandni's little girl, Meena, to prepare refreshments.

The local ladies all worked together to make preparations for dyeing the clothes. A brick-built *chulha* or semi-circular hearth was set up in the courtyard of the Lawyers' Den and filled with logs. Then a heavy, two-handled *karah* or iron cauldron was brought out, placed on it, and filled with water. The log fire beneath the *karah* was lit and when the water was hot enough, green dye was added to it. The shirts were then left to soak in the water. Meanwhile, with Azizah's help, the ladies knotted the *dupattas* to create a variety of designs in different shades of green. The shirts were put out on lines to dry and the *dupattas* placed into the dye solution. When the *dupattas* were ready, they were hung out to dry, and everyone enjoyed refreshments served by Qulfi and Chandni. They brought freshly made *samosey* and *pakorey* from Ram Das, together with *sharbat* and cold water scented with rose petals.

On the first day of Muharram, Qulfi, Chandni and Meena were invited to join the ladies in the Lawyers' Den to offer *fatiha*. The ladies were plainly dressed in keeping with tradition due to the solemnity of the occasion, and their children wore freshly dyed shirts and *dupattas*. Everyone sat in a room specially cleaned for the occasion with a white sheet on the floor. On it were a jug of *sharbat* or sweet drink with glasses and also bowls of *revri*, a kind of sweet only made during Muharram. The ladies offered *fatiha* over the *sharbat* and *revri*. Then they recited the first chapter of the Holy *Quran* as a prayer for the souls of the dead. Afterward, *revri* and *sharbat* were offered to everyone present. A pot of burnt wood aloe sent out thick smoke and the air was perfumed with the heavy scent of sandalwood coming from thin sticks of *agarbatti*.

During the first ten days of Muharram, *sabils* or drinking posts were set up in various Muslim localities in Ujjain. Scented iced water and *sharbat* were served to passers-by, who were encouraged to drink as much as they wanted, free of charge. Some families prepared ice cold milk with crushed pistachio nuts and cardamom seeds, which they then blessed and offered to friends and relatives.

The men and boys in Mirzawari always walked from Camel Courtyard to the Chowk Bazaar, the main shopping center in Ujjain, taking a short cut through the red light district to get there. This was the only red light district in Ujjain, where the lady singers, dancers, and prostitutes lived.

These Muslim working ladies had set up their own *sabil* for Muharram at the spot where they usually waited for business at night. An older lady stood there wearing a white *kameez* over narrow white cotton trousers, her head covered with a green *dupatta*. She called out to a group of boys and young men walking past, "Come on, you boys from the Lawyers' Den! Come and have a drink!"

The group saw that she was holding out a clay mug. On

the *sabil* behind her was a large clay *matka* or pot full of ice cold water with a ewer of *sharbat* and several small clay mugs nearby.

"Would you like to drink water or *sharbat*?" she asked.

"Water, please," said one boy shyly.

"I'll have *sharbat*," said a young man.

"Drink! Drink!" the working lady urged them. "Don't go thirsty to Chowk Bazaar." As soon as each one had finished his drink, she insisted on offering them a refill.

Mrs. Waheeda Begum together with Qulfi and Chandni prepared ice cold water and *sharbat*. Then the three of them blessed the water and *sharbat* before offering them to everyone in the Lawyers' Den, together with a bowl of *batashe*, small round white sugar puffs. Kausar prepared cold water by leaving two large clay *matkay* or pots of water wrapped in thick wet hessian out in the courtyard overnight in the cold breeze. The ladies in the Lawyers' Den also cooked brown lentils according to tradition at least once during the first ten days of Muharram.

- - - - - - - - - - - - - - - - - - - -

During Muharram, men in different localities made taziyeh or replicas of the tomb of the martyr Imam Hussain in various styles and colors, using a bamboo framework covered with paper to build a structure with a dome on top of it. There were colorful displays in Muslim localities all over Ujjain.

A large *taziah*, provided by the Maharajah of Gwalior, was exhibited in a prominent position in the town center. Near the boundary of Ujjain was another display that also came from the Maharajah of Gwalior. This featured a life-sized replica of a *dul dul*, the horse ridden by Imam Hussain, together with a *buraq* of similar size next to it. This *buraq* had a woman's face with long black hair and beautiful eyes outlined with *kajal*. Its body was that of a horse with four legs, a long tail, and two large wings. The *buraq* was believed to run more swiftly than the wind and fly faster than light.

Every evening from the second to the ninth of Muharram, processions from different localities made their way through the main streets of Ujjain toward the Chowk Bazaar. Each procession was led by men beating drums in rhythm. After them came more men bearing green banners, followed by others carrying a *taziah*, and maybe also a *dul dul* or a *buraq*. Then came men bearing the ancient weapons of war -- *firshey*, *dharye* and *nezey*, and also swords. Two drummers headed a group of stick fighters, sword fighters, jugglers, and acrobats. Several devotees followed the procession. Men holding *chaarye* and gas lamps illuminated the whole procession. From time to time it stopped. A crowd gathered to watch performers staging mock fights with swords or sticks, re-enacting scenes from the battle of Karbala. They were followed by jugglers and acrobats. The performance marking the grand finale was held in the Chowk bazaar in the town center.

On the evening of the fifth of Muharram, the boys from Mirzawari joined the procession from Gharib Colony together with Jugnu Khan and Gulzar Khan. Talib Sahib joined Waqar Hassan, Anwar Ali, Diwan Khan, and Halim Nawaz to walk from the Lawyers' Den to Chowk Bazaar to watch the displays being put on by the people in the procession from Gharib Colony. Before he left, Halim Nawaz promised to tell his wife and the other ladies all about the displays the following evening.

As the men from the Lawyers' Den were walking through the red light district, some of the older working ladies smiled at them and respectfully raised their hands in *Salam*.

"Why are these working ladies greeting us?" asked Anwar Ali, feeling slightly uncomfortable. "Do they know us?"

"I worked for them once when they were involved in a lawsuit," replied Waqar Hassan.

"Which lawsuit was that?" asked Anwar Ali intrigued.

"It all happened about 15 years ago," Waqar Hassan began. "The people living next to the red light district wanted to close it down. The singers, dancers, and working girls sent representatives to Qazi Sahib seeking help and he directed them to my office. I took down the details and Shakil Sahib agreed to plead their case in court. This case was most unusual and the first of its kind in the whole area."

"It was much talked about at the time," said Halim Nawaz.

"What happened in the end?" asked Diwan Khan.

"Oh, the ladies won their case and the red light district remained open for business," answered Waqar Hassan.

The men had reached the Chowk Bazaar. They were a little early, so they had time to take up a good position from which to watch the displays. The beating of drums announced the arrival of the procession. The men admired the *taziyeh* and the *dul duls* and marveled at the performances of the jugglers and the acrobats. The high point of the evening came when the stick fighters and sword fighters began their display. Afterward, the group from the Lawyers' Den drank tea at the Chand Hotel and had a lively discussion about the show they had just seen. Anwar Ali and Diwan Khan commented on the remarkable sight of a stick flying through the air during the stick fight between Jugnu Khan and Gulzar Khan.

"This is the best display of stick fighting you will ever see anywhere," remarked Halim Nawaz. Waqar Hassan and Talib Sahib agreed. Everyone was full of praise for the boys from the Lawyers' Den for learning stick fighting so well in such a short time. They had been amazed by the breathtaking display of the man from Gharib Colony on sword points, where a false move would have led to serious injuries or even death.

The following evening after everyone had eaten, the ladies were sitting on *charpoys* in the courtyard of the Lawyers' Den. Mrs. Waheeda Begum saw Halim Nawaz standing on the verandah of their house.

"Come and tell us about the Muharram procession," she called to him. "Bring a chair with you."

"Our boys showed off their skills very well," said Halim Nawaz, seating himself near the ladies. "First came display stick fights between Mehboob and Aftab. Mehboob sent Aftab's stick flying into the air. Then Nazir and Arif gave a display of stick fighting. They were hitting each other's sticks very fast."

"What happened next?" asked Kismet.

"There were sword fighting displays, first by Mehboob and Aftab using real swords. Then came Nazir and Arif with blunt swords and they finished by bowing to each other. Afterward, the professional stick fighters Gulzar Khan and Jugnu Khan demonstrated some interesting variations of display stick fighting. In one of them, Gulzar Khan gave a quick twist of his stick and Jugnu Khan's stick suddenly left his hand and flew up high behind the crowd. There was laughter and someone quickly brought the stick back to Jugnu Khan. Then they resumed the stick fight, circling each other slowly, their eyes locked on each other. Suddenly, Jugnu Khan attacked and put Gulzar Khan's stick behind his neck so that it held both his arms up in the air. Gulzar Khan was unable to release his arms and had to wait for Jugnu Khan to free him. The crowd laughed in amazement."

"What about Umer and Tiddi? Did they give a display of stick fighting?" asked Mrs. Adiba Hassan, smiling at the thought of the two small boys wielding their long sticks.

"They certainly did," replied Halim Nawaz. "It was a most original display. Umer struck Tiddi's stick so that Tiddi lost hold of it. Then, using his own stick, Umer quickly pushed Tiddi's stick beneath one of Tiddi's arms and behind Tiddi's neck and then pushed Tiddi's other arm behind the stick with his other hand. Tiddi was trapped by his own stick with both hands up in the air. Jugnu Khan quickly set Tiddi free and Tiddi and Umer shook hands."

The ladies leaned back on their *charpoys*, sighing with satisfaction at the part played by their people in the Muharram procession. Mrs. Adiba Hassan in particular, felt very proud of her son Umer's performance.

During the late afternoon of the ninth of Muharram, Diwan Khan and Anwar Ali built a semicircular wall of bricks about two feet high in the center of the Lawyers' Den courtyard. Tiddi and Umer brought logs and placed them inside the wall. Then Diwan Khan and Anwar Ali hauled out an empty *karah* or cauldron and placed it on top of the bricks. The women brought a cooking pan filled with onions, garlic, ginger, and spices fried in *ghee* and poured the contents into the *karah*. Next, meat and several types of split lentils were added together with water.

Diwan Khan lit the fire and a couple of people stirred the ingredients together thoroughly, using two wooden ladles each four feet long. Everyone was preparing *khichra*, a dish that took all night to cook. Throughout the evening, men, women, and children came out into the courtyard to stir the *khichra*, the women lifting the smaller children up so that they too could touch the handle of one of the ladles. From time to time someone added more water to the *khichra*. Late at night, the heat beneath the cauldron was reduced and the *khichra* was left to simmer. During the night, someone would come out into the courtyard occasionally, to give the *khichra* a stir. By the morning of the tenth day of Muharram, the *khichra* was ready and the mouth-watering smell of the mixture filled the courtyard in the Lawyers' Den. After it had cooled down, some of the *khichra* was put into large dishes and *fatiha* was offered over them. Afterward, Diwan Khan and Anwar Ali collected pans from all the houses around the courtyard and the ladies filled them with *khichra* for each family in the Lawyers' Den.

About 60 years after the Prophet Muhammad (peace be upon him) moved from Mecca to Medina, his grandson, Imam Hussain, was martyred in Karbala, Iraq. On the tenth day of Muharram (*Yom-e-Ashura*), the Muslims in Ujjain commemorated the martyrdom of Imam Hussain. A procession went through Ujjain carrying some replica *taziyeh*, *dul duls,* and *buraqs*. As the people made their way along the streets, they were joined by others from various localities, also bearing *taziyeh, dul duls,* and *buraqs.* The procession walked to the outskirts of the town and through the jungle to the river Shipra, to a point where there were no *ghats* for swimming. A ritual took place on the river bank to prepare for the respectful commitment of the replicas to the flowing water. Strong swimmers from each group took some of the replicas into the middle of the river, where the current was fast and the water was deep. Then they gently released them into the river and swam back. A separate ritual was held for some of the larger, well-made replicas, in which they were sprinkled with water from the river Shipra. Afterward, they were covered with white sheets and brought back to be stored for display the following year.

Shaukat Ali, a distant relative of Waqar Hassan, invited some of the families from the Lawyers' Den to watch the Muharram processions making their way down to the river Shipra during the night. Shaukat Ali and his wife lived in a house by the spot where the main road from Ujjain ended and became a wide track leading on through the jungle to the river Shipra. It was a hilly area. Their house was about ten feet above the main road with stairs leading to the front door. Along the front of their house was a separate room with two windows at the side and a flat metal roof on top, from which the ladies and children were able to watch the Muharram procession making its way to the river Shipra.

The ladies took along a pot of freshly made *khichra* in the *tongas* with them as well as kebabs, *samosey, pakorey,* and *dopurti rotis,* two thin *chapatis* sandwiched together with *ghee* and baked on a *tawa.*

Shaukat Ali's wife had laid mattresses on the roof and provided thick quilts for the ladies and children, so that they could sit and watch the processions in comfort. In the evening, they took their places on the roof and watched a small procession walk quietly past toward the river Shipra. The gentlemen had assembled downstairs. When they heard the first procession coming, they went outside to stand on the open verandah on the ground floor, beneath the metal roof, to watch it pass by.

Soon afterward, the distant beat of drums was heard. A wave of excitement ran through the ladies and children. The sound of the drums became louder. Men appeared carrying *taziyeh*, followed by the drummers. They stopped outside the front of the house and were joined by more men bearing old-fashioned weapons, storm lanterns, and *chaariye*. More processions from different parts of Ujjain joined them in front of the house, all carrying replicas of *dul duls*, *buraqs*, and *taziyeh*. The drum beats were silenced, the men started to move slowly toward the river Shipra. Night began to fall. A cold breeze rose. The ladies drew the quilts over themselves and the children and took turns preparing hot tea for everyone on the roof. The occasional sound of drums in the distance signaled the arrival of another procession. It was after midnight when Mrs. Adiba Hassan and some of the other ladies took their children and went into the bedrooms to sleep.

In the morning, Umer went for breakfast and saw Tiddi sitting there, his clothes crumpled, yawning and holding a cup of tea.

"When did you go to bed?" he asked his friend.

"We didn't," answered Tiddi sleepily. "We spent all night on the roof, watching the stars. I don't remember whether any more processions came along after you left."

Later that morning, Akram and Jugnu Khan came with their *tongas* to collect the ladies and children and bring them back to the Lawyers' Den. On her return, Mrs. Adiba Hassan told her mother, Mrs. Waheeda Begum, about the procession. "Shaukat Ali and his wife sent you *Salam*," she added.

"I remember Shaukat Ali when he came here to see us just after graduating from Aligarh University," said Mrs. Waheeda Begum. "As soon as he arrived, all the men, women, and children crowded round him. He was like a being from another world. He was wearing trousers with his shirt tucked inside just like an Englishman, although he went to Aligarh University wearing *pajamas* and *kameez*."

"Oh yes, I remember," said Mrs. Adiba Hassan, smiling. "I made him a cup of tea. He stood by the door, leaning against the door frame chatting, holding the cup in one hand and drinking tea from it. He never poured the tea into the saucer in his other hand to drink it, like he used to do before he went to university."

"This is an English custom adopted by the professors and teachers at Aligarh University," replied Mrs. Waheeda Begum.

--- --- --- --- --- --- --- --- --- ---

Milad-un-Nabi, the birthday of Prophet Muhammad (peace be upon him), fell on the twelfth of Rabi-ul-Awwal and was a special day for the ladies of the Lawyers' Den. They all put on new clothes, contributed money, and arranged for freshly made *kalakand* and *sohan halwa* to be bought for them in the morning from Ram Das the sweet merchant. Chandni and her daughter, Meena, came with Qulfi early in the day to cook carrot halva under the guidance of Mrs. Nafisa Begum. They were then invited to join in the celebration together with Tara Bibi.

First, they lit sandalwood *agarbattis* and *loban,* a kind of incense, and set the sweets out next to them -- two large metal dishes containing *kalakand* and *sohan halwa* and a large china dish of carrot halva. Then they performed *wuzu,* washing their hands, face, and feet before sitting down on a carpet in the private courtyard of the house belonging to Anwar Ali.

Everyone covered their heads and chanted together loudly in praise of Prophet Muhammad (peace be upon on him). Perfume from the *agarbatti* and *loban* wafted across the courtyard. Afterward, Mrs. Waheeda Begum offered *fatiha,* reciting the first chapter of the holy Qur'an in a clear voice with her hands open palms upward, while the others joined her in silent prayer with closed eyes. The blessed sweets and carrot halva were then distributed to all those present and also to each house in the Lawyers' Den.

--- --- --- --- --- --- --- --- --- ---

Fasting during the month of Ramadan forms one of the five pillars of Islam. It enables Muslims to practice self control, cleanse the body and mind, and also think of all the hungry people in the world. During Ramadan, Muslims get up in the night to eat *sahri*, a meal that is eaten before sunrise. Afterward, they practice *sawm* or fasting and do not eat, drink, or smoke between sunrise and sunset.

In Mirzawari, a group of young men would get up two hours before dawn to chant a call to wake people in all the Muslim houses for *sahri*. At daybreak, a *mu'azzin* would go to the Qazi Mosque opposite the Lawyers' Den and sound the *azan* or call to prayer from the tower of the mosque. When they heard the *azan*, the Muslim men and women would stop eating and quickly drink a glass of water, hoping to keep their thirst at bay until sunset. During Ramadan some men and women recited the Qur'an each day.

During the day, the ladies in Mirzawari gave much thought to devising delicious dishes for their families to enjoy, spurred on by the knowledge that all their good deeds in this month would be doubly rewarded in heaven. Fasting sharpened their palates, so that they were able to produce much better meals than usual.

After sunset, the fast was broken with a meal known as *iftar*, for which the ladies had prepared dates and savories -- *samosey*, *pakorey*, and *namkeen* (savory crisps) -- known as *iftari*, the food for *iftar*, which was served in large dishes together with water and cold drinks to family and friends. The main meal came later.

After *iftar*, the men gathered in large numbers for the evening prayer in the Qazi mosque. They came from the Lawyers' Den and the Criminals' Den and stood side by side to offer prayer in the mosque. After praying, they held up their hands and begged Allah for forgiveness. The ladies in the Lawyers' Den went to Anwar Ali's courtyard and lined up behind Mrs. Waheeda Begum, who acted as their Imam or spiritual leader, and prayed together for forgiveness.

- -

Eid-ul-Fitr follows after Ramadan. On the evening of the twenty-ninth of Ramadan, some men from Mirzawari climbed to the top floor of the Qazi mosque to view the sky. It was cloudy, so they were unable to see the new moon. They joined others outside the Qazi's residence and debated whether *Eid* would fall on the following day or not. Suddenly, the sound of horses' hooves was heard and a couple of horseback riders drew up. They had come from a distant village outside Ujjain, where the moon had been sighted and the village headman had sent them to inform the Qazi. The Qazi then declared that *Eid* would fall on the following day. This news soon spread all over Ujjain and the surrounding areas. Some shops remained open throughout the night. There were three days' official holiday to celebrate *Eid-ul-Fitr*.

Everyone wore new or clean clothes for *Eid*, strongly perfumed with scent bought especially for the occasion from Nazar Bhai *atterwala*, who sold top-quality perfume at his shop in Chowk Bazaar. Many ladies in the Lawyers' Den left pistachio nuts and almonds to soak in water overnight for *Eid*. For breakfast the following morning, everyone had a bowl of hot milk with pistachio nuts and almonds followed by a bowl of *siwayyan*, sweet home-made vermicelli, together with cardamom seeds and raisins boiled in buffalo milk and finished with a cup of tea.

Afterward, the men left the house to perform the *Eid* prayer. This was held at the *Eidgah*, a special mosque in Ujjain, which was only used once a year at *Eid-ul-Fitr*. As they entered the *Eidgah* the men paid *fitrah*, alms for the poor, to a representative of the Qazi.

The *Eidgah* was in the middle of the jungle about four miles from Ujjain. It was set on a slight rise next to a lake with *singharey* or water chestnut plants growing all over the surface. The prayer area was partly roofed over and was completely surrounded by a whitewashed wall about six feet high with a single entrance. Inside the wall was a line of water taps for the men to perform *wuzu*. Beneath the roofed section was an arch facing the *Ka'aba*, before which the Qazi stood to lead the *Eid* prayer. There were stone slabs on the ground and these had been covered with long cotton sheets. Up to 100 people could offer *Eid* prayer there.

On *Eid* day, Akram *tongawala* drove Qazi Sahib along the broad track from Ujjain to the *Eidgah* by *tonga*. The lawyers, teachers, and businessmen had booked *tongas* to take them to the *Eidgah* as soon as the Qazi announced the start of *Eid*. Some people traveled to the *Eidgah* by donkey cart and people from the surrounding villages arrived there in bullock carts and on horseback.

There was also a short cut to the *Eidgah* along a narrow track through the jungle. A group of men and boys from Mirzawari assembled in the Qazi football ground beneath the *kabeet* tree to walk together along this track. Among them were Mehboob, Nazir, Arif, Tiddi, and Umer, all wearing their best *Eid* clothes of *kameez* and *pajamas* with an Afghan hat or cap on their heads and *Bata* shoes or *chappals* on their feet.

The walkers from Mirzawari were soon joined by others on their way to the *Eidgah*, among them Arif's friend, Bhura. Gulzar Khan and Samosa Khan from Gharib Colony came on bicycles toward their group.

"Our business is doing so well that I am now employing two other women to help my mother to make *samosey*," Samosa Khan told everyone with pride. "I have just bought a new bicycle as an *Eid* present to myself."

Everyone admired Samosa Khan's new bicycle and Bhura eyed it in a calculating way. As a professional cycle thief, Bhura never left the house without the tools of his trade inside a secret pocket of his *kameez*, even on *Eid* day. These were a bunch of keys that could open most cycle locks. He saw that Samosa Khan had a chain with a lock on it dangling from his handlebars for securing the bicycle and noted that he had a key capable of opening that lock. Gulzar Khan and Samosa Khan set off to cycle along the broad track to the *Eidgah*, while the others started to walk toward the track leading through the jungle.

Many boys carried sticks to protect themselves against snakes and some of them also had knives. These could be used in case of attack by wild animals or to cut into the skin to release the poison if bitten by a snake. As the men and boys walked through the jungle, they heard foxes barking from time to time. Thick vegetation lined the track on both sides. This often concealed poisonous snakes such as cobras and vipers. Umer threw some stones into a bush. A snake appeared and made for Mehboob, who was walking nearby. Mehboob fled with the snake in hot pursuit. As it drew near, one of his friends shouted, "Turn left!" Mehboob obeyed. Unable to turn quickly, the snake continued on, before slithering back round to come back and attack Mehboob. Meanwhile, the others picked up stones and flung them at the snake, which swiftly disappeared into the bushes.

Some boys spotted hoopoes or hud hud birds with crowns digging into the ground for worms. Weaver birds were building their two-roomed nests on the lower branches of the trees and the boys were able to peer inside the tiny compartments that had been so carefully constructed. The smaller boys chased chameleons as they ran along the ground and escaped up a tree. In the distance, peacocks stood or danced beneath the trees. The jungle was quite safe as there were no lions or tigers in that area.

Clumps of small bushes dotted the open ground near the *Eidgah*. These often concealed snakes. As they walked, the boys threw stones into the bushes until a snake appeared. Then they would start aiming stones at the snake and one of them would run away from it. The snake would immediately set off in pursuit and was followed by the other boys. As the snake drew near its quarry, the boys behind it shouted, "Turn left!" The first boy immediately obeyed and another boy took his place. The snake, unable to react so quickly, slowly slithered to a halt and then started to follow the second boy. The same game was repeated until the snake got tired and escaped into the jungle.

As the group entered the *Eidgah*, Bhura dropped behind, telling his friend Arif that he was feeling unwell. He soon found

Samosa Khan's bicycle, which had been locked to a tree by the *Eidgah*. He unlocked it and concealed it in a bush some distance away. Bhura then entered the *Eidgah* and stood in the back row to offer *namaz*.

After prayers, everyone got up and embraced each other before going home to have *Eid* dinner and exchange *Eid* presents with their families and friends. The group from Mirzawari waited outside the *Eidgah* for Bhura, so that he could walk back with them. However, he had disappeared and so had Samosa Khan's new bicycle.

"Has anyone seen my bicycle?" asked Samosa Khan. Mehboob, Nazir, Tiddi, Arif, and Umer all shook their heads.

"It's that cycle *chore,* that bicycle thief, Bhura!" said Gulzar Khan angrily. "He's taken it. When I get ahold of him, I will break both his legs so that he will never steal a bike again. He will sit and beg like Ghinwa did, outside the Chand hotel in the Chowk Bazaar, with his broken legs dangling in front of him."

"There's Bhura, there he is!" shouted one of the men and pointed. Everyone was surprised to see Bhura running toward them from the far side of the clearing, shouting "Snake! Snake!" Behind him was a four-foot-long cobra in hot pursuit. The men and boys threw stones and the snake slithered away into the bushes.

Gulzar Khan seized Bhura firmly by the arm. They were soon surrounded by the boys from Mirzawari and a lot of other people who had just come out of the *Eidgah*.

"Where's Samosa Khan's bike? What did you do with his new bicycle?" demanded Gulzar Khan and struck Bhura's head hard with his fist. Bhura began to cry and pointed toward a bush at the far side of the clearing.

"Ah! That's why the snake was running after you," said Gulzar Khan. Everyone laughed. "Serves you right!"

Tightening his grip on Bhura's arm, Gulzar Khan walked

toward the bush, followed by all of the boys and most of the men. They threw stones into the bush until the snake reappeared and disappeared into some other bushes nearby, followed by five baby snakes. Samosa Khan recovered his new bike, which was undamaged. Gulzar Khan released Bhura, who slipped away toward the back of the crowd. He was never again seen at *Eidgah*.

- - - - - - - - - - - - - - - - - - - -

Meanwhile, the women from the Lawyers' Den were offering *Eid* prayer in the courtyard of Anwar Ali's house. They had invited Tara Bibi to join them. Everyone gave her money, food, and clothes for *Eid*, for distribution to the poor families of Gharib Colony. Then Mrs. Waheeda Begum led the ladies in prayer. Afterward, they embraced each other, saying "*Eid Mubarak*," drank *sharbat* together, and then dispersed to prepare food for their families and friends. Everyone was busy all day with guests coming and going.

Later that day, Tara Bibi went in Jugnu Khan's *tonga* to Gharib Colony to visit Khatoon Bibi. Jugnu Khan agreed to return in the evening to take Tara Bibi back to Mirzawari and then went to visit his friend, Gulzar Khan.

Khatoon Bibi took Tara Bibi to the house of the widow who lived with her daughter, Shakuri. Ill-treated by both her husband and mother-in-law, Shakuri was granted a divorce from Murad and was now back living in her mother's hut. Shakuri and her mother embraced Khatoon Bibi and Tara Bibi, wished them "*Eid Mubarak*," and offered them *siwayyan* and tea.

"How are you both keeping?" Khatoon Bibi asked.

"I am very happy now that I'm no longer living with Murad and his family," Shakuri said with satisfaction.

"Do you have work?" asked Tara Bibi.

"Yes, I do," answered Shakuri happily. "About a year ago, a woman living nearby died after a long illness, leaving two young children aged six and three. Her widowed husband goes out to work each day. He has no one to look after the children, so he asked us to take care of them. He is a good man and the children are sweet. Recently, I became engaged to him and we are now saving for our wedding." Her face glowed with joy.

"Congratulations!" Tara Bibi and Khatoon Bibi said in unison. Shakuri blushed, suddenly feeling shy, then with a little encouragement, told the ladies more about her new fiancé and the children.

"Here is something for you from the ladies in Arithewaley," said Tara Bibi, and gave them some money, food, and clothes. The two ladies thanked her.

"I know of someone who needs your help," remarked Shakuri's mother. "There is a young family with five children. One of them, a four-year-old boy, is sick and needs special medicine and hospital treatment. I am not sure where they live, though."

"I will make enquiries and then go and visit them," said Tara Bibi.

Tara Bibi and Khatoon Bibi returned to Gulzar Khan's hut, where he was sitting outside with Jugnu Khan. They told them about the poor young family with five children.

"I know the family you mean," said Gulzar Khan. "I'll take you there."

They went by *tonga* with Gulzar Khan sitting in front next to Jugnu Khan and the two ladies in the back. The family was overwhelmed to receive a visit from both ladies. The children's mother wept when Tara Bibi gave them money, food, and clothes.

"I will arrange for you to take your sick child to the hospital, so that the doctors can find out what treatment he needs," Tara Bibi told the mother.

"May Allah bless you for the kindness you have shown us." Her voice choked with sobs.

Jugnu Khan took Gulzar Khan and Khatoon Bibi back to their huts and then drove Tara Bibi back to Mirzawari. Before she got down from the *tonga*, Tara Bibi arranged for Jugnu Khan to come and collect her after the third day of *Eid*, so that she could take the young mother and her sick child from Gharib Colony to the hospital.

During the *Eid* holidays, the people in the Lawyers' Den found many pleasant ways to pass the time. In the evenings, some men and women gathered in the courtyard of the bungalow of Yousuf Ali Sahib, the retired lawyer, to enjoy readings of poetry by local poets and famous Urdu poets. Some men played chess or cards in one room of the bungalow. Meanwhile, the women relaxed on *charpoys* in the courtyard of the Lawyers' Den and told stories.

On the second day of *Eid*, the women and children from the Lawyers' Den went for an outing in the country, in three bullock carts escorted by two horse riders. They stopped by a well in a meadow and climbed down the steps inside the well to fill their jugs. Then they sat beside the well to have lunch. Afterward, the carts continued to the river Shipra and everyone got out to walk along the bank. Someone spotted a crocodile and shrieks of excitement filled the air. Some of the women waded in the shallow water, raising the bottoms of their loose trousers to keep them dry. The children played by the river bank and the women sat down after a while to enjoy the fresh breeze and watch the birds and small animals. That evening, they returned to the Lawyers' Den tired and happy.

- -

Occasionally, there was a water shortage and the water levels were low in the river Shipra and the big water tank in the town center. The reservoir started to dry up. Crops were withering and the fruit was shriveling on the trees. It was then that the Muslims in Mirzawari gathered to form a procession to the *Eidgah*, to pray for rain. Old and young men joined the procession, bareheaded and chanting loudly:

We are walking bareheaded for rain,

Please God give us a lot of rain

Or as much as you can.

We hope our prayers won't be in vain.

The rain procession was well known in Ujjain. All along the route, Hindus and Muslims would come out to the street to cheer on the procession. Some people also threw flower petals at the procession.

"We will offer prayers for rain at the *Eidgah* and we are sure to get rain falling soon," the people in the procession shouted again and again, as they made their way to the *Eidgah*. Strange to say, nearly every time there was a rain procession, the skies would open and rain would fall on the people in the procession as they walked back from the *Eidgah* and they would reach home soaking wet.

- - - - - - - - - - - - - - - - - - - -

Eid-ul-Adha, the festival of sacrifice, is celebrated by all Muslims each year to remind them of their submission to God. In Ujjain, it is known as *Bakra Eid*, literally Billy-goat *Eid*, as the majority of Muslims there sacrifice billy-goats for this festival.

A few months before *Eid-ul-Adha*, Diwan Khan's work contract ended and he was unemployed. "Can you buy me a young billy-goat from the monthly cattle market?" he asked his father, the Rent Collector, Haider Khan.

"You already have a cockerel and several hens and chicks," his father replied brusquely. "It's too early to buy a billy-goat now. We'll buy it a couple of weeks before *Eid-ul-Adha*."

"I want to look after the billy-goat, feed him well, and give him a happy life in order to prepare him for sacrifice at the next *Eid-ul-Adha*," pleaded Diwan Khan.

"You must also exercise him regularly on the Qazi football ground during the day when not many people are around," his father replied, his tone softening.

"Yes, father, I will."

Haider Khan and his son visited the next farmers' market and soon found where the goats were being offered for sale. Diwan Khan began to pick out possible billy-goats for purchasing. Haider Khan examined each goat with great care. He looked at its teeth to find out its age and check that none of them was broken. Then, putting one hand under its neck and the other beneath its body, he lifted the billy-goat to check its weight and also to make sure that its legs were uninjured, as it is forbidden to sacrifice an animal with a broken limb. When father and son had agreed on their choice of animal, Haider Khan began to haggle about the price with the seller. They finally bought a healthy young billy-goat and arranged for a local farmer to supply them regularly with fodder.

Each day, Diwan Khan took his billy-goat out onto the Qazi football ground. He soon became very popular with the children in Mirzawari. About two months before *Eid- ul-Adha*, some other families in the Lawyers' Den also bought billy-goats. Umer's and Tiddi's families and Anwar Ali had one billy-goat each. Shakil Sahib's family bought two billy-goats. Arrangements were made for Diwan Khan to feed all six billy-goats, and the boys from the Lawyers' Den helped him to take them to the Qazi football ground for daily exercise.

One sunny Thursday morning, Diwan Khan was looking after his poultry. He had cleaned out the chicken house and collected the eggs and was feeding the birds when Umer and Tiddi came by, leading their billy-goats to the football ground.

"Are you coming along with your billy-goat?" Umer called to him.

"Not yet," answered Diwan Khan. "You go on ahead. I'll join you later."

When Umer and Tiddi reached the football ground, they saw two more boys from Mirzawari with their billy-goats.

"Let's have a fight between our billy-goats," suggested one of the boys from Mirzawari. "Mirzawari against Lawyers' Den, see who wins."

Umer and Tiddi thought this was a great idea. Umer grasped his billy-goat firmly and a Mirzawari boy hit it hard on the forehead. The infuriated billy-goat took a few steps back, lowered its head, and rushed forward to butt its tormentor. Meanwhile, the Mirzawari boy struck one of their own billy-goats and the two billy-goats were soon locked in battle.

Suddenly, there came a loud voice. "Stop that fight at once! Those billy-goats will get hurt."

The boys looked around startled. Diwan Khan was coming toward them, holding his billy-goat by its rope.

"What's the matter?" asked one of the Mirzawari boys.

"Don't you know that if a billy-goat loses one of its horns in a fight, it cannot be sacrificed on *Eid-ul-Adha*," Diwan Khan said sharply. "Also, if it is injured in a fight, it won't be suitable for *halal* either." The boys immediately stopped the contest.

Eid-ul-Adha was celebrated for three days in Ujjain. The day before *Eid-ul-Adha*, the courtyard in the Lawyers' Den was cleaned. When all the men had returned from *Eid* prayers, two professional butchers from the slaughterhouse, who had been engaged by Diwan Khan a month earlier, arrived to perform the sacrifice of each billy-goat in turn, according to ritual. The butchers were surrounded by men and children as they took hold of each billy-goat to *halal* it and kill it according to Islamic law. Some of the ladies watched from a distance, but others went to their rooms to weep, covering their eyes with their *dupattas*.

Each animal was then skinned and the meat was divided into three portions. A third of the meat went to the family, a third to friends, and a third to the poor. The skin was given to charity.

The charity collected the skins and sold them giving the money, together with one portion of meat from each household, to poor people so that they could celebrate *Eid*. The people of the Lawyers' Den feasted on meat curry, kebabs, and *rotis* during the following week.

Kites circled the sky above the Lawyers' Den courtyard while the butchers were slaughtering the billy-goats. When the butchers had gone and the meat had been taken by each family to be distributed, Diwan Khan and the young boys fed the remaining scraps of meat to the kites. As Diwan Khan flung a piece of meat into the air, one of the kites dived down and caught it. Other kites joined the first one, sweeping over the people below and swooping down to seize the scraps of meat being thrown up at them by the boys. Half an hour later, all the meat was gone.

Akram *tongawala* took Tara Bibi from the Lawyers' Den to Gharib Colony with the meat for the poor, where Khatoon Bibi, Gulzar Khan, and Samosa Khan helped them to distribute it among the poor people living in the huts there.

Halim Nawaz, a teacher at the Urdu Middle School, had gotten together with another teacher from Freeganj School, to arrange for teams from each school to play a hockey match, on the last day of the holiday for *Eid-ul-Adha*. This event was held at the Qazi football ground. Among the local Hindus and Muslims watching the match were the three *tongawala* friends, Fazal *cyclewala*, his business partner Nazir, Mehboob, Arif, Umer, Tiddi, and Anwar Ali. Ram Das and two *baniye* grocers, Ashok Kumar and Premji, were also there.

As the match drew to a close, Halim Nawaz' school team was winning two to one. Gitta and Tinka had each scored one goal for the Urdu Middle School. Gitta's friend Bihari Lal had scored one goal for Freeganj School. The referee put the whistle in his mouth and looked at his watch. Everyone's eyes were on him, waiting for the signal to end the match. The goalkeeper of the Urdu Middle School team was moving forward to celebrate, just as Bihari Lal came running toward him with the ball and swiftly struck it with his hockey stick straight into the net. Immediately afterward the referee blew his whistle and the match ended in a draw.

All the onlookers clapped and shouted and there were loud cheers from the students at Freeganj School, as their team lifted Bihari Lal onto their shoulders and paraded him all round the Qazi football ground. Afterward, the players from each team shook each other's hands and then gathered around their teachers, who gave them cold, scented *sharbat*.

At the end of the match, Ram Das and the two *baniye* grocers approached Halim Nawaz and asked him to send some boys to their shops, to collect *diye* clay lamps and oil to illuminate the Qazi mosque during the forthcoming *Diwali*, the Hindu festival of light. Halim Nawaz thanked the Hindu gentlemen and promised to do so. Then he went over to the winning players, who were still drinking *sharbat*, surrounded by all their supporters who were congratulating them and clapping them on their backs.

"Well done, team!" said Halim Nawaz cheerily to the boys. "Let's keep practicing and make sure that we win next time. Now, off you go when you're ready!" Turning to Mehboob and Arif, who had been standing on the sidelines watching the match, he asked, "Could you please take some boys with you on *Diwali* to collect *diye* from Ram Das and the two *baniye* grocers, and bring them over to light the mosque?"

Chapter 10: Hindu Festivals and Celebrations

Hindu festivals have an extra radiance when held in Ujjain, one of the four cities made sacred by the nectar of immortality being spilled on it from a *kumbh* or pitcher.

During *Diwali* -- the Hindu New Year celebrations -- the Maharajah of Gwalior sent a band of Indians wearing Scottish tartan kilts to march all around Ujjain playing the bagpipes and drums. As they passed, people came out of their houses and thronged the streets to witness the spectacle and join in the celebrations. The front doors of the Hindu houses in Ujjain had been freshly painted and decorated with flowers. *Diye* had also been placed on the walls around the open roofs, on the sills beneath the windows of the houses, and by the front doors.

Umer and Tiddi were kicking a football around the Qazi football ground, when they heard someone calling them. "Hey boys, *idhar ao*, come over here!"

Mehboob, the messenger, was standing at the edge of the field together with Arif, the petty thief from the Criminals' Den. The two boys ran over.

"After the hockey match at the end of *Eid-ul-Adha*, Ram

235

Das, the sweet merchant, and two *baniye* grocers, Ashok Kumar and Premji, asked Halim Nawaz to send someone to their shops to collect *diye* and oil to light the Qazi mosque during *Diwali*," said Mehboob. "Will you come and help us?"

The boys and young men collected nearly 50 *diye* and cans of oil from the three shops. Soon afterward, the *diye* were casting their light around from the windowsills and the tops of the walls surrounding the flat roof of the Qazi mosque.

After work, Hira Lal *tongawala* joined his *tongawala* friends Jugnu Khan and Akram in front of Akram's house. "Tomorrow is *Diwali*," he announced with a happy smile. "Let's celebrate."

"*Charas piyo*," said Jugnu Khan. "Here is *charas*. *Charas piyo, maza karo*, let us smoke and enjoy our lives."

The three friends sat contentedly, watching the clouds of smoke swirling in front of them. Eventually, Akram broke the silence.

"Tomorrow evening, the s*ingharey* women will bring *diye* for our house," he said.

Some of the women from the Hindu families living near Akram *tongawala's* house regularly walked to the lake opposite Eidgah, the mosque where Muslims went to offer Eid prayers. When the *singharey* were ripe, the women went out on the lake, in boats, to collect the abundant harvest. If any one of the three friends saw these women walking to or from the lake with their wickerwork baskets, he would give them a free ride in his *tonga*. In return, the women would give them *singharey*.

"Let's clean the front of the house this evening, to welcome them when they come," said Hira Lal. "*Jharu kidhar hay*, where's the broom?"

The friends searched the house for a broom without success.

"Qulfi always hides the broom now, ever since we broke it

by accident the last time we took it to do some cleaning," complained Akram.

"We could borrow a broom from the graveyard," suggested Jugnu Khan. "Some people leave brooms by the graves of their relatives." This was so that they could sweep around the sides of the grave before sitting down to pray for the souls of their loved ones, a ritual habitually carried out on Thursdays. It is generally believed by Muslims that the souls of the dead visit their relatives every Thursday. Then, when relatives visit the graveyard on Thursdays, they can sweep around the sides of the grave before they sit down to pray for the souls of their loved ones. "We can put the broom back when we've finished."

The *tongawalas* found two brooms. Jugnu Khan and Hira Lal started to sweep in front of the house while Akram took a cloth to dust the door.

When Qulfi came home, all three men were busy sweeping, cleaning, and singing cheerfully. Her eyes widened at this unusual sight.

"Why are you cleaning the front of the house and where did you get the brooms?" she asked Akram suspiciously.

"We are preparing for *Diwali*," her husband replied. "We got the brooms from the graveyard."

Qulfi went into the house and burst out laughing.

The *Diwali* celebrations in Ujjain continued for about five days. During that time all Hindus, rich and poor, young and old, wore new clothes, and sweets were distributed among family and friends. On the first day of *Diwali*, Hira Lal arrived at Akram's house in the evening wearing a clean white *dhoti* and a new *kameez*. Later, the *singharey* women from the Hindu families living nearby brought several *diye* across to Akram's house. The three *tongawalas* gave them boxes of sweets from Ram Das, set the *diye* along the front of the house, and lit them, so the house glowed with light. Hira Lal then went onto the football ground and offered sweets to the boys playing there.

Late one afternoon during *Diwali*, Umer sat in the gallery on the first floor of his house reading a book. The gallery wall was unique in Mirzawari. It was composed of glass in many different colors set into window frames and faced on to the courtyard. Suddenly, Umer heard Tiddi calling him from below. He opened a window and looked out. "What is it, Tiddi?" he asked.

"Let's go along the street by the mosque where the Hindu families live and look at their *Diwali* lights," his friend suggested.

The two boys made their way along the street, admiring the *diye* lights shining along the front of each Hindu house. Tables had been set out on the verandah of one house and they could see men sitting around them playing cards.

"I've heard from Mehboob that men sometimes play cards for money," Umer said.

"I don't believe you," scoffed Tiddi. "It's just a story. Gambling isn't allowed."

"They still do it, though. Shall we go and see? Then you'll believe me."

The boys climbed the stairs to the verandah and stood by one of the tables watching the card players. The men held cards in their hands. There were small piles of coins and rupee notes in front of each player and a larger pile of money in the center of the table. "See! I told you! They're playing for money," whispered Umer.

Just then, the organizer of the game came out from an inner room. He was tall and slim with a *tilak* mark on his forehead and was wearing a cream silk shirt over a white *dhoti*. Spotting Umer and Tiddi, he asked, "What are you boys doing here? Young children are not allowed to come to this place."

The two boys looked up at him, tongue-tied. The games

organizer took them to one side. "I know you boys," he said. "You're from the Lawyers' Den. I know your father as well," he added turning to Umer. "He's a respectable lawyer. He wouldn't be happy if he found out that you boys had come to a place like this."

"We don't have any money to gamble," Umer replied, his confidence suddenly returning to him. "We would like to watch and if we find it interesting, we will go and get some money to play with."

"Muslim boys are not allowed to play here or to watch," the games organizer told Umer.

"We'll keep it secret. We won't tell anyone," Umer assured him.

"Oh! So you are the lawyer's son after all, trying to win the argument," the games organizer replied with some amusement. "Your pocket money would be too little to gamble here. Since this is *Diwali*, our festival of goodwill, I will give you boys each some money each to play, on three conditions."

"What are they?" asked Umer.

"One: that you both keep quiet about it and don't tell anybody -- ever. Two: you will only be allowed ten minutes or a maximum of three bets to play and then both of you will go home, win or lose. Three: you must promise me that you will never gamble again or ever come here again."

Both boys willingly accepted these three conditions. The games organizer took some money from the side pocket of his *kameez* and gave it to them. Then he led them into a room where a game of roulette was in progress, on a table just inside the door.

"You may let these Muslim boys from the Lawyers' Den have three bets each," he told the croupier. All the men round the table looked up in amazement.

"What are they doing here?" asked one of the players.

"They have never seen gambling before, so I am letting them find out about it."

"You boys may place three bets each on any of these numbers," the games organizer told Umer and Tiddi. Then he watched while Umer and Tiddi placed their bets. Tiddi lost all three bets, but Umer managed to win back his money on his third and final bet. The games organizer picked up Umer's winnings and handed the money over to him. Umer quickly pocketed it.

"*Ab gher jao* -- now you go home and never come here again, otherwise I will tell your father," said the games organizer to Umer.

Both the boys thanked him for allowing them to take part in the *Diwali* gambling. Then they went home with the words of the games organizer etched into their memories. They kept the secret of their *Diwali* gambling for a long, long time, in accordance with the promise they had made to him.

- - - - - - - - - - - - - - - - - - - -

The Rakhi Bandhan festival brings brothers, sisters, friends, and neighbors closer together. This is when Hindu women tie a colored sacred thread or *rakhi* to the wrists of their brothers or close male family friends, to ensure that they are protected from evil spirits.

One evening, Akram *tongawala* was driving home when he saw two of the *singharey* women walking toward Mirzawari at the side of the road, their heavy wickerwork baskets balanced on their heads. He drew up alongside them. "Climb up into my *tonga*, ladies!" he called. "Climb up and I will bring you back to your homes."

"Thank you very much," answered one of the *singharey* women. "We have been gathering water chestnuts all day and we are very tired."

As they got down from the *tonga*, both women thanked Akram once again. "It will be our Rakhi festival in a few days," said the older woman. "We will visit you and your friends and reward you for your continuing kindness to us, by tying *rakhi* threads around your wrists."

"This is our Hindu custom," Hira Lal told Akram afterward, when he and Jugnu Khan joined Akram to smoke and chat as usual. "These ladies are doing us a great honor. We must get sweets for them when they come to tie the *rakhi* threads around our wrists."

Some days later, after taking his evening meal, Akram *tongawala* was sitting outside his house with both his friends when they saw their four *singharey* women neighbors coming toward them carrying a basket of *singharey* and a bunch of red and yellow threads. The three men rose to welcome them.

"We have brought you *singharey* from the lake near the Eidgah," said the eldest of the four women. "You are all like our brothers," she added, coming toward Akram and holding out a red thread. "Here, give me your wrist and I will tie this *rakhi* thread to it." The three men held out their wrists to each of the four women in turn and the women tied red and yellow *rakhi* threads to their wrists.

"You ease our burden whenever you can," the eldest *singharey* woman told them. "At the start of the day, you bring us to the lake near the Eidgah so that we can begin our work sooner. On our homeward journey, when we are weary and our loads are heavy, you take us up in your *tongas* without asking for payment and swiftly bring us back to our families."

The *singharey* women finished tying the red and yellow *rakhi* threads to the men's wrists. "Now you are all our adopted brothers," the eldest woman told them with satisfaction.

"We also have something for you," said Akram. He went into the house and came out bearing four paper packets of *imarti* and *sohan halwa*, one for each *singharey* woman, which he and his friends had bought earlier that day from Ram Das, and presented one to each of them with a friendly smile.

Holi, the Spring Festival or festival of colors, usually lasts for three days and is the second main festival after *Diwali*. It is celebrated one day after the full moon in early March according to the Hindu calendar. Hindus prepared various dyes at home including *gulal* powder, which was brilliant yellow, orange, or red, and was also supposed to be good for the skin. Bonfires were lit on the second day, bringing some welcome warmth to the evening, and images of Holika, a female demon, were burned as people danced around the fires to welcome the spring. On the third day of Holi the Hindus added dye to buckets of water, which they then sprinkled over family and friends, who wore special clean clothes for this occasion. Then the men and boys went on the street outside their houses armed with red *gulal* powder and buckets of colored water, which they flung over each other and anyone else lucky enough to be passing by at the time. For several days afterwards, their skin glowed in remembrance of their celebrations.

Umer ran through the Elephant Gate into the courtyard of the Lawyers' Den and stopped outside Gul Bhai's house. "Hey Tiddi, are you there, Tiddi?" he called.

Gul Bhai's son Tiddi, appeared on the verandah. "What is it?" he asked.

"The Hindus living near the Qazi mosque are all throwing colored water over each other for the Holi spring festival. Do you want to come and join in?"

"I'll be right down," Tiddi cried.

The next moment, Umer and Tiddi had raced out of the courtyard.

Meena was playing hopscotch with a couple of other girls in the courtyard while her mother, Chandni, and her mother's friend, Qulfi, were doing housework. She watched sulkily as the boys rushed off through the Elephant Gate, in high spirits. "It's not fair!" she said loudly. "The boys have all the fun! They can throw colored water over each other with our Hindu neighbors. We can't do anything."

Kismet, the Rent Collector's wife, her daughter-in-law, Karima Bibi, and Kausar, Tiddi's aunt, were also in the courtyard sitting on *charpoys*.

"Our house is just opposite the Qazi mosque," said Kismet. "Would you all like to come with me and watch the Holi celebrations from our balcony? We can see everything going on in the street outside the Hindu houses near the mosque."

"Ooh, yes, please!" chorused the three girls.

"I'd love to see the celebrations," added Kausar.

Everyone immediately followed Kismet and Karima Bibi and crowded on to the balcony of their house.

Hindu women wearing white saris were grouped on their verandahs, laughing and rubbing *gulal* powder into each other's faces and clothes.

"Some of the women are throwing mugs of colored water over each other," said Meena with astonishment.

"Their saris are getting all wet and brightly colored," laughed one of the girls.

"They're enjoying it," Kausar said smiling. "See, they are all laughing. The *gulal* and the colored water make the saris come up in such pretty colors and *gulal* is also good for the skin."

"Look between the houses," said Kismet. The women and girls saw small groups of smartly dressed men and boys, their clothes already stained with dye. They were standing quietly in the passageways with buckets of colored water beside them.

"That's Hira Lal's *tonga* coming along!" exclaimed Karima Bibi suddenly.

Two men came and stood in the middle of the road and

held up their hands for the *tonga* to stop. The women watched as Hira Lal drove toward the men. Siddique Bhai and Diwan Khan were sitting in the back of the *tonga* and Hira Lal wore a white shirt over a freshly laundered *dhoti*. Hira Lal stopped near the men and leaned down to speak to them. The next moment, the men had dragged him down from the *tonga* and more men and boys had rushed from the passageway into the street bearing buckets of water.

Umer and Tiddi were hurrying along the road toward the Qazi mosque.

"What's going on in the street by the Hindu houses?" asked Tiddi.

Umer told him then added suddenly, "Oh, look! It's Hira Lal with Siddique Bhai and Diwan Khan. Let's go and see what's happening."

As they approached, they heard loud shouts of *"Bura na mano yeh Holi hai*, please don't mind, it's Holi," from the men and boys. Their three victims joined in the laughter.

Umer and Tiddi stopped and watched. Some of the Hindu boys in the group turned and spotted them. "Umer! Tiddi! Come over here!" they called.

Umer and Tiddi came closer. Two of the Hindu boys flung red *gulal* powder over them and followed it up with mugs of colored water. Umer and Tiddi thought it was great fun to be soaked all over in Holi water of different colors. When both boys were soaked, the Hindu boys offered them mugs and invited them to join in the fun.

The women and girls were watching the activity outside the Hindu houses when Kismet heard a woman clearing her throat behind them. She turned to see Qulfi. "What is it, Qulfi?" she asked.

"Mrs. Waheeda Begum and Mrs. Adiba Hassan have news for you," answered Qulfi.

"Nafisa's baby is due any moment," said Kausar immediately.

Kismet and Kausar went quickly with Qulfi into the courtyard and were met by Mrs. Waheeda Begum. "Nafisa has just brought her child into the world," she announced. "It's a fine and healthy little girl." There were exclamations of delight.

"How is Nafisa?" asked Kausar.

"She is resting. The midwife is with her. You can come and see them," came the reply. "Qulfi, could you please boil dried dates, raisins, sultanas, ground almonds, and ground pistachio nuts in buffalo milk to make *achhwani* for the new mother to drink."

"The new baby will bring more color into all our lives," said Kismet.

Suddenly, they heard the sound of children's voices. A moment later, Umer and Tiddi burst breathlessly into the courtyard. Their shirts and trousers were streaked with red, yellow, and orange dye.

"Now there is an interesting pattern of colors," remarked Mrs. Adiba Hassan. "Did you enjoy your Holi celebrations?"

"Your clothes are a mess," Kausar scolded Tiddi. "Go and change them at once."

"Don't worry, the dye will wash out," Mrs. Waheeda Begum assured her.

"You always say that we should try to get on with everyone, regardless of religion," Umer reminded his mother.

"Yes, yes, it's all right," Mrs. Adiba Hassan quickly answered. "Go and have a bath and change your clothes. Then I'll come and get your evening meal."

As soon as Umer and Tiddi had left to change their clothes, all the ladies started to laugh. "Those children had a good Holi celebration," Mrs. Waheeda Begum chuckled.

- - - - - - - - - - - - - - - - - - - -

A road coming from Milkipura led directly to the Qazi mosque, past a row of Hindu houses. During Holi, Muslims attending Friday prayers at the Qazi mosque avoided this road by taking a longer route through the graveyard, past the Qazi's house, to reach the mosque.

One Friday, Mehboob the messenger and his friend Nazir *cyclewala* were standing outside the Qazi *Masjid* dressed for Friday prayers, watching the Holi celebrations in the distance. Suddenly, Mehboob spotted one of his friends hurrying along the road from Milkipura, on his way to Friday prayers. He was immaculately dressed, as usual, in starched white *pajamas* and a long-sleeved, starched white *kameez,* with his head covered by a white handkerchief and Bata *chappals* on his feet. The Hindu men and boys saw Mehboob's friend coming and quickly hid in a passage between the Hindu houses with *gulal* powder and buckets of colored water standing ready beside them.

Mehboob waved frantically to his friend, pointing toward a street leading toward the graveyard and indicating that he should take that route. Mehboob's friend returned his wave and, thinking that Mehboob was trying to indicate that he was late for Friday prayers, started to walk faster. Suddenly, powder was flung over him and he was drenched with colored water. He gasped and spluttered. His clothes were stained bright red, orange, and yellow.

"*Bura na mano yeh* Holi *hai,* please don't mind, it's Holi," came a shout. He heard laughter and saw several Hindu men and boys surrounding him.

"Oh yes, of course, I quite forgot," answered Mehboob's friend, joining in the laughter.

"Don't worry, I'll lend you some clothes," Mehboob told his friend when he reached the Qazi mosque. "There's still time to change and prepare for Friday prayers."

Mehboob went home quickly and returned with clean clothes. Mehboob's friend had a shower in the mosque and changed into them before joining in the Friday prayers.

The festival of Dussehra celebrates the triumph of good over evil and lasts for ten days. On the tenth day, young men and boys dressed as various characters in the life of Lord Rama, one of the Hindu gods, to march in procession through the streets of Ujjain. Afterward, actors re-enact the battle between Rama and the demon king Ravana, finishing with the death of the demon king, when the actor playing Rama shoots flaming arrows at life-sized effigies, accompanied by loud cheers from the audience.

The three *tongawalas* Akram, Jugnu Khan, and Hira Lal went to watch the final day's celebrations for Dussehra together with Mehboob the messenger, Nazir *cyclewala*, and Arif, a petty thief. Gulzar Khan, a retired security guard, and Samosa Khan, a *samosa* seller, came from Gharib Colony to join them. Everyone stood chewing *paan* by the *paanwala's* shop at the corner of the Chowk Bazaar.

Suddenly, there was a loud shout. "Ey, Arif!" Everyone turned to see the cycle *chore*, Bhura, coming toward them. "*Salam!*" he called, waving his hand.

"Are you coming to watch Rama shooting flaming arrows at the effigies?" asked Mehboob.

"Yes, I am," answered Bhura. He turned to Samosa Khan. "I want to ask your forgiveness for trying to steal your new bicycle from outside the Eidgah, when we went there for Eid prayers."

"You had your punishment, don't do it again," came the reply.

"I have stopped stealing bikes," Bhura told him. "I am now doing honest work in a cycle shop in Musaddipura."

"You know what will happen if you ever try to steal a bike again," said Gulzar Khan.

"I learned my lesson on that Eid day," said Bhura. "I will never steal a bike again."

Everyone was very pleased to hear this and asked him to come with them to watch the fight between Rama and the demon king. Good had finally triumphed over evil.

- - - - - - - - - - - - - - - - - - - -

During Dussehra, Bengali Hindus decorated the entrances of their houses with flowers. Many of them were professional classical musicians, dancers, and singers and ran the only academy of classical music and dance in Ujjain. Madhav Sahib, a mathematics teacher and colleague of Halim Nawaz, went there after school to give the students music lessons. He also owned a shop selling musical instruments, which was run by an assistant during the day. Madhav Sahib was often heard playing the piano there in the evenings.

On the last day of Dussehra, students from the academy of classical music and dance formed a procession to take small clay statues of the goddess, Durga, from Gonde-ki-chowki down the main road out of Ujjain, and then along a wide track through the jungle and down to the river Shipra. The dancers wore colorful clothes and were accompanied by musicians playing various instruments. From time to time, they stopped to give performances of music and dance to the delight of the people thronging the streets.

Some days earlier, Halim Nawaz had spoken to Madhav Sahib about this procession. "The ladies from the Lawyers' Den have heard a lot about the music and dancing of the students from the academy of classical music and dance," he said. "They would love to be able to watch one of the live performances themselves. Would you be able to arrange this for them somewhere along the route?"

"Where would be the best place?" asked Madhav Sahib.

"One of our relatives, Shaukat Ali, has a house where the main road out of Ujjain finishes and the jungle track begins. Your procession will be taking this route down to the river Shipra. They could stop in front of the house and give a performance there. Then the ladies and children can watch from the flat roof upstairs while the men and boys gather downstairs."

"Very well, then," Madhav Sahib agreed. I will arrange for them to put on a special performance in front of the house."

The following day, Madhav Sahib informed Halim Nawaz of the special show planned, and Halim Nawaz passed this news on to Shaukat Ali and his wife. Delighted by this honor, Shaukat Ali's wife immediately asked him to invite the ladies in the Lawyers' Den to come and watch it.

Mrs. Adiba Hassan, her mother Mrs. Waheeda Begum, Kismet the Rent Collector's wife, Kausar, Tiddi's aunt, Qulfi, Chandni, and little Meena all assembled with Shaukat Ali's wife on the flat metal roof over the verandah along the front of the house. They were all talking and enjoying light refreshments of *pakorey* with tea and *sharbat* when they heard the distant sound of music and chanting.

"The procession is coming!" exclaimed Mrs. Waheeda Begum.

On the verandah downstairs, Halim Nawaz, Waqar Hassan, Diwan Khan, and Anwar Ali were standing with Umer and Tiddi.

"They're coming! They're coming!" shouted Tiddi.

"They're here!" Umer yelled. Both boys began to jump up and down with excitement on the stone floor.

The procession made its way down the road and stopped in front of the house, which stood high above the road. The men and children waved down at them.

"Welcome! Welcome!" shouted Halim Nawaz.

Madhav Sahib held up the clasped palms of his hands in greeting. Then everyone gave a performance of the music and dancing that had been rehearsed for this special occasion. When they had finished, the audience clapped enthusiastically. The performers waved farewell and continued on toward the river. The little clay statues of Durga were carefully carried down the river bank and gently placed on the waters of the holy river Shipra.

- - - - - - - - - - - - - - - - - - - -

The Kumbh Mela is the largest of all Hindu festivals celebrated in India. Ujjain is one of only four cities throughout the whole of India to have the honor of hosting this festival. The other three are Prayag (Allahabad), Nasik, and Hardwar. These four cities, which are sacred for Hindus, each host the Kumbh Mela in turn.

Hindu pilgrims come to Ujjain from all over India, once every 12 years, to celebrate the Kumbh Mela. On one such occasion, there were Sadhus, holy men wearing saffron robes, yogis who lived in caves in the Himalayas, and many pilgrims from different parts of India wearing colorful robes. During the celebrations for the Kumbh Mela, pilgrims bathed in the sacred river Shipra according to status, to wash away their sins. First came the Sadhus and yogis. They were followed by the ordinary pilgrims, who dipped into the river several times -- once to wash away their own sins, then one time each to wash away the sins on behalf of their loved ones and friends.

On one such occasion, the pilgrims came, as usual, in chariots and in bullock carts, on horseback, and on camels. Many of them were sounding gongs, beating drums, blowing conch shells, and ringing bells. The long procession moved slowly through the streets of Ujjain, stopping from time to time so that the musicians and dancers could give performances for the crowds thronging the streets and the people looking down from the houses. The people in the procession eventually congregated on the banks of the sacred river Shipra, where tents had been provided for their stay.

A group of men and boys stood in the street, in front of the Qazi Mosque, to watch the Kumbh Mela procession go by. Among them were Mehboob, Nazir *cyclewala*, and Anwar Ali, together with Umer and Tiddi. Nearby were the three *tongawalas* Jugnu Khan, Hira Lal, and Akram. More Muslim men and children from Mirzawari were also gathered on the other side of the street. A little away from them was a large group of local Hindu men, women, and children, eager to see the holy men and yogis passing by.

The Muslim women living close to the Qazi mosque stood by the windows of their houses or peered through their front doors, to watch the Kumbh Mela procession. The women from the Lawyers' Den, together with Qulfi and Chandni, gathered on the balcony above the reception room of the Rent Collector's house by the Elephant Gate. The group included some of the younger girls, including Meena, and the boys too small to go out with the older men.

Everyone cheered as the magnificent procession began to pass in front of the Qazi mosque. People watched in awe as the pilgrims and devotees, Sadhus, and holy men from all over India slowly walked by. Suddenly, the line of people came to an end.

"Is that all? Has the procession finished already?" asked Tiddi.

"Wait and see," said Mehboob.

"I'm hungry, I'm going home to eat something before the rest of the procession comes," said Tiddi and slipped off. His father Patwari Sahib, an estate manager, was due back at any time.

There were loud murmurs of excitement and anticipation as people looked down the road to see what was coming next.

When Tiddi entered the house, his father was sitting at the

table and his mother was starting to prepare a meal.

"What are you making, *Ammi*?" Tiddi asked his mother.

"Your father's favorite *pakorey*," his mother replied.

"Did you like the procession, Tiddi?" his father asked. "Has it finished yet?"

"No! I think there's much more to come," answered Tiddi. "I'm feeling hungry, so I want to eat *pakorey* quickly and then go back to watch."

"Sit down quietly and wait. Your mother is just starting to cook the food," his father told him.

"But I want to eat now and then see more of the procession," protested Tiddi.

"All right, go back now and come back later for the *pakorey*," said his mother.

Tiddi started crying. "Sit down quietly and wait or go back and watch the procession," said his father sharply.

"Hot *pakorey* coming up in a minute," announced his mother brightly.

Tiddi sniffed hungrily. The scent of fried onions, all hot and spicy, came wafting over to him. He sat down quietly. His mother put a plate of *pakorey* before him and Tiddi tried to eat them as quickly as possible without burning his tongue. However, they were very hot, so it was some time before he was able to finish them, despite his gulping down some water at the same time.

Meanwhile, the rest of the procession began to appear. A line of Sadhus in rows of three was moving forward at a fast and steady pace. They had long, shoulder-length hair, thick moustaches, and long beards flowing down over their chests. Most of them were tall and deeply tanned, with strong, healthy-looking bodies, and pleasant, serious expressions on their faces.

All of them were completely naked.

The crowds on both sides of the road fell completely silent. One or two boys began to whisper to each other. The procession passed solemnly through Mirzawari and down the street in front of the Qazi mosque. As the Sadhus passed the Rent Collector's house, the women on the balcony laughed nervously and turned away, drawing their *dupattas* over their faces.

"Look *Ammi*, those men aren't wearing any clothes," Meena shouted. Her mother quickly grabbed Meena, put her hand over the little girl's mouth, and pulled her inside the room.

"That's not a sight for little girls," she told Meena.

The little boys on the balcony watched quietly, wide-eyed, as the Sadhus marched past.

By the time Tiddi rejoined Umer and the others, the naked Sadhus had already passed by and an elephant was coming toward them. On its back was a plump young man with light brown skin wearing a white *dhoti* and cream silk *kameez*. He was sitting cross-legged with a *pankhawala* standing behind him waving a fan over him.

"Who's that man? Is he a Maharajah?" the boys asked.

"He's a holy Sadhu," answered Mehboob. "His status is as high as that of a Maharajah. He eats no food at all and drinks only buffalo milk."

After the procession had passed, one or two Sadhus rushed by at intervals, trying to catch up with the others. The local Hindus offered them food and water. Some of the Sadhus were pleased to accept and take a break in their journey.

Later, Umer and Tiddi joined the older boys on the Qazi football ground and stood listening to them talking about the procession earlier that day.

"Those Sadhus! They were marching in military style, just like an army," said one boy.

"They were walking so fast," another boy commented. "It was easy for them, though -- nothing to carry and not wearing any clothes."

Tiddi turned to Umer. "Were there really naked Sadhus?" he asked.

"Yes, a whole troop of them," his friend answered. "You missed them." He paused. "Anyway, you saw the man on the elephant."

"How could he be so fat if he eats nothing at all and drinks only milk?" asked Tiddi.

"Oh, that's just one of Mehboob's stories," Umer replied.

Tiddi went straight to his father, when he got back home, "I missed the best part of the procession this afternoon," he complained. "There were a whole lot of naked Sadhus marching together like soldiers. Everyone else saw them. I want to see them as well. They have all gone down to the river Shipra. Will you take me to the river Shipra to see the naked Sadhus?"

"I'm not walking all that way," Patwari Sahib told his son. Then he saw Tiddi's sad face, thought for a moment, and said, "You can see a naked Sadhu too. Go into your bedroom, take off all your clothes, and look at yourself in the mirror. Naked Sadhus are just like that."

Tiddi went to his bedroom, flung himself on his bed, buried his face in his pillow, and burst into sobs. His mother heard him crying and came into his room. "What's the matter, Tiddi?" she asked. Tiddi didn't answer. "There are some *pakorey* in the kitchen. Go and help yourself," she said gently. Then she left the room.

The next morning, Umer went to Tiddi's house and spoke to Tiddi's mother. "My father is taking me to see the Kumbh Mela today," he said. "Can Tiddi come with us?" Tiddi was delighted to be invited.

After lunch, Umer's father, Waqar Hassan, the solicitor, set off from home with Umer and Tiddi. The crowds increased as they came closer to the river Shipra. Groups of men and women were going to visit the Sadhus in their holy tents, to seek their blessings and also to ask the Sadhus to pray for them and help them to make their wishes come true. Both boys were very excited, looking around everywhere and pointing at the variety of clothes being worn by the pilgrims from different parts of India.

As they approached the bridge over the river Shipra, they were met by a throng of people moving toward them and were shuffled about by the crowds coming from both directions. Suddenly, Umer was pushed apart from his father and Tiddi and was swept along by the crowd going toward the bridge. Umer knew the area well. He had learned to swim from the opposite bank on the shallow side of the river just across the bridge, while his friends took turns warning those in the water of approaching crocodiles. Umer tried to go back and find his father, but he was unable to move against the oncoming tide of people. He pushed his way to one side and grasped a strut of the bridge.

A large group of people spotted the little boy desperately clinging to the bridge, looking lost and helpless. Five strong men from the group surrounded Umer to prevent him from being swept away by the crowd.

"What is your name?" one man asked him gently.

"My name is Umer," he said in a little voice.

"Umer, what are you doing alone in this huge crowd?"

"I was with my father and a friend. We got separated. I want to find my father."

"Don't worry, we will find your father for you," one of the men assured Umer.

Another man lifted Umer onto his shoulders. "Look around and see if you can spot your father anywhere," he told Umer.

Among the crowds visiting the Kumbh Mela were some policemen. However, the visitors were all very peaceful.

One of the men in the group saw a policeman, raised his hand, and shouted for help. The policeman thrust his way through the crowd toward them.

"This little boy has lost his father," said the man.

"Thank you for bringing him to me," said the policeman. "I'll find his father for him."

"What's your father's name and where do you live?" the policeman asked Umer.

"My father's name is Waqar Hassan and I live in Mirzawari," answered Umer.

"I know your father" said the policeman. "I know him very well. He is a solicitor from the Lawyers' Den. We'll go and see if we can find him in the crowd."

They began to walk toward a nearby restaurant, which was situated on higher ground and had a good view of the bridge over the river and the road leading up to it. "If we don't find your father, I will take you back to your home in Mirzawari," the policeman told Umer. As they were walking toward the restaurant, a slim, smartly dressed man stopped them and addressed Umer.

"Ey Umer, what's the matter, are you lost?"

"Do you know this man?" the policeman asked Umer.

"He is our relative, Shaukat Ali Sahib. He's a writer," Umer replied, cheering up a little, and turned to Shaukat Ali. "I have lost my father in the crowd and the policeman is helping me to find him."

When Waqar Hassan realized that Umer had become separated from him, he grasped Tiddi firmly by the hand and tried to turn back. The stream of people coming toward them was very strong and it took some time before they were able to move further away from the bridge. Waqar Hassan decided to make straight for the restaurant above the road and look for Umer in the crowds down below. He strode quickly through the dining area and stood outside, his hands on the railing, anxiously scanning the throng of people. Tiddi stood beside him looking subdued.

There were tents everywhere, as far as the eye could see. They extended down both sides of the river bank from the bridge. The tents were illuminated by storm lanterns, hurricane lamps, and *diye*. Suddenly Waqar Hassan caught sight of Shaukat Ali together with a policeman. Umer was walking between them.

"Shaukat Ali! Shaukat Ali Sahib!" called Waqar Hassan. The small group looked up.

"*Peerji! Peerji!*" shouted the policeman.

"*Abba! Abba!*" cried Umer excitedly.

"Waqar Hassan Sahib! Thank goodness we've found you!" called Shaukat Ali.

All three went into the restaurant to join Waqar Hassan and Tiddi, where Waqar Hassan invited everyone to take refreshments. The policeman and Shaukat Ali then accompanied Waqar Hassan and the two boys back to the bridge so that the boys could see the rest of the Kumbh Mela.

- - - - - - - - - - - - - - - - - - - -

Hira Lal had never married. He was charming to the *singharey* women to whom he regularly gave free rides in his *tonga*, but he always fell silent and changed the subject as soon as they tried to find out why he had never wanted to take a wife. Many years ago, when Hira Lal was young and handsome, he had met an upper caste girl. She was slender and fair-skinned and they were instantly attracted to each other. Time seemed to stand still whenever they met and started to talk and laugh together. These meetings were all too few and all too brief for Hira Lal. He wanted to see her more often and tell her how much he loved her.

One day, her mother came along with her to one of their meetings. "My daughter tells me that you are both in love," her mother said to Hira Lal.

"That is so," answered Hira Lal. "She is my *Maharani*, my princess, and I will do everything in my power to make her happy if she chooses to share her life with me."

"Alas, that cannot be," said the girl's mother gently but firmly. "You are not of our class and background. She is my eldest child. If she marries you, no one will marry her two younger sisters or her brother. Our whole family will become outcasts."

Hira Lal felt tears coming to his eyes and raised a hand to his face. His heart was filled with sadness. His *Maharani* quietly wiped her tears away with the corner of her *sari*. "There is but one way in which you can show your love for my daughter," said the girl's mother. Hira Lal lowered his hand and looked at her, his eyes shining with hope. "Go from here and think no more of marriage with my daughter. Do not speak her name to anyone and promise that you will never try and see her again. Only in this way can you hope to bring her happiness."

Hira Lal never found another girl to match his *Maharani*. The girl and her sisters and brother all made good marriages. One day, when driving his *tonga* around Ujjain, Hira Lal happened to pass a house and saw his *Maharani* standing by the door with her husband, holding a small boy by the hand. The years went by. Hira Lal's love for his *Maharani* was a secret sorrow of which he never spoke, not even when smoking *charas* with his friends Akram and Jugnu Khan *tongawalas*.

Three months before the Kumbh Mela, Hira Lal drove past the house of his beloved once again. He saw a lady standing by the door, gazing down the street. Despite the changes made by time, he recognized the face and form of the girl he had once loved. Stopping the *tonga*, he got down and stood before her.

"My *Maharani*, it is you," he said.

She started and gazed at him wonderingly. Then, recognition dawned.

"Hira Lal, how are you? Are you married?"

"No. There has never been anyone but you," answered Hira Lal, igniting the *phuljharian* in his heart.

Hira Lal learned that his beloved was now a widow. She had a son and a daughter, both married and living far away. Her mother and father had passed away some time ago and her husband had died four years earlier.

"Soon it will be the Kumbh Mela in Ujjain," Hira Lal told her. Maybe when it is here, it will work a miracle and bring us together. When can we meet again?"

"Go now to the *tonga* stand and wait for me," said the widow. In an hour, I will bring something nice for you."

"Yes, my *Maharani*. For you, I will wait forever," answered Hira Lal, only with effort, managing to contain his happiness at seeing his *Maharani* again.

The widow went into the house and mixed together barley and seven different types of lentils. Next, she ground them into a powder or *sattu* between two millstones and put the powder into a packet. Then she went to the *tonga* stand and handed the packet to Hira Lal.

Hira Lal thanked her, his eyes shining with joy. "Will you consider sharing my life and bringing to me some of the joy of the Kumbh Mela?" he asked.

"Yes, I will," the widow replied, sensing the embers being rekindled of a fire that she had thought would never be lit again. "When you go home, mix the *sattu* with water and think of me when you drink it. Then let us meet by the *tonga* stand three days after the Kumbh Mela and we will speak of this again."

However, it was the younger sister of the widow who met Hira Lal three days after the Kumbh Mela. "My elder sister died last week," she told Hira Lal. "Before she died, she whispered in my ear and asked me to tell you that she has always loved you."

Hira Lal left his *tonga* with his employer and went to join his friends Akram and Jugnu Khan outside Akram's house to smoke *charas*. He was overwhelmed with shock and grief that his *Maharani* had now left him forever. With hesitation, he began to speak of his lost love for the first time. His friends listened in silence, letting their sympathy reach out to him through the clouds of *charas*. Suddenly, Hira Lal got up and told them that he was going to Anwar Ali's shop to get *sattu*.

Hira Lal came to the open gutter at the corner near Anwar Ali's shop. Overwhelmed with sadness, he sank to the ground by the gutter, his head resting on his hands and his elbows pressed to his knees. His brain was a fog of sadness and misery. Some time later, Jugnu Khan came to Anwar Ali's shop.

"Have you seen Hira Lal?" he asked.

Silently, Anwar Ali pointed to Hira Lal sitting by the gutter.

"He has just had bad news," Jugnu Khan told him.

"He'll be all right in a while," said Anwar Ali cheerfully. "I have seen others come to that corner weighed down with sorrows, only to have their burden lightened by the soothing flow of the stinking water from the nearby houses."

Jugnu Khan stood some distance from Hira Lal, watching him in silence. The stench of the hot water flowing gently through the gutter was engulfing Hira Lal's sorrows and the sad sound of his singing could be heard.

"Where have you gone to, my *Maharani*? Why have you left me alone, my *Maharani*?"

The passers-by glanced over at the figure wearing a dirty white *dhoti* huddled by the open gutter singing sadly to himself. Most of them recognized Hira Lal and smiled with sympathy at this expression of his drug-induced sorrow. Among them were Nawab, Rashid, Rabia, and Gulshan. They were returning home from the monthly poetry reading at the bungalow of Yousuf Ali Sahib, the retired lawyer who lived next to the Qazi Mosque. Nawab was the spoiled only son of a property tycoon and had met his friend, Rashid, at the local boys' school that they both attended. Rashid's sister, Gulshan, had invited her school friend Rabia to join them for the poetry reading. Their father worked for Nawab's father as a property manager.

"That poor man," said Gulshan, "to have lost everything that gave color and meaning to his life."

"There must have been much sadness in his life," said Rabia sympathetically.

"Maybe there was a woman whom he once loved very deeply and Fate kept them apart," commented Rashid.

"I don't think so," Nawab replied. "He is just singing some sad film song very badly."

All four friends were standing on the threshold of their lives, the hope of everything they wished for shining brightly before them. Little did they know that they too would someday come to experience similar depths of loss and sorrow.

The smell from the gutter passed through Hira Lal's nose into his brain and lightened his sadness. He looked up. Jugnu Khan moved towards Hira Lal and held out his hand. Hira Lal grasped it and Jugnu Khan helped him to rise. Hira Lal stood gazing down into the open gutter.

"*Gham na kar*, don't grieve," said Jugnu Khan. "*Chalo charas piyo*, let us smoke."

Hira Lal walked away with Jugnu Khan with a feeling of lightness, freed from the heavy burden of his sadness, free to seek happiness elsewhere. They went to join Akram *tongawala* and indulge in their usual smoking session by the graveyard.

Chapter 11: Bombay Fever

Nawab walked home with his usual duck-like waddle. He knocked loudly at the front door of the house and then inserted his key in the lock. "I'm back now!" he announced to his father, Faqiruddin, who had come into the hall in response to the knocking. He joined his father in the reception room, where his mother Sakina was sitting with some sewing.

"Everyone loved my poetry," he told his mother proudly. "I read them one of my favorite compositions." Without waiting for her reply, he launched into a recitation:

"One day I was free / I climbed a tree / The branch broke beneath my weight / I hurt my leg and I am late." Then he recited a couplet: "A buffalo wanders round on his hoof / That buffalo jumped from the roof."

"How was the poetry reading?" asked Sakina.

"Very enjoyable," answered Nawab. "Some people read

their own poems, others read the work of well-known poets. We sat in the courtyard of Yousuf Ali Sahib's bungalow. Afterward, we stayed on and talked a bit."

Nazaruddin or Nawab was the only child of Faqiruddin, a self-made, rags-to-riches property tycoon, and his wife Sakina. Nawab was happy-go-lucky, but also very lazy, and often missed school. He wore expensive clothes, had expensive tastes, and was given a lot of pocket money. He and his friend Rashid went to the same local boys' school.

When both boys took the Urdu Middle School Examination, Rashid got good marks, but Nawab only just managed to scrape through, thanks to the private tuition he had been given. This was sufficient to establish his family's standing in the social circles they moved about in, as it was the minimum qualification the children in their middle-class area achieved. This also ensured that Nawab could continue to mix with the children with a similar social status.

Rashid and his younger sister, Gulshan, reached home and went to the kitchen, where their mother, Batul, was preparing supper for them, as usual.

"Did you both enjoy yourselves?" she asked, looking up at them with a smile.

"Yes, the poetry reading was very interesting," answered Rashid.

"Gulshan, please help me to bring the *pakorey* and plates into the other room," said her mother.

Batul's husband, Kaleem Beg, worked as a property manager for Faqiruddin, Nawab's father. Kaleem Beg had come to Ujjain with his family from Gaunkrigaon, a village outside Ujjain. They lived in a small rented bungalow near the residence of Bashir Ali, the father of Gulshan's friend, Rabia Begum.

"*Ammi*, will you show me how to make *pakorey*?" Gulshan asked her mother.

"Yes, I will," answered Batul. "Next time we go to Gaunkrigaon, I will also show you how to milk a cow and how to make *gaunkris*. When I was 14, I gained a certificate with distinction in the annual *gaunkri*-making examination in Gaunkrigaon."

Once at home, Rabia Begum helped herself to snacks in the kitchen and then joined her chaperone, Nur Jehan Begum, in the reception room. "After the poetry reading, I had an interesting conversation with Mrs. Adiba Hassan, Mrs. Farah Begum, and some of the other ladies from the Lawyers' Den," she told her chaperone.

"These people are well-educated, even though their speech and tastes are somewhat provincial," remarked Nur Jehan Begum.

"Mrs. Adiba Hassan explained to me many different ways of dyeing cloth," said Rabia Begum.

"Those are not fitting occupations for someone like yourself!" came the response. "Your father is an aristocrat from Bhopal with royal connections. He has done everything possible to ensure that you learn the social etiquette befitting someone of your station and have the best possible education. You speak Urdu with an upper-class accent and also fluent English. It is more important for you to develop the good dress sense you have learned in Bhopal, so that you can wear the right outfits for every occasion."

Bashir Ali, Rabia Begum's father, had married a beautiful woman from a wealthy family without royal connections. Afterward, he felt it would be wiser to set up his business outside Bhopal, so he moved with his family to Ujjain, a small town completely unlike the bustling metropolis of Bhopal, and started a jewelry business there. Bashir Ali's wife was unhappy there, far away from her family and friends, and died five years later. Rabia Begum had few memories of her mother.

After his wife's death, Rabia Begum's father employed a nanny to care for her and sent her to the only school for Muslim girls in Mirzawari, where she met Gulshan. When she was eight, her father took Rabia Begum to Bhopal and left her with a sister of her mother's, who had a daughter about the same age. He arranged for tutors to the Bhopal royal family to give both girls private lessons not only in academic subjects, but also in etiquette. In their spare time, the girls learned to play chess, which Rabia Begum really enjoyed.

Rabia Begum was ten years old when she returned to Ujjain to live with her father, accompanied by a chaperone, Nur Jehan Begum, who was a well-educated widow from a good family. She rejoined the Mirzawari Muslim girls' school and renewed her friendship with Gulshan. Two years later, Rabia Begum and Gulshan took the Middle School Examination of the Ajmer Board. Both girls passed and Rabia Begum went on to study for the Intermediate Examination at the Maharajwada High School.

One day, Gulshan met up with Rabia Begum. "Mother and I have just been to the annual Gaunkri Festival at Gaunkrigaon," she said enthusiastically.

"What's that?" asked Rabia Begum.

"Each year, there is a one-week festival in an open field near the village. Farmers from the surrounding villages bring their produce and animals to the field to sell in the *haat*, the open-air market. On the last day of the festival, there is a *gaunkri*-making examination for unmarried girls in and around the village."

"How do you make the *gaunkris*?"

"First, we knead flour with water until it is ready to shape into round balls a little larger than tennis balls. After flattening them slightly, they are ready to be placed in the ashes of fires made of dried *gober* or cow dung," Gulshan replied. "Mother has registered me to take part in this examination next year. She is teaching me how to make the dough for *gaunkris* and cook *toor dal* or yellow lentils to go with them. I can't bake the *gaunkris* properly here, as there aren't many cows in Mirzawari."

- - - - - - - - - - - - - - - - - - - -

At one of the monthly social gatherings at Yousuf Ali Sahib's bungalow, Gulshan's parents, Kaleem Beg and Batul, invited everyone there to visit them in Gaunkrigaon on the last day of the Gaunkri Festival, to watch Gulshan taking part in the *gaunkri*-making examination.

"I should love to go to the Gaunkri Festival," said Rabia Begum to Nur Jehan.

"Very well, you may go with the ladies from the Lawyers' Den," answered her chaperone.

On the day that Gulshan was due to take part in the festival, a group of people from the Lawyers' Den and Mirzawari joined Kaleem Beg and Rashid at the Ujjain railway station, to take the small steam train to Gaunkrigaon. The group included Yousuf Ali Sahib and his wife, Mrs. Waheeda Begum, Mrs. Adiba Hassan, Tara Bibi, Rabia Begum, Kismet, Kausar, Umer, and Tiddi. A couple of teachers and Nawab also decided to go. The 24 mile journey took two and a half hours, with stops at every small village station. Refreshments of tea and *pakorey* were offered, and were very popular with the passengers.

The villagers at Gaunkrigaon had arranged front row seats on the open field for Batul's party from Ujjain, so they had a good view of the *gaunkri*-making examination.

"I have to go and help Gulshan make the final preparations for her examination," Batul explained, as she and Gulshan got ready to leave the group.

"What sort of preparations does she have to make?" asked Kismet.

"We came to Gaunkrigaon two weeks ago, so that Gulshan could collect fresh *gober* or cow dung, shape it into round slabs, and leave it to dry on the mud walls of our family's house. Today, we are going home so that she can prepare *toor dal* or yellow lentils to cook in front of the judges. This is part of the examination. Later, she will serve the *toor dal* to the judges together with eight freshly baked *gaunkris*, small round cakes of dough about one and a quarter inches thick and three inches in diameter."

The Ujjain party watched the activities on the competition field with mounting interest, as the girls each built a pyramid of dry cow dung slabs and burned it under the supervision of two female and two male judges, all of whom had many years' experience in tasting *gaunkris*. When the fires had burned down, each girl buried the round uncooked *gaunkris* in the hot ashes, first poking each one on top with her index finger to form a navel, and then left them there for about 20 to 25 minutes.

"Look! The girls are taking the *gaunkris* out of the cow dung ashes with tongs and putting them on plates to cool," said Kausar to Kismet.

"Some of them are dusting the ashes off each *gaunkri* with their bare hands," said Kismet.

"There's Gulshan!" exclaimed Mrs. Waheeda Begum. "She's taking a large plate of *gaunkris* and yellow lentils to the judges for tasting,

"I do hope she passes," said Mrs. Adiba Hassan.

Some time later, Batul came over to the group from Ujjain smiling happily. "She's passed! Gulshan has passed the *gaunkri*-making examination with distinction," she informed them with pride. "She got 80 percent and she will be awarded a certificate."

"How do the judges decide whether the *gaunkris* are well made?" asked Yousuf Ali Sahib's wife.

"Each *gaunkri* should be brown on the outside and cooked right through inside," replied Batul. "*Ghee* is poured over them and they are served with cooked *toor daal* to which *ghee* and fried garlic have been added. The fried garlic should be brown but not burned. This dish is very popular here."

"What about the girls who fail the examination?" asked Kausar.

"If they get less than 30 percent, they can take the examination again the following year," answered Batul.

Later, the judges sent over plates of *gaunkris* and yellow lentils to the people from Ujjain, so that they could try this village specialty for themselves. Afterward, several village women came over to speak to the ladies from Ujjain. "Gulshan passed the examination with distinction just like her mother Batul," one told them.

The villagers took the Ujjain party to see the *haat* and the fields around Gaunkrigaon. The people from Ujjain returned home loaded with *gaunkris* made by the villagers for all the guests from Ujjain, and many happy memories. Batul was satisfied that Gulshan would now have a better chance of getting married.

However, when Batul took Gulshan for another visit to Gaunkrigaon for a couple of weeks to look for a suitable marriage partner, she was unable to find anyone. Despite Gulshan's success in the *gaunkri*-making examination, the village boys and their families considered Gulshan to be too well educated to fit in with them.

- - - - - - - - - - - - - - - - - - - -

Rabia Begum showed a keen interest in jewelry from an early age. Her father Bashir Ali taught her the names of the precious stones and how to recognize them. When she was older, Rabia Begum visited her father's shop in Ujjain and attended to his lady customers, advising them on jewelry to suit their particular styles. Rabia Begum had impeccable taste in fashion and the ladies were more than happy to let her help them choose gold and silver jewelry for engagements and weddings.

Bashir Ali was now highly successful, with a jewelry shop in the main shopping center of Ujjain, which he managed personally, as well as a large chain of jewelry shops all over Central India. These were run by reliable local employees, their relatives, and family friends.

When Rabia Begum visited Bhopal with Bashir Ali, her

extensive knowledge of precious stones and jewelry made her popular with aristocrats and members of the royal family. The ladies at the social gatherings at Yousuf Ali Sahib's bungalow were equally interested in hearing Rabia Begum talking about jewelry and called her "Nagina" -- precious stone.

In due course, Bashir Ali went to Bhopal to ask his sister there to make inquiries on his behalf for a suitable husband for Rabia Begum. He wanted someone who would live in Ujjain with Rabia Begum after marriage and eventually take over the jewelry shop in Ujjain as well as managing the chain of jewelry shops in Central India. Bashir Ali's sister did as she was asked, but without success.

- - - - - - - - - - - - - - - - - - - -

When Yousuf Ali Sahib's social gatherings and poetry readings were not being held, the young men and boys in Mirzawari used one of two adjoining rooms in the bungalow for regular meetings of their chess club. At one of the social gatherings, Rabia Begum spoke to the ladies and suggested that they too should start their own chess club. It was decided that the women and girls could play chess on the same day as the men and boys, in the room next door to them. Halim Nawaz and a teacher from the girls' school agreed to come and referee the games.

Some time later, one of the teachers came up with the idea of chess tournaments between the men's and women's chess clubs. This proved to be very popular and the membership of both clubs increased. People from the clubs began to drift together after the games and groups with common interests gradually formed.

Rabia Begum and Gulshan regularly attended the women's chess club meetings. Gulshan's brother Rashid and his friend Nawab played chess in the men's club. All four met up after the meetings and walked home together. Rabia Begum had grown into a tall, slim, elegant young woman. Gulshan was also slim and beautiful, of medium height, and fair skinned. Rashid was taller than Rabia Begum with fair skin like his sister. He always wore a silk *kameez* over a plain cotton *shalwar* with a small black hat on his head. Nawab was the complete opposite to Rashid. He was fat and dark-skinned, slightly shorter than Gulshan, and wore glasses with thick frames and lenses.

The two sets of friends were drawn together by their common interest in chess. After the meetings, they would discuss the various games and tactics used. Gradually, they began to find out more about each other's interests.

Rashid enjoyed listening to Rabia Begum's descriptions of precious stones and watching the way her face lit up when she spoke about jewelry. He was also fascinated by her Bhopal accent acquired in royal circles. Rashid spoke little and to the point, in a village accent picked up at home from his parents. His interests included sports, particularly football and hockey. Rabia Begum felt relaxed with Rashid. She found herself becoming increasingly attracted to him and gradually became aware of an understanding growing between them.

Nawab spoke at length to Gulshan about the attractions of Bombay and his trips there. "There are many fine shops in Bombay selling goods from all over India and other countries. The night life is great -- bright lights, restaurants, and hotels, always lots going on, not dead like Ujjain."

Nawab rubbed his stomach and smacked his lips with relish.

Gulshan described the various dishes she enjoyed cooking, particularly *gaunkris* and yellow lentils. Nawab was less interested in hearing about the relatives she met on her trips to Gaunkrigaon.

- - - - - - - - - - - - - - - - - - - -

Bashir Ali was starting to think seriously about Rabia Begum's marriage prospects and discussed it with her chaperone, Nur Jehan Begum. "We need to find a boy with the right background and of a similar social standing to our family," he told her. "None of the boys in Bhopal wants to come to Ujjain.

Do you know anyone suitable here?"

"I will ask the go-between, Tara Bibi, if she knows of anybody suitable," replied Nur Jehan Begum.

The next day, Nur Jehan Begum went to see Tara Bibi and posed the question to her.

"There is only one boy of the right age and status here in Ujjain," replied Tara Bibi after some thought.

"Who is that?" asked Nur Jehan Begum.

"Nazaruddin, also known as Nawab. He is the son of Faqiruddin, the property tycoon."

"Can you tell me more about him?"

"He loves eating and hates working."

Nur Jehan's face fell. "Do you think he might change after marriage?" she asked.

"*Kuttey ki dum ko bhonglee mein daalkar bara saal baad nikalo phir bhee tairhee rahaigee*," replied Tara Bibi. "You can keep a dog's tail in a straight tube for 12 years and it will still stay crooked. He will never change. However, he will inherit his father's money and a good business, so your girl will always be well off."

That evening, Nur Jehan Begum informed Bashir Ali of a possible match for Rabia Begum. "His name is Nazaruddin or Nawab. His father Faqiruddin is a property tycoon and he is the only son, so he will be very wealthy one day."

"Yes, I have heard of his father," replied Bashir Ali. "He owns many properties and commercial buildings in Ujjain. Tell Tara Bibi that I would be interested in this match for my daughter."

Nur Jehan Begum went to see Tara Bibi once again. "Please inform Faqiruddin and his wife that it would give Bashir Ali great pleasure to strengthen the bonds of friendship between his family and theirs," she said to Tara Bibi. "You may also let them know that any approach to Bashir Ali regarding his daughter Rabia Begum would be favorably considered."

In due course, Nur Jehan Begum received the following verbal message from Faqiruddin through Tara Bibi: "We are greatly honored to learn that your family wishes to become more closely linked with ours. Our son Nazaruddin is in Bombay at present. We will send you our formal reply in writing as soon as we have spoken to him."

Bashir Ali assumed from this that Faqiruddin's family was in favor of the engagement and immediately asked Nur Jehan Begum to help him draw up a guest list of his close relatives and friends for the engagement party of Rabia Begum and Nawab.

- - - - - - - - - - - - - - - - - - - -

On Nawab's return from Bombay, his parents called him into the sitting room. The maidservant brought them tea and left. "Nawab, we have some very good news for you," said his father Faqiruddin, beaming happily. "Tara Bibi, the go-between, has informed us that Bashir Ali, who owns several jewelry shops, would be in favor of a proposal on your behalf for the hand of his daughter Rabia Begum in marriage."

"He is an aristocrat and has royal connections in Bhopal," his mother Sakina put in. "We will rise socially through our connection with him."

"Oh no!" groaned Nawab. "I can't possibly marry Rabia Begum."

His parents were aghast. "Why not? This is a golden opportunity for us to establish ourselves in the upper level of society here," said his mother.

"I want to marry Gulshan," replied Nawab.

"You mean Gulshan, the daughter of my employee Kaleem Beg?" asked his father, amazed.

Nawab reddened. "Yes," he answered quietly.

"Rabia Begum has a far better family background than Gulshan," said Sakina. "She will also inherit her father's jewelry empire later on."

"Rabia Begum and Rashid like each other," Nawab replied. "I want to marry Gulshan," he repeated.

"Oh dear, what will we do?" wailed Nawab's mother. "What can we possibly say to Bashir Ali's family?"

"Gulshan's father works for me in my property business. His social level is much lower than ours," said Faqiruddin. "My standing in society is high. I cannot possibly allow you to marry Gulshan. Think about it overnight."

Nawab rose and left the room without speaking.

Nawab did not join his parents for breakfast the following day and his mother went to his room to speak to him.

"Have you thought about your future?" she asked.

"I want to marry Gulshan," stated Nawab.

"I'll tell your father," said his mother.

Sakina came downstairs just as Faqiruddin was about to leave for the office.

"Has the boy seen sense yet?" he asked her.

"He still wants to marry Gulshan," she replied.

Faqiruddin sighed. "I suppose we'll just have to accept it."

He went to his desk, took out some paper, and clumsily penned the following letter to Bashir Ali, in his uneducated scrawl:

My Dear Sir,

We are honored that you consider joining our two families together. However, I regretfully inform you that my son Nazaruddin is not yet ready to settle down, as he is immature for his age. We appreciate once again your kind offer.

Yours very sincerely,

Faqiruddin

Faqiruddin put the note into an envelope, addressed it, and passed it to his wife. "Call the go-between, give her this letter, and ask her to take it to Bashir Ali," he said.

When Tara Bibi arrived, Sakina gave her the letter for Bashir Ali and asked her to have a quiet word with Nur Jehan Begum. "Please tell her that we are very conscious of the chance being offered to our son to make such a fine marriage. However, he is unlikely to settle down for several years."

Tara Bibi passed on Sakina's verbal message to Nur Jehan Begum together with Faqiruddin's letter for Bashir Ali. Nur Jehan Begum made no reply.

The day after Tara Bibi's visit, Nur Jehan Begum invited some ladies from the Lawyers' Den around for tea.

"I have heard that Nawab, Faqiruddin's son, wants to marry Gulshan, the daughter of Kaleem Beg, his father's employee," she announced.

Everyone was surprised.

"Gulshan comes from a nice family and she is educated," said Mrs. Adiba Hassan. "She will fit in well with that family."

"Nawab will enjoy eating *gaunkris* made by someone so well qualified," Mrs. Waheeda Begum added.

"Yes, you're right," said Nur Jehan Begum. She began to feel a little happier.

- - - - - - - - - - - - - - - - - - - -

Word of the hoped-for engagement between Nawab and Gulshan gradually spread around Mirzawari.

One day Faqiruddin came home from the office and told Sakina to ask Nawab to join them in the sitting room. "Someone has spoken of our private family business outside this house," Faqiruddin said, looking at Nawab. "Everyone in our neighborhood seems to know that we hope to arrange a match between you and Gulshan."

Nawab shifted uncomfortably in his chair, reddening slightly, and looked down.

"Your mother and I have been discussing this matter," his father continued. "Gulshan is educated just like Rabia Begum and also has domestic skills. She knows how to mix in good society, so she would fit in well with our family."

Nawab's face lit up. "Then will you let me marry Gulshan, father?"

"Yes, we will agree to this marriage," his father replied. His mother nodded her head.

Faqiruddin sent a message through Tara Bibi to Kaleem Beg asking if he and his wife Batul would agree to marry their daughter Gulshan to his son Nawab. Their reply soon came. "We are delighted to accept your proposal for the marriage of your son Nazaruddin to our daughter Gulshan," Kaleem Beg wrote.

Later, Sakina invited some ladies from Yousuf Ali Sahib's monthly social gatherings to her house. After tea and light refreshments had been served, she announced her good news: "Kaleem Beg and his wife Batul have agreed to the marriage of their daughter Gulshan to our Nawab. We are arranging their engagement and wedding parties and you and your families are all invited."

There was a buzz of congratulations.

Shortly afterward, Faqiruddin was in the office with his

property manager, Kaleem Beg. "The forthcoming marriage of Nawab and Gulshan will bring happiness to both our families," he said. "I have heard that your son Rashid is also ready for marriage."

"What do you mean?" asked Kaleem Beg.

"Rashid is very friendly with Rabia Begum, the daughter of Bashir Ali."

Kaleem Beg was taken by surprise. "I didn't know that."

"Speak to your son tonight," Faqiruddin urged. "See what he says. If he loves the girl, then you can send a marriage proposal to her father."

"Rashid is looking for a job," said Kaleem Beg.

"Let's interview him tomorrow, and if it goes well, he can start work here tomorrow," replied Faqiruddin. "You can teach him the property business. This will reduce your workload."

"He will be delighted to work for you. I will tell him the good news tonight."

"Don't forget to ask Rashid about Rabia Begum at the same time."

"Yes, Faqiruddin Sahib."

That evening, Kaleem Beg told Rashid that Faqiruddin had offered to hire him if his interview goes well. "There's one more thing," Kaleem Beg added. "I've heard that you are friendly with Bashir Ali's daughter, Rabia Begum."

"Yes, father," replied Rashid.

"Let's see how your job interview goes, then we will speak of this again," his father answered.

The following day, Rashid accompanied his father to the office wearing his best suit, shirt, and tie with brightly polished shoes. They arrived half an hour early. Kaleem Beg showed his son around the office where he would be working and learning the property business if his job interview with Faqiruddin was successful.

Rashid was very nervous about the coming interview and went to the toilet to put some last-minute touches to his appearance. First, he looked into the mirror above the washbasin and adjusted his tie. Then he patted his shoulders to remove any particles of dust, shook the dust off his hands, and looked down at his shoes. Their shine was slightly clouded.

"No problem," said Rashid to himself. He took an old handkerchief from his left hand trouser pocket and rinsed one corner under the tap. Then he put each foot in turn on the side of the toilet seat, dusted the shoe with the dry part of the handkerchief, wiped it with the damp part and then wiped it once again with the dry part. Finally, he spat on each shoe and gave it a last wipe with the handkerchief to bring out the shine. He left the toilet with confidence, completely satisfied that his whole appearance was immaculate for this, the first and most important career interview in his life.

At about 10 a.m. Faqiruddin came to his office, ordered the messenger to bring *chai*, and sat down at his desk. Kaleem Beg knocked at the door and entered.

"My son Rashid is here," he said.

"Good," answered Faqiruddin. "Send him in on your way out."

Rashid entered the office.

"*Salam*, Faqiruddin Sahib," he said.

"Come here, Rashid," came the reply. "Take a seat."

Faqiruddin leaned back in his chair. "Your father has been working with me for many years," he said. "I hope you will be as hard working as he is. You will have to go out a lot to visit the clients. You must also keep the records of all my properties fully updated and coordinate your work with my accountant and the rest of the office staff. Do you think you can do this job?"

"Yes, sir," said Rashid.

"Very good," said Faqiruddin. He rose and shook hands with Rashid. "You can start work now. Go to your father in his office and send him in to me."

"Yes, sir, thank you, sir," replied Rashid.

"Ah, Kaleem Beg," said Faqiruddin, as he entered the room. "Did you speak to your son regarding Rabia Begum?"

"Yes, Faqiruddin Sahib. Rashid is very friendly with her, but I am not sure whether her father would accept a marriage proposal for Rabia Begum from our family on his behalf."

"Rashid is now working for me as an assistant property manager," replied Faqiruddin. "He is in a good position for Bashir Ali to consider him as a suitor for Rabia Begum."

"Very well, I will write to Bashir Ali."

- - - - - - - - - - - - - - - - - - - -

Kaleem Beg accordingly sent a message to Bashir Ali through Tara Bibi asking for the hand of Rabia Begum in marriage to his son Rashid, assistant property manager in Faqiruddin's property business.

When he received Kaleem Beg's letter, Bashir Ali was furious. He showed it to Nur Jehan Begum.

"These people are only villagers and live in a rented bungalow," said Nur Jehan Begum scornfully. "What makes them think that their son is a match for our Nagina?"

Bashir Ali sent the following reply to Kaleem Beg: "I will never marry my daughter to your son, so do not approach me again." Then he asked Nur Jehan Begum to speak to Rabia Begum about this matter.

Nur Jehan Begum went to see Rabia Begum in her bedroom. "I believe you have been meeting Rashid at the chess club," she said.

Rabia Begum lowered her eyes. "Yes, it is true," she replied.

"Your father wants to speak to you about this."

Nur Jehan Begum immediately informed Bashir Ali of what Rabia Begum had just said. He stormed upstairs, banged on Rabia Begum's bedroom door, and burst into the room. She was sitting on the edge of her bed. "Nur Jehan Begum tells me that you have been seeing Rashid," he said. "This is most unbecoming behavior for a lady of your family background. You are an aristocrat in every way. Rashid's father is just a villager who is employed by Faqiruddin. He has no standing in our society. You have brought shame on our family name. There is also one more thing. "

Rabia Begum looked up at her father and waited, biting her lip.

"Recently, I approached Faqiruddin to propose a marriage between you and his son Nazaruddin. He sent me a refusal. It would be degrading for me to accept this proposal from Kaleem Beg on behalf of his son Rashid. It is a conspiracy by Faqiruddin to insult me and my family."

Rabia Begum lowered her eyes and drew her *dupatta* over her head.

"What do you want of me, father?" she asked in a low voice.

"Promise me that you will never marry Rashid," came the reply. "Always remember, we come from a royal family."

"I promise, father," Rabia Begum answered solemnly. "I will always strive to keep our family honor intact."

Faqiruddin invited several families from Yousuf Ali Sahib's social club to attend the wedding of his son Nazaruddin to Gulshan, the daughter of Kaleem Beg, his property manager. "Your relatives from Gaunkrigaon will also be most welcome," Faqiruddin graciously informed Kaleem Beg. "Please do not hesitate to invite them."

"Gulshan is a most accomplished girl," Sakina told her friends. "She is educated and her domestic skills will be an asset to our family."

"We will not attend the wedding of Nazaruddin," Bashir Ali informed Nur Jehan Begum. "His father is an arrogant social climber who has insulted our family by his refusal to marry his son to our Rabia."

Rabia Begum selected a beautiful necklace from the jewelry shop and quietly gave it to Gulshan after one of the meetings at the social club. "This is a wedding present from me to you," she told Gulshan. "I am very sorry that I will be unable to attend your wedding."

"Thank you, Rabia," said Gulshan. "I will miss you at my wedding but I fully understand your circumstances."

- - - - - - - - - - - - - - - - - - - -

Soon after the wedding, Faqiruddin spoke to his son. "Now you are a married man with responsibilities. You must come and work in my office."

"I'll start next month," Nawab replied.

"You'll come in to the office first thing on Monday morning," Faqiruddin said firmly.

Faqiruddin showed Nawab the property books and explained which properties were likely to increase in value and which ones should be sold when the time was right. "Always look out for any property for sale in the commercial area," Faqiruddin told his son. Consult the accountant and the property managers before buying or selling any properties. Learn as much as you can about the property business from them. When you and Rashid have gained enough experience, you will both be working together with the accountant. However, the final decision will always be yours."

Nawab was happy that his father thought so highly of him and went regularly to work each day.

Gulshan adjusted well to married life and willingly did her share of the household chores. She enjoyed cooking and supervised the kitchen staff very well. The visitors to Faqiruddin's house frequently complimented their hostess on the good food they were served. Sakina came to realize that, although Gulshan came from a village background, she was indeed an asset to their family due to her education and domestic skills.

- - - - - - - - - - - - - - - - - - - -

Rashid settled down well in his new job. He visited clients with properties for sale and kept the records up-to-date. He was soon able to describe in detail the localities of properties available for sale or rent. Clients visiting the office would speak to Rashid before making a final decision.

"Your future is well assured," said Kaleem Beg to Rashid one day as they were walking home. "Have you thought about getting married? Your mother will make inquiries in Gaunkrigaon on your behalf if you wish."

"I have no plans for marriage at the moment," came the reply.

Kaleem Beg remembered Bashir Ali's refusal to marry his daughter Rabia Begum to Rashid and said no more, struck by the sadness in Rashid's voice.

Soon, Gulshan was expecting a baby. Nawab accompanied his wife and her mother Batul to Gaunkrigaon to stay with relatives for the birth of the child and was back at work a week later.

A month later, Gulshan gave birth to a healthy baby boy, Fahim, and remained in Gaunkrigaon for a further two months with her mother. During that time, Nawab and his mother Sakina visited them regularly.

"How would you like us to have a place of our own in Gaunkrigaon?" Nawab asked Gulshan on one of his visits.

"That would be lovely," she replied. "Then I wouldn't have to stay with my relatives each time I come there."

"There is a two-bedroom house for sale in the village. Come and see it with me tomorrow."

The following day, Nawab and Gulshan looked over the house and liked it. That evening they mentioned it to Gulshan's relatives.

"We will look after the house for you when you are not there," said one of her uncles.

Nawab spoke to the man selling the house and made him an offer subject to his father's approval. The seller agreed, as everyone in Gaunkrigaon knew of his father, Faqiruddin the property tycoon.

On his return to Ujjain, Nawab told his mother that he had made an offer for a house in Gaunkrigaon. "It was very cheap," he said with satisfaction.

"I will speak to your father tonight," his mother replied. "That house can be your holiday home. Property prices in most villages are much cheaper than in Ujjain."

That evening, when Faqiruddin learned that Nawab had made an offer on a house in Gaunkrigaon subject to his approval, he was somewhat hesitant, fearing that Nawab would spend more time there and less time in the office. However, he finally agreed with Sakina that it would be a good holiday home for Nawab and his family, as Gulshan's relatives were prepared to keep an eye on the house when no one was there. Soon afterward, the house purchase was completed on behalf of Nawab.

A year later, Gulshan was expecting her second child. Nawab suggested that she might like to stay in their holiday home in Gaunkrigaon with Fahim and Batul and be near her relatives when the child was born. He told his parents of his plan.

"I will go to the village two weeks before Gulshan, Batul, and Fahim," he said. "Then I can have the house repaired and decorated in preparation for their arrival and come back afterward to fetch them. I will need money to have this work done."

"That is not a good idea," his father replied. "You should all go together to Gaunkrigaon. I will give you money for the house renovations. Gulshan, Batul, and Fahim can stay with their relatives, while you stay in the house and supervise the property repairs and decoration. When the work is complete, you will come straight back to the office."

- - - - - - - - - - - - - - - - - - - -

"I need to go to Bombay to look for business opportunities," Nawab told Gulshan soon after their arrival in Gaunkrigaon. "I'll be back in a couple of weeks. Then I'll see to the house repairs."

"Does your father know about this?" asked Gulshan.

"No, I want to give him a surprise," Nawab replied. He took a thick bundle of rupee notes from his leather bag and handed them to Gulshan for household expenses.

Nawab was not there when Gulshan's second child was born a week later and only returned to Gaunkrigaon two weeks after the birth of his child.

Gulshan greeted him. "We have a fine healthy son," she said. "His name is Amir."

"Good, good," answered Nawab. "Let us go to Ujjain and introduce him to our family."

"What about the decorations to our house here?" asked Gulshan.

"Never mind that now. It can be done later."

When Nawab and his family arrived home, his mother was there to greet them. After admiring little Amir, she asked a servant to take their luggage upstairs. "Join me in the reception room when you are ready," she told Nawab. "Gulshan, you can take the children into the kitchen and feed them there."

"What's been happening?" demanded Nawab's mother when he entered the room. "Your father is very angry. He has heard rumors that you went to Bombay, leaving Gulshan and Fahim in Gaunkrigaon; and that you were in Bombay when your son was born. He has told you so many times, 'Don't go to Bombay.' He also wants to know what you did with all the money he gave you for repairs and decorations to the house in Gaunkrigaon. Has this work been done?"

Just then Faqiruddin stormed into the reception room. "What's all this I've heard about you?" he burst out, addressing Nawab. "You leave your wife and son in Gaunkrigaon and you travel to Bombay. Why did you go to Bombay?"

"I went to look for a business opportunity in Bombay, so that we can expand our business there," replied Nawab calmly. "I have found a two-bedroom flat in Bombay. It will be a very good investment. We can buy it now and sell it later at a profit."

"This is the most foolish business talk I have ever heard," shouted Faqiruddin. "Tell me, where do you think you can get the kind of money you need to buy a flat in Bombay?"

"Oh, we can sell those two large buildings next to your office."

"You fool, if you sell those buildings, you will destroy our business."

Nawab's mother interrupted them. "You have not

answered my question yet, Nawab. What did you do with all the money you took to Gaunkrigaon?"

"I had to stay in Bombay to look for a business opportunity, so I spent it there," replied Nawab.

Faqiruddin was furious. "Who asked you to look for a business opportunity in Bombay and who would look after a flat for us in Bombay?"

"I will live there in one bedroom, rent the other for income, and look for more opportunities to expand your business," replied Nawab.

"There are many opportunities in Bombay, but only for spending money, not for earning money," said Faqiruddin. "What do you want to do in Bombay? It is a very expensive city to live in, and who will run our property business?" he asked angrily.

"But father, I want to buy this flat in Bombay. Bombay is expanding fast and there are a lot of really good openings in Bombay. This is the best chance to start up a business in Bombay."

Faqiruddin was infuriated to hear "Bombay, Bombay, Bombay" again and again from Nawab. "Don't you ever mention Bombay to me again, *sower ka bacha*, you piglet," he shouted. "Get this Bombay fever out of your body and out of your brain. You abandoned your wife and family in the house in Gaunkrigaon and you were not even there for the birth of your second child. You are never ever going to Bombay again. Leave this house at once and never set foot in it again, otherwise I will break your legs, you *kuttey ka bacha*, you puppy."

Nawab and his mother were stunned. Nawab immediately left the room and went to his bedroom.

"There is no transport to Gaunkrigaon at this time of night," said Sakina to her husband. "Let the boy stay here overnight and I will make sure that he gets up in time to take the first train to Gaunkrigaon tomorrow morning."

"I don't want to see him in this house again," shouted Faqiruddin.

Sakina went upstairs to speak to her son. Nawab was packing his bag. "The first train to Gaunkrigaon leaves Ujjain at 7 o'clock in the morning," she told him. "The servant will see that you get up in time to catch it." She took some money from the *batwa* (cloth bag) in her hand and gave it to him. "Here is money. Make sure that all the work on the house in Gaunkrigaon is completed in the shortest possible time."

On his arrival in Gaunkrigaon, Nawab spoke to one of Gulshan's uncles and asked him to arrange for the necessary repairs and decorations to be done to his family's holiday home there. The men knew Gulshan's relatives, so they worked well and soon completed all the work. Afterward, Nawab brought Gulshan and their sons to join him in the house in Gaunkrigaon and provided for them with money given quietly to him by his mother.

Some time later, Sakina persuaded Faqiruddin to go with her to Gaunkrigaon to see their grandchildren. Nawab apologized to his parents for his behavior and Faqiruddin asked him to come back to the office and make a fresh start. A few days after Faqiruddin and Sakina returned home, Nawab brought his family back to Ujjain to live with his parents.

Before Nawab started work, Faqiruddin called him into his office. "You must come in to work punctually each day," he told his son. "You will also get a fixed salary for the days you work and no more holidays."

Nawab agreed to these requirements. He went regularly to the office each day, due largely to the efforts of Gulshan and Sakina to ensure that he left the house on time. Faqiruddin was pleased to see that Nawab appeared to have changed his ways.

Rabia continued to visit her friend Gulshan accompanied by Nur Jehan Begum. She loved playing with Gulshan's little boys Fahim and Amir, and brought them each a set of beautifully sewn clothes for *Eid-ul-Fitr*.

The parents of Gulshan's father, Kaleem Beg, moved to Jalgaon to live with one of their sons. When Amir was two years old, they invited Nawab, Gulshan, and their two boys to stay with them. Sakina mentioned the invitation to Faqiruddin and he agreed to let Nawab accompany his family on the three-day train journey to Jalgaon, stay there for a week, and then bring them back to Ujjain.

"I will expect you back in the office in two weeks' time," Faqiruddin told his son.

Nawab looked forward to visiting Jalgaon, as he had heard that the village was not far from Bombay.

Gulshan's grandparents were delighted to see their great grandchildren and proudly showed them off to everyone who came to visit them. Their friends and relatives also invited Gulshan and her sons to their homes. All the women made a fuss over Fahim and Amir and the other children loved playing with them. Nawab had never been to Jalgaon before and spent a lot of time exploring the village with Gulshan's cousins.

One day, while wandering around Jalgaon with one of Gulshan's cousins, Nawab saw a group of people on a patch of open ground. They were watching a man selling *kajal*, a black paste smeared inside the eyelids. "Use this regularly and it will improve your eyesight within a week," he was telling the crowd.

"That's all lies," shouted a man at the back. He pushed his way forward. "I bought this stuff from you a week ago," he said holding up a small tin. "It's made no difference to my eyesight, none at all."

"Come here," said the salesman. "Open both this man's eyes, one at a time" he told his assistant. The salesman examined each eye thoroughly.

"Did you put a drop of camel's milk in each eye before using my *kajal*?" he asked the man. (Camel's milk was not available in that area).

"No," came the reply. "You never told me that before."

"You didn't tell me your problem," replied the salesman. He turned to his audience. "Look, this man has a big problem with his eyes and he's trying to blame me."

Everyone started to laugh and the man quickly fled.

Another man stepped forward. "I can't get ahold of camel's milk for my eyes," he said.

The salesman examined the man's eyes. "You don't have the same problem as that stupid man. Just use this *kajal* each morning for two weeks and you will be able to see all the seven skies." The crowd laughed.

"Any one else want their eyes examining?" asked the salesman. He sold four more tins of *kajal* and then packed up his goods and left.

Two weeks later, Nawab brought his family back to Ujjain and returned to work. He began to take a particular interest in the sales side of the property business, as he felt that selling property would be the best way to achieve his dream of returning to Bombay.

- - - - - - - - - - - - - - - - - - - -

Bashir Ali's health began to fail. He was no longer able to spend so much time on running his shops outside Ujjain and business started to fall off. He was forced to sell his shops one by one. Once more, his thoughts turned to finding a suitable husband for Rabia Begum. He traveled to Bhopal and stayed with his sister who, once again, made inquiries on his behalf, to no avail.

Rabia Begum took over her father's business in Ujjain. She set up a section of the jewelry shop for ladies only and engaged two ladies part-time to attend to the clients. Rabia Begum was always on hand to offer advice when needed and deal with special clients. This innovation was the first of its kind and was very popular with the ladies in Ujjain and the surrounding area. They felt more at ease when buying jewelry in a ladies-only section and business soon began to increase.

Some time after her father had left for Bhopal, Rabia Begum received the following telegram from her aunt: "Last night your father had a stroke and died. Please come."

When Rabia Begum informed her of this sad news, Nur Jehan Begum expressed her condolences. "I will come with you to Bhopal," she said. "However, I am getting older and I would like to remain there now. I have a friend in Bhopal who could come and live with you as a chaperone in my place."

After the funeral, Nur Jehan Begum sent a message to her friend Khalida, who came to visit Rabia Begum at her aunt's house. Khalida was a widow, a retired nurse who had worked in the local hospital for many years. She agreed to take on the duties of chaperone to Rabia Begum and live with her in Ujjain.

On her return to Ujjain, Rabia Begum continued to run her father's jewelry business. She also attended the ladies-only social club from time to time together with Khalida. The club members all knew of the long-established friendship and unspoken love between Rabia Begum and Rashid and felt the deepest respect for feelings so pure that were doomed to remain unfulfilled. Many of them invited both Rabia Begum and Rashid to their houses. One lady, Mrs. Adiba Hassan, once offered to act as mother to Rabia Begum and make arrangements for her marriage to Rashid.

"Thank you for your kind offer," Rabia Begum replied. "However, I made a solemn promise to my father many years ago that I would never marry Rashid for the sake of our family honor. I love him, but I cannot break this promise."

"Why did you make such a promise?" asked Mrs. Adiba Hassan.

"This is a deeply private family matter," replied Rabia Begum.

"I understand and I respect your silence," said Mrs. Adiba Hassan. "Come to my house tomorrow afternoon."

The following day, Rabia Begum went to the house in the Lawyers' Den. Mrs. Adiba Hassan and her little son Umer met her at the door and took her upstairs to a large room on the second floor that was not overlooked by any of the other houses. Rashid was already there, sitting motionless and gazing sadly at an empty chair directly opposite him. As Rabia Begum entered the room he rose, greeted her, and indicated the place opposite. Then he slowly took his seat once again.

Mrs. Adiba Hassan and Umer left them and went downstairs. A little later, Mrs. Adiba Hassan made a pot of tea and asked Umer to take it upstairs on a tray along with two cups, milk, sugar, and biscuits. When Umer arrived at the room, the door was open. He saw Rashid and Rabia Begum still sitting on their chairs opposite each other. They were holding hands and whispering together. Umer stood silently watching them. Both turned their gaze toward him and smiled. Then Rashid quickly rose, took the tray from Umer, placed it on a small table at one side, and asked him to thank his mother for the tea and biscuits.

Umer had heard much about the unspoken love between Rabia Begum and Rashid. However, it was the first time that he had seen it for himself. He quickly went downstairs and excitedly told his mother all about it. She smiled and told him not to speak of this to anyone else.

Rabia Begum never married, even though in the following years she received a couple of proposals through Nur Jehan Begum in Bhopal. Some families in Gaunkrigaon approached Rashid with proposals on behalf of their daughters. These were never accepted and Rashid remained single for the rest of his life.

- - - - - - - - - - - - - - - - - - - -

Following the visit to Jalgaon with his family to see

Gulshan's grandparents, Nawab's enthusiasm for his father's property business seemed to be renewed. He reached the office at the same time as the property managers and the accountant each day and carefully studied the lists of properties on his father's books. Many of them were in prime locations in Ujjain, and he went to see some of them. Kaleem Beg and his friend Rashid, his father's property managers, were happy to answer all Nawab's questions concerning the buying and selling of property. Faqiruddin was satisfied that Nawab was finally taking a real interest in his property business, so he decided to take Sakina to Kashmir for three weeks' holiday.

Some days later, Nawab was sitting in his father's office when the accountant entered. "There is a businessman here who wants to buy two of the commercial properties on our books," he told Nawab. "He comes from one of our rivals. Don't sell him the properties now. If you wait, he will make you a better offer. You sold him some property cheaply last time and he knows your father is away on holiday. Wait until your father returns and ask him what he wants to do.

"Send the man in and let me talk to him," said Nawab.

The accountant looked uneasily at Nawab, but he obeyed and left the office, closing the door behind him.

"My father is making me waste my life here in Ujjain," Nawab said to himself. "There are so many properties on his books. If I sell only one or two of them, it won't make the slightest difference to his business here in Ujjain. This is the best time to take the first steps to increase and expand our business in Bombay. I know the value of these properties and I know the property business. I can look around for properties in Bombay."

The businessman entered the office carrying a leather bag.

"I believe you wish to buy two of our commercial properties," Nawab said to him.

"Yes, indeed," answered the businessman. He gave the addresses of both properties, which were in prime positions. "I have the cash here," he added, putting the heavy bag on the table and saying how much it contained. "If you agree, we can complete the deal right away."

Nawab opened the bag and quickly counted the thick rolls of rupee notes. "Very good, I agree," he said. He rose and both men shook hands. Then the businessman handed the money over to Nawab and Nawab gave him a receipt.

"Come back in three days and our accountant will give you the deeds to the properties," Nawab told him.

The following day, Nawab took the overnight train to Bombay, traveling first class. He sat in the compartment tightly clutching a leather bag with the money from the sale of the two properties. He was, as always, immaculately dressed in an expensive suit. "I must get my father to see that if we buy a commercial property in Bombay, it will be far more profitable than a property in Ujjain," he said to himself.

Nawab leaned back in his seat and closed his eyes. He opened them some time later to find that his bag with all the money in it had disappeared. He informed the railway guard, for whom this was a common occurrence and who could do little other than report the theft to the police as usual. Nawab still had a return rail ticket to Ujjain in his pocket and sufficient money to stay in a hotel in Bombay for a few days.

On reaching Bombay, Nawab booked himself into a top class hotel for a few days and sent telegrams to the accountant at his father's office and to Gulshan at home, giving them his address and informing them that he lost his leather bag with the money from the sale of the properties in Ujjain. He wandered the brightly lit Bombay streets in a daze, marveling at the variety of shops with their tempting displays of goods. Rich people and foreigners thronged the paths. He wanted to belong to this place where fast cars drove along the streets, and not bullock carts or camel carts, like on the streets of Ujjain.

On learning of the sale of the two properties, the accountant informed Faqiruddin in Kashmir by telegram.

Faqiruddin immediately returned to Ujjain with his wife. He went to the office in a rage, heard the details from the accountant, and suffered a heart attack.

Nawab's mother sent Nawab a telegram. "Your father has had a heart attack. Come and see him before he dies."

"Coming home now," came Nawab's reply.

Nawab and Gulshan sat with their children and Sakina by Faqiruddin's bed.

"Forgive me for all my mistakes," said Nawab with sincerity to his father, holding Fahim in his arms.

"You must take over the property business now," Faqiruddin replied faintly, gently pinching Fahim's cheeks. "Listen to the advice of the accountant and the property manager." He lay back, exhausted.

Faqiruddin signed to Gulshan to come closer with Amir. He put his hand on her head and pinched Amir's cheeks.

"Thank you for everything," he whispered to her and was still. Sakina gently straightened his pillow and she and Gulshan started to weep loudly.

Nawab took over the property business. Kaleem retired to Jalgaon and Rashid became property manager. Nawab sold some large properties, bought a new leather bag, and asked Aftab, an ex-pickpocket, to come with him on his next business trip to Bombay to ward off thieves.

"I will come with you to Bombay," Aftab told him, "but I want to take the next train back to Ujjain."

As the train drew into Bombay station the following morning, Aftab leaned across to Nawab. "There are two thieves following you," he whispered. "I think you should return to Ujjain with me."

Nawab did not heed this advice. As soon as he left the

station, three men surrounded him. One of them pulled out a knife and another one snatched his bag. Nawab made no resistance and fled empty-handed to a hotel. When his remaining money was gone he returned to Ujjain. Gulshan was angry and sad to see that Nawab's trips away from home simply fed his Bombay fever to spend, spend, spend and brought in no extra income whatsoever. Nawab's mother was also upset to see her only son squandering the family fortune. Soon afterward she died of a broken heart.

On returning from one of his regular trips to Bombay, Nawab arrived at Elephant Gate by *tonga,* wearing a gold wrist watch and carrying a black leather overnight bag. He got down from the *tonga* and paid a generous *bakhshish* to the *tongawala.* Then he entered the Lawyers' Den, smiling to show two gold teeth in the front of his mouth. People crowded around to greet him and Nawab walked around the courtyard a few times. He raised his right hand in greeting, saying "*Salam, Salam, Salam,*" while chewing *paan* and occasionally spitting on the ground.

Contrary to the advice of Rashid and the accountant, Nawab gradually started to sell more properties. When their business rival offered the accountant a job in his business, he accepted. During the following year, Nawab's friend Rashid was forced to sit by and watch as Nawab gradually started to sell off all the properties on his father's books well below their market value. Once he had the money in his hands, Nawab would lavish cash on Gulshan and his family and make regular trips to Bombay. Once there, he didn't do any business. He simply went on spending sprees, living it up in top class hotels, wearing expensive top quality clothes, eating fine food, and traveling everywhere by taxi. When the money ran out, he returned to Ujjain and remained there until he had sold another property. This pattern continued for a couple of years until all the properties had been sold. After that, Rashid accepted a job working for their business rival.

Nawab sent Gulshan and his two sons to their house in Gaunkrigaon. Then he sold his family house, went to Gaunkrigaon to give Gulshan part of the proceeds, and took the next train to Bombay, where he remained until all his money was gone. Rabia regularly arranged for Gulshan and her sons to come and stay with her and Khalida in Ujjain and she would give them clothes and presents.

Eventually, Nawab's money ran out. He was forced to sell the house in Gaunkrigaon. He returned to Ujjain and made arrangements with Aftab to sell all the fine clothes belonging to him and Gulshan. Rabia offered to adopt his elder son, Fahim, and pay for his education. This offer was gratefully accepted by Gulshan, although she was broken hearted at having to part with her firstborn. Fahim slept in Rabia Begum's residence with Khalida looking after him. Nawab knew that if he stayed in Ujjain for a few years, he would be penniless as he was unable to do any sort of work. He therefore left India with the rest of his family to go to Karachi in the newly formed state of Pakistan, hoping to get some sort of clerical work which he would have been ashamed to do in Ujjain.

- - - - - - - - - - - - - - - - - - - -

Nawab earned his living in Karachi sitting on the footpath by the passport office every day, filling in passport application forms together with others competing for the same task. Each morning, he came there by rickshaw with his typewriter and set it on a small wooden box outside the entrance, with a small sheet over some cardboard on the path behind it, for him to sit on. Afterward he would stand nearby, wearing spectacles with tortoiseshell frames on his round, dark, unshaven face, shouting, "Eh, *chaiwala*! Bring tea! *jhannat chai*, boy! *jhannat chai*! --half tea and half milk boiled together, with two spoonfuls of sugar!"

A young boy standing outside the nearby tea house would then run inside and bring him tea. Nawab would rub his hand around and around his belly beneath his dirty, slightly torn shirt, smiling and shouting, *"Pahlay pait pooja baad mein kaam sujha.* First fill your tummy, then think of work." Then he would laugh loudly.

Rabia, Fahim, and Rashid visited Nawab and his family in

Karachi. Each time, Rabia quietly gave money to Gulshan before they returned to Ujjain.

- -

After some months, Nawab found that he was unable to support his family in Karachi from his earnings, as he typed much more slowly than the other men sitting near him. So he took Gulshan and Amir to Shikarpur, a small village in the hottest part of the Sindh desert, in Pakistan. A poor family who had migrated to Shikarpur, from the servants' quarters of Nawab's father's house in Ujjain, allowed Nawab's family to share their single-storey house. Nawab returned to Karachi and managed to keep himself somehow from the money he made typing forms outside the passport office.

There was a small milk bar just outside the house in Shikarpur, where Gulshan and Amir both worked to earn their keep. Amir collected the used glasses and took them to Gulshan, who washed them in the kitchen behind the shop. Outside the living quarters of the house was a small courtyard with a bathroom in one corner. The bathroom had a stone floor with a well and a hand pump at the center. This provided ice cold water for bathing and washing clothes.

A year later, Nawab developed arthritis and was unable to continue working, so he joined his family in Shikarpur. Shortly afterward, he died penniless. Gulshan followed him a few months later. Amir left Shikarpur and found a job in a shop in Clifton, an upper-class area in Karachi. He rented a small one-bedroom house on the outskirts of Karachi and traveled to work each day by motorbike.

Rabia Begum gave her adopted son Fahim a very good education. He eventually became a prominent and very successful lawyer in Ujjain. Fahim did not attend his parents' funerals, as he had struggled to overcome the sense of rejection at being "farmed out", as he saw it, despite now being old enough to understand the financial difficulties brought upon his family by his father's behavior. He now saw Rabia as his mother. Later,

Fahim went to Karachi to see his younger brother Amir. Amir was living in rented rooms in a poor locality on the outskirts of Karachi, and working as a salesman in a very posh area. Each day, he took two buses to travel to work. Fahim gave his younger brother money to buy a small house in that area, and also a motorcycle to commute to work.

The Indian tapestry is now complete. It will hang forever in the corridors of time, its bright pictures an everlasting memory of events in Mirzawari, Ujjain, and the surrounding area during and after the Second World War up to Indian independence and the founding of Pakistan.

LIST OF CHARACTERS

Chapter 1 – Background

Mrs Adiba Hassan – wife of Waqar Hassan living in the
Lawyers' Den
Blue Silk Lady - a traveling seller of fabrics
Kamal Hammal - a self-made businessman originally from Gharib
Colony
Kausar - a widow living in the Lawyers' Den, Gul Bhai's sister
Khatoon Bibi - a widow and go-between living in Gharib Colony
Kismet - wife of Haider Khan, the Rent Collector living in the
Lawyers' Den
Tara Bibi - a girl from Ghanswara, who later becomes a
go-between
Tara Bibi's parents - outsiders from Aligarh living in Ghanswara
Umer – son of Waqar Hassan and Mrs Adiba Hassan
Mrs Waheeda Begum – mother of Shakil Sahib, Mrs Adiba Hassan
and Halim Nawaz
Waqar Hassan – a solicitor, husband of Mrs Adiba Hassan

Chapter 2 - Shabnum's Wedding

Ahmed Ali Sahib – a rich landlord
Akhtar – son of Shakil Sahib and Mrs. Farah Begum
Akram *tongawala* – *tonga* driver
Asma and Salma – Shabnum's friends
Mrs. Delara Begum – wife of Mirza Sahib
Mr D'Silva – secretary to Governor of Ujjain, Shakil Sahib's friend
Fatima – a widow living in Gharib Colony
Mrs. Farah Begum – wife of Shakil Sahib
Gulzar Khan – a retired security guard living in Gharib Colony
Halim Nawaz – a teacher from the Lawyers' Den
Hasina – a bride-to-be, daughter of Fatima
Mrs. Khadeeja Begum – wife of Ahmed Ali Shah
Khatoon Bibi – a go-between
Mehboob – Talib Sahib's messenger

Mirza Sahib – a rich landlord from Mirzawari
Murad – a bridegroom living in Gharib Colony
Nazir - son of Akram *tongawala*
Samosa Khan – a *samosa* seller
Shabnum – daughter of Mirza Sahib and Mrs. Delara Begum
Shakil Sahib - a prominent lawyer
Shakuri – Murad's bride-to-be, also living in Gharib Colony
Shandar Ali – son of Ahmed Ali Shah and Mrs. Khadeeja
 Begum
Talib Sahib – a lawyer, brother of Mrs. Delara Begum

Chapter 3 - Bride Swap

Adam Beg – bridegroom from Ujjain
Anwar Ali – bridegroom from Ujjain
Bamboowala – a businessman living in Ghanswara
Fayyaz - nicknamed *Machhanddar* (monkey)
Mrs. Jamila Begum – wife of Bamboowala
Latifa Bibi – second wife of Saeed Khan
Niaz – brother of Fayyaz
Nuri – daughter of Saeed Khan's first wife (deceased)
Saeed Khan – landowner living in Ghanswara
Shahida – Nuri's friend
Sara and Rani – daughters of Bamboowala and Mrs. Jamila
 Begum
Shukri Bibi – Nuri's aunt, sister of Nuri's mother

Chapter 4 - Time out with the Tongawalas

Akram *tongawala* – *tonga* driver
Bashira – Chandni's sister living in Khajurpur village
Chandni – Qulfi's friend from Khajurpur village, a
 domestic servant working in the Lawyers' Den
Fazal *cyclewala* – husband of Chandni
Hira Lal *tongawala* –*tonga* driver
Jawwad – Chandni's elder brother living in Khajurpur
 village
Jannat – Nazir's future wife living in Khajurpur village
Jugnu Khan *tongawala* – *tonga* driver

Meena – daughter of Fazal *cyclewala* and Chandni
Nazir – son of Akram *tongawala* and Qulfi
Qulfi – wife of Akram *tongawala*, a domestic servant working in
the Lawyers' Den
Yousuf Ali Sahib – a retired lawyer

Chapter 5 - Elephant Gate

Anwar Ali – a businessman living in the Lawyers' Den
Aunt Moomani – Nafisa Begum's aunt
Diwan Khan – bridegroom, with a mild learning disability, Haider
Khan's son by his first wife
Faiz Khan – bridegroom, footballer
Gul Bhai (Patwari Sahib) – an Estate Manager
Haider Khan – Rent Collector
Halim Nawaz – bridegroom, a teacher, son of Mrs. Waheeda
Begum
Karima Bibi – bride to Diwan Khan from *Nunga Sadhu Gaon*
(Naked Sadhu Village)
Maimuna – Mansur Sahib's wife
Mansur Sahib – a businessman
Nafisa Begum – bride to Halim Nawaz
Sitara Banu – bride to Faiz Khan
Tiddi – son of Gul Bhai
Zaheer, Gitta, Tinka and Kana – 4 footballers

Chapter 6 - Life in the Lawyers' Den

Afaq Hassan – Police Inspector, brother of Waqar Hassan
Azizah - wife of a dyer from Bhairugarh
Mrs. Farah Begum – wife of Shakil Sahib
Fasiuddin – Guard at Kaliadeh Palace
Mrs. Firdaus Begum – aunt of Waqar Hassan and Afaq Hassan
Karima Bibi – wife of Diwan Khan
Shakil Sahib – a prominent lawyer
Hashim – one of Shakil Sahib's sons
Izhar – Gul Bhai's second son
Khatoon Bibi – a voluntary worker in Gharib Colony
Lalu nicknamed *Kaam Chore* (work shy) – Gul Bhai's eldest son

Moon Khan – a solicitor
Murad – a mill worker
Qutub and Raunak - two brothers involved in litigation

Chapter 7 - Next Door Neighbors

Aftab - a professional pickpocket
Arif – a petty thief, Aftab's brother
Ashraf Babu –a ticket collector, son of Kausar
Bohri – businessman
Bhura –a *cycle chore* (bicycle thief)
Fida Hussain Bhai *Topeewala* - hat seller
Ghaffar *dabbawala* - a tiffin carrier-delivering their own home
 cooked lunches to office workers.
Hoshiar Gul – a drug dealer
Lohar *Ghundah* - organized illegal cock fights
Major Sahib – a retired Major
Sher Khan - killed a rival in a cock fighting dispute
Siddique Bhai – a mill worker, wore a black cap for 22 years
 during all weather
Zamir Khan – son of Sher Khan, killed a drug dealer

Chapter 8 - Glimpses of the Unseen

Deenar Sahib – an unsuccessful treasure hunter, Qazi's relative
Rizwan Sahib – communicated with *genies*

Chapter 9 - Events and festivals during the Muslim year

Ashok Kumar and Premji - two Hindu grocers
Shaukat Ali – a writer and poet, a distant relative of
 Waqar Hassan

Chapter 10 - Hindu festivals and celebrations

Madhav Sahib – a mathematics teacher

Chapter 11 - Bombay Fever

Amir - younger son of Nawab and Gulshan
Bashir Ali – a businessman from Bhopal's Royal family living
  in Ujjain
Batul – wife of Kaleem Beg
Fahim – elder son of Nawab and Gulshan
Faqiruddin – a property tycoon
Gulshan – wife of Nawab, daughter of Kaleem Beg and Batul
Kaleem Beg – Property Manager to Faqiruddin
Khalida – replacement chaperone to Rabia Begum
Nazaruddin (Nawab) – son of Faqiruddin and Sakina
Nur Jehan Begum – chaperone to Rabia Begum
Rabia Begum (Nagina) – daughter of Bashir Ali
Rashid – son of Kaleem Beg and Batul
Sakina – wife of Faqiruddin

GLOSSARY

abba - father

ab gher jao - now go home

achhwani - a gruel comprising a mixture of dried fruit and ground almonds boiled in goats' milk usually given to women after childbirth

agarbatti - incense stick

ammi or *amma* - mother

aqd-e-nikah - marriage certificate

aritha - soap nut used for washing clothes

Arithewaley - people dwelling by the aritha tree

Assalam-o-Alaikum - greeting, peace be with you, good morning

atterwala - perfume seller

ayat - a verse of the holy *Quran*

azan - call to prayers, the summons to prayers

Babu - title of respect for a man, a clerk

bakhshish - tip

bandar tamasha - monkey show

baniya (plural, *baniye*)-shopkeeper, grocer

bara karah - a deep-two handled iron pot

barkat - blessing

bas - enough, stop

Bata - a popular brand of shoes

batashe – small, round, white sugar puffs

batwa - a purse, cloth bag with strings to open and close it

bengan bhaji - cooked eggplants

bhag - run

bhaji - cooked or uncooked green vegetables

bhishti - professional water carrier

bhoot - ghost

bindi - brightly colored dot on the forehead
Bismillah - in the name of God
Bohri - a businessman
buraq - the winged horse on which the Holy Prophet ascended
  to Heaven
bura na mano yeh Holi hai - please don't mind, it's Holi
buri nazar - evil eye
burqa - a veil covering the whole body from head to foot
chaarya (plural, *chaariye*)- round iron brazier of burning coal
chadar - sheet
chai - tea
chaiwala - waiter serving tea
chakki pisna - to grind with a millstone
chalo charas piyo - come smoke hashish
chambeli - jasmine
chapati - a thin pancake of unleavened dough
chappal - sandal, slipper
charas - hashish
charas piyo, maza karo - let us smoke hashish and enjoy life
charpoy - string bed
charsi - one addicted to smoking *charas*
charya - habitual hashish smoker
chavanni – four annas – an anna was a currency unit formerly
used in India equal to 1/16 of a rupee
chhachh - buttermilk
chilam pio - come and smoke a pipe
chilam pio, khush raho - smoke and be happy
chimta - tongs
chore - thief, robber
chowkidar - guard
chulha - fire place
chunri - a multi-colored scarf of a female
chup chaap - be quiet
compowder - a pharmacist who dispenses medicines
cycle chore - bicycle thief
cyclewala - bicycle shop owner
daal - lentils
dabbawala - (also known as *tiffin carrier)* person delivering home
  cooked lunches to office workers

dahi barey - vegetarian curd pie
dharye - lances
dhoban - washerwoman
dhobi - washerman
dholak - drum
dhoti - cloth worn around the waist by a Hindu man
Diwali - Hindu New Year
diya (plural, diye) - oil lamp

do purti roti - two *chapatis* with *ghee* in between them, cooked
  together
dul dul - horse ridden by Imam Hussain
dupatta - long scarf worn by women
durries - small carpets
Eid – a Muslim festival
Eid-ul-Adha - Muslim festival of sacrifice
Eidgah - place where Muslims offer prayers on *Eid* day
eidi - A present given for *Eid*
Eid namaz - *Eid* prayer
Eid-ul-Fitr - Muslim festival following *Ramadan*, the month of
  fasting
Eid Mubarak - Muslim greeting during the festivals of *Eid-ul-Adha*
  and *Eid-ul-Fitr*
fatiha - first chapter of the Holy *Quran* recited when praying for
  the souls of the dead
firsha - battleaxe
fitrah (plural, fitrana) - alms given on *Eid-ul-Fitr*
gaunkri - a ball of dough baked in the hot ashes of a fire made
  from dried cow dung
genie - spirit
ghaiver - crown-shaped sweetmeat, an Ujjain specialty
gham na kar - don't grieve
gharara – baggy, wide-bottomed trousers
ghat - stone-built section on the river bank
ghee - clarified butter
ghundah - a bad character
gober - cow dung
gulab jamun - a round sweetmeat soaked in sugar syrup
gulal - red powder

gupa - cave

gur - raw sugar

haat - open-air farmers' market

halal - the slaughter of an animal in the prescribed Islamic way, legal, lawful

haram khor - a lazy person living off his family

haveli - mansion

hijra - professional male dancer in women's clothes

Hoshiar Gul ka bachcha - son of *Hoshiar Gul*

idhar ao - come over here

iftar - meal eaten after sunset to break the fast

iftari - food for *iftar*

Imam - religious leader

imarti - a sweetmeat made of pulses

imli - fruit of the tamarind tree

jalebi - a sweetmeat

jhannat chai - half tea half milk boiled together

jharu kidhar hay? - where's the broom?

Ka'aba - the house of Allah at Mecca

kaam chore - workshy person

kabaddi - an Indian game

kabeet - wood apple

kajal - soot from lamps used in the same way as an eye pencil

kalakand - a sweetmeat

kameez - loose top

karah - a two-handled cauldron

katchori - savory pie

khajur (plural, khajurein) - date

khamosh - silence

khas - sweet scented grass

khasta kachori - a cooked cake made of pulses

kheer - rice pudding

*khich*ri - a dish made of split pulses and rice boiled together

khichra - a dish made from meat, rice, wheat and various pulses

khon khon - sounds made by a monkey

khuda hafiz - farewell, may God protect you

khutbah-tun-nikah - marriage sermon

kon hai? - who is there?

kumbh - pitcher

kuttey ka bacha - puppy
laddu - a sweetmeat rolled into balls
langot - a loincloth
loban - a kind of incense
lota - a water pot
maandey - large thin circular *chapatis* about 18″ in diameter
machhanddar - monkey
mashq - water carrier's large bag for carrying water made of two
  goatskins sewn together
mangni - engagement ceremony
masjid - mosque
matka - clay pot
mehndi - henna, a red dye
mehr - marriage gift, dowry
mirasan - woman singer who sings only in front of women
miswak - toothbrush
mu'azzin - man who summons people to prayer
naan - bread
nahi maar - don't kill
namakpare - small salty savory crisps
namaste - Hindu greeting
namaz - prayer
namkeen - savory crisps
neem - a tree, the twigs of which are used as a *miswak* or
  toothbrush
neza - spear
paan - betel leaf with condiments for chewing
paandan - metal box containing betel leaf and the condiments used
to prepare *paan*
paanwala - seller of betel leaves, who also prepares *paan* for
  chewing
paisa – a monetary unit equal to 1/100 of a rupee
pajama - cotton trousers worn beneath a shirt by men of all classes
pakora (plural, *pakorey*) - fried gram-flour paste mixed with onions,
  spices and greens
Panjab - old spelling for Punjab
pankha - a fan
pankhawala - servant waving a fan
paratha - bread made with *ghee*

patloon - wide-legged trousers
patti - broad strip of cloth bound round the legs as leggings
Peerji - spiritual guide
phuljharian - sparklers
pilla - puppy
pulao - rice cooked with meat or vegetables
puri bhaji - fried cake and vegetables
qasam khaa - solemnly swear
Qazi - Muslim priest and judge who also performs wedding
 ceremonies
raitha - yogurt mixed with finely chopped onions and cumin seeds
rajgareh kay laddus - sweetmeats in round balls
rakhi - colored sacred thread given by Hindu girls
revri - a kind of sweet only made during Muharram, a Muslim
 festival
roti - thick *chapati*
saag puri - small fried pancake and cooked vegetables
sabil - drinking post
sadhu - holy Hindu man
safah - a strip of cloth wound round the head, turban
sahib - a gentleman
sahri - meal eaten before sunrise when fasting during the Muslim
 month of *Ramadan*
Salam - Muslim greeting
samosa - a triangular pie containing spiced potatoes, peas and
 mince meat
sari - length of cloth worn by a woman in folds round her body
satta - speculation on future prices on the cotton market
satte baz - a speculator
sattu - powdered lentils
sawm - fasting, not eating, drinking or smoking between sunrise
 and sunset
seekh kebabs - meat with spices barbecued on long metal rods
sehra - veil made of flowers
shahnai - flute
shaitan ka bachcha - son of Satan
shalwar - baggy trousers, fitted at the ankle
sharbat – a sweet drink made from sugar and water

sherwani - a long coat
shikari - hunter
singharey - water chestnuts
siwayyan - sweet home-made vermicelli
sohan halwa - sweetmeat made with corn flour, ghee and dried
 fruit
sower ka bacha - piglet
surma - also known as kohl or kajal - eye makeup worn by women
tamasha - an impromptu entertainment, show
tawa - an iron plate on which *chapatis* are baked
taziyeh - replicas of the martyr's tomb
thaal - a large metal plate
tiffin - lunch, midday meal
tilak - colored mark on the forehead of Hindus
tonga - a small, open, two-wheeled, horse-drawn carriage
tongawala - *tonga* driver
toor daal - yellow lentils
topeewala - hat seller
ubtan - a perfumed yellow paste rubbed all over the body
vakil - lawyer (*Sahib* added after the name out of respect).
victoria - an open horse-drawn four-wheeled carriage with or
 without a hood
vizier - a minister of state in a Muslim government
Walaikum assalam - response to the greeting *Assalam-o-Alaikum*
walimah - wedding feast
wazu - ritual of washing hands, face and feet before offering
 prayers
zardah - sweet yellow rice with saffron, containing pistachio nuts
 and dried fruit

ABOUT THE AUTHOR

Syed Abdul Majid Quadri was born in Ujjain, Central India in 1935. When he was 14, civil war broke out in India, forcing him to flee Ujjain, leaving his family and friends and breaking off his education at Maharajwada High School. Three years later he was reunited with his family in Karachi, Pakistan. They had lost their home and all of their possessions. He passed his matriculation examination from the Panjab University, Lahore in 1953, and obtained a Bachelor of Commerce degree from Karachi University in 1958.

After working for an American firm in Iran for a year, he travelled from Tehran to London via Istanbul and Paris by coach, train, the Orient Express, and boat. He is now retired and resides in Derby, England with his wife Ann, and his memories of a bygone era. *Indian Tapestry* is his first book.

www.ingramcontent.com/pod-product-compliance
Lightning Source LLC
Chambersburg PA
CBHW070220260626

47160CB00002B/625